Breeding

PEDIGREED

CATS

Breeding

PEDIGREED

CATS

Carolyn Vella and John McGonagle, Jr.

With photos by the authors

HOWELL
BOOK
HOUSE

New York

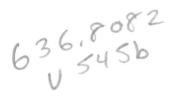
Howell Book House
A Simon and Schuster Macmillan Company

1633 Broadway
New York, NY 10019

Library of Congress Cataloging-in-Publication Data
Vella, Carolyn M.
    Breeding pedigree cats / by Carolyn Vella and John McGonagle: with photos by the authors
        p.   c.m.
    Includes index.
    ISBN 0-87605-698-2
    1. Cats—Breeding.   I. McGonagle, John, Jr.   II. Title
SF447.5.V44   1997
636.8'082—dc21   97-5549
                                                        CIP

Manufactured in the United States of America

99 98 97   9 8 7 6 5 4 3 2 1

Editor: Beth Adelman
Production Editors: Beth Mayland, Virginia Noble
Book Design: Scott Meola
Cover Design: Heather Kern & Scott Meola
Photography: Carolyn Vella

TABLE OF CONTENTS

ACKNOWLEDGMENTS

A Special Thank You!

Terry W. Stanglein is a graduate of the University of Pennsylvania School of Veterinary Medicine, member of the American Veterinary Medical Association and member of the Association of Feline Practitioners. He has been a practicing veterinarian in Northampton, Pennsylvania. He has a general practice that includes many dog and cat breeders. Terry has been our veterinarian—and our friend—for many years. His advice is invaluable and his care for animals is unsurpassed. To see him hold one of your precious kittens is to see a skilled veterinarian who also has a special love for that little life he has in his hand. Terry is the veterinary consultant for this book, and his conservative approach, his love for cats, his respect for breeders of pedigreed cats and his oath to do no harm to any animal is the essence of this book. Thanks, Terry!

Many thanks are also due to the following groups, individual breeders and "cat people" who contributed to this book through their kind cooperation and suggestions:

American Cat Fanciers Association Inc. (ACFA)

Kitty Angell

Janet Bassetti

Lynn Berge

Deanna Carroll

Cat Fanciers' Association Inc. (CFA)

Cat Fancy magazine

Cats magazine

Cat World International Magazine

Tom Corn

Cornell Feline Health Center

Ellen Crockett

Laura Cunningham

P. Decano

Rosaline DeDan

John A. DePlanque, DVM

Jean Marie Diaz

Helen Dohrmann

Gail Dolan

Donna Ellison, PhD

Barbara French

John & Rebecca French

Kitty Goodwin

Lorraine Jarboe, DVM

Carol W. Johnson, DVM, PhD

Lara Keyser

Susan Little, DVM

Ashley D. Loomis

Jean Lorah

Kerrie Meek

Ginny Molloy

Sonja Moscoffian

Leigh Polli

Cathy Rokaw

Jody Rugenstein

Anna Sadler

Lorraine Shelton

Tord Svenson

The International Cat Association Inc. (TICA)

Betsy Tinney

University of Pennsylvania School of Veterinary Medicine

The Winn Foundation

Janet Wolf

Specifically, we wish to acknowledge that the authors have received permission from ACFA, CFA and TICA to reprint their forms, logos and other copyrighted, trademarked or propriety materials. All are reprinted with permission. All rights are reserved.

The quotes from *101 Ways to Know You're a Cat Fancier* were originally produced by the members of fanciers@fanciers.com. They are reprinted with permission. All rights are reserved.

The authors would like to thank the cats of Jacat Cattery who were volunteered to serve as models for many of the photographs. All photographs were taken by Carolyn Vella, are copyrighted by her and reprinted with permission. All rights are reserved.

Particular thanks are due to each and every member of the Fanciers List, whose e-mail "conversation" has enhanced this book. Being able to discuss various aspects of kittens with experienced breeders of every breed of pedigreed cat is invaluable. Discussing the husbandry techniques necessary to maintain a healthy cattery is critical. Spending time on the Fanciers List is one of the most important and enjoyable aspects of our day. All this, and we still have fun!

ABOUT THE AUTHORS

Carolyn Vella and John McGonagle have been involved with pedigreed cats since 1982, and with cats of all sorts for over 25 years. They own Jacat Cattery, specializing in Japanese Bobtail Cats. They are also active cat exhibitors, and are cat show judges for the American Cat Fanciers Association, Inc. In addition to managing their own breeding program since 1988, they have assisted many other breeders in delivering and caring for their kittens.

Carolyn and John are co-authors of *In the Spotlight: A Guide to Showing Pedigreed and Household Pet Cats* (Howell Book House 1990). They have written dozens of articles and columns for cat-related publications, and are award-winning professional members of the Cat Writers' Association.

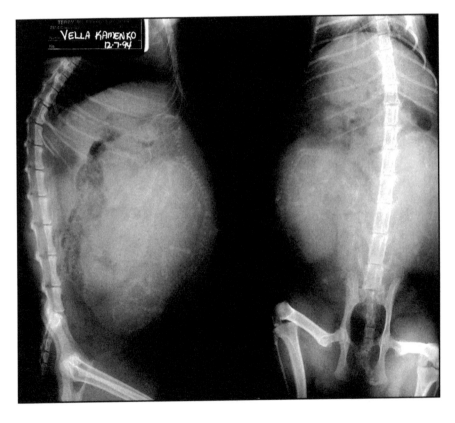

A litter of kittens at 55 days.

INTRODUCTION

BREEDING

Breeding pedigreed cats can be wonderful and rewarding, heartbreaking and frustrating. Holding a newborn kitten in your hand makes you appreciate miracles. Having a young kitten die makes you more sad than you ever thought you could be. But at the end of the day when one of your favorite cats comes up to you and sits in your lap, every care is forgotten because you are with a very special friend.

Is breeding pedigreed cats worthwhile? Without question! As a breeder, you will be part of promoting, protecting and preserving the breed you find so special. Without responsible breeders, there would be no pedigreed cats. You are part of a very special group of people who are doing a very important job. No matter how difficult it gets, other responsible breeders will be there for you to help you and encourage you. You will not be alone in this endeavor, as breeders form a community of people who are dedicated to pedigreed cats. If you want to be part of this very special community, you will be part of a growing family sharing a mutual interest. Welcome to the wonderful world of breeding pedigreed cats!

ABOUT THIS BOOK

Many of the photographs in this book follow one kitten. You can watch him throughout the book as he is delivered and as he grows. He was a singleton kitten and was born in the middle of the night in a record-breaking blizzard when we were unable to get out to our veterinarian and he was unable to get to us. Jasmine, the kitten's mother, had a hard labor, and the kitten was a breech birth. Fortunately, she was able to deliver the kitten without veterinary intervention.

After 12 hours Jasmine rejected the kitten, so the bottle feeding and all the kitten care you see were really done. This hand-raised kitten is now strong and healthy. He is called, appropriately enough, Blizzard, and this, in a way, is his biography. We have written this book as if we were sitting down and talking with you. This means we have tried to avoid technical language, but we cannot always avoid it. As a breeder, you will have to become familiar with these terms, too.

Also, the book is arranged so that you can (and should) read it from start to finish if you are considering becoming a breeder of pedigreed cats or want to use it as a refresher course. However, once you have done that, you will find that you can dip into it to refresh your understanding of an issue. For that reason, from time to time we have repeated something we said elsewhere, to avoid making you flip back and forth between chapters.

You will find out that, as a breeder, you should never stop learning. As Rosaline Dolak DeDan of Ardee Cattery, our own mentor, once said, "If you're in this long enough, you'll see everything." So be as prepared as you can be.

ABOUT CAT GROUPS

In this book we have often referred to two different groups: *cat registries* (also called *associations* or *fancies*) and *breed societies*. Let us try to tell you the key differences.

Cat registries are permanent groups, established to register pedigreed cats and to license shows at which cats compete for titles in that registry. Registries also license judges and maintain written standards against which these cats are judged in their own shows. Some of them have cattery inspection programs; others have voluntary ethical standards. However, none of them involve themselves in what they classify as "breeder disputes," that is, conflicts between breeders arising out of the sale, lease, showing, breeding, etc., of cats and kittens.

Breed societies are groups that are made up of breeders (and sometimes simply owners) of a particular breed of pedigreed cat. They usually publish a newsletter. These newsletters can be an invaluable source of information on the history of the breed, genetic and health issues, who is actively breeding and showing that breed, etc. Some of the breed societies also give annual awards. Unlike the registries, the breed societiesare getting more and more involved in developing form contracts for their members to use, requiring adherence to a written set of ethical standards and providing ways to resolve complaints about their members.

Breed societies should not be confused with breed clubs. Breed clubs are cat clubs, carrying the name of a breed, which are associated with only one registry and are permitted to put on shows for that registry. They are not independent groups.

At present, there are a number of cat registries. We have chosen to divide them into two groups: national and regional (which includes local and state groups).

By *national cat registries*, we mean those established groups in the United States that run a full-time registry office, have an established record dealing with registering cats and licensing (sanctioning) shows, and currently license shows throughout most of the U.S. (and occasionally in Canada). At this time there are three:

- American Cat Fanciers Association Inc. (ACFA)

- Cat Fanciers' Association, Inc. (CFA)

- The International Cat Association, Inc. (TICA)

Their addresses, telephone numbers, fax numbers and Internet sites are listed in the Appendix.

State and local registries are those that typically meet one or more of the following criteria:

- They hold shows in one state or in a small number of adjacent states.

- Their registry office is not staffed full time.

- Their registration paperwork is not accepted by all of the national registries.

In order to give our readers as accurate a summary as possible of the rules and policies covering the registration of cats and kittens, cattery names and how owners list themselves, we sent each of the three national registries (ACFA, CFA and TICA) an identical letter asking specific questions about these very subjects. Each registry answered us, in writing. These answers formed the basis for our comparative summaries of their rules. Since the underlying rules and policies dealing with these matters can and will change over time, always check with the registry *before* you plan to do anything that involves such critical, technical matters.

You know you are a cat breeder when . . .

A purr is the ultimate accolade.

You think people who don't adore cats are emotionally damaged and culturally deprived.

You search out the softest pillow in the house, and it's not for you.

Ailurophile is your favorite word.

When you wish for something you cross your paws.

You buy tuna flavored toothpaste.

You sleep without turning over for fear of waking the cats and put off going to the bathroom when you have a cat sleeping on your lap.

You find it impossible to sleep without a cat purring in your ear.

Adapted from *101 Ways to Know You're a Cat Fancier.*

CHAPTER ONE

Before You Begin

WHAT ARE PEDIGREED CATS?

A pedigreed cat is, to put it simply, a cat that is registered with a cat registry so that you can be sure of its heritage. That, in turn, means the breeder of that cat has filed a registration certificate with the registry certifying that the kitten in question is the result of a breeding between female cat A and male cat B, and that these cats are also pedigreed members of the correct breed. If the male and female cats are not owned by the same person, both the female's owner and male's owner must sign the registration certificate.

The result is a history of that individual cat's lines, going back generation after generation. The reason this is done is to ensure that the cat you have is really a member of that breed.

Very often you will hear someone say that they have a "purebred" cat, say a Siamese. Unless that cat is registered and therefore is actually pedigreed, what that person has is a cat that looks like a Siamese or that the cat's seller said was a Siamese. To put it bluntly, you cannot be sure you have a purebred cat unless you have a pedigreed cat. This is why we use the term *pedigreed* rather than *purebred* throughout this book.

WHY DO WE BREED PEDIGREED CATS?

While cats are abundant in nature, pedigreed cats are not. Without dedicated, responsible breeders, many of the beautiful breeds that exist today would not be here. Many natural breeds, or those native to a certain environment that have existed for hundreds of years, have almost been decimated by wars or just by people themselves. It took many years

Pedigree for: Jacat Breaking The Close
Common Name: Blizzard
Color: Red Spotted Tabby & White
Breed: Japanese Bobtail   Sex: M
Breeder: C.Vella/J.McGonagle
Owner: C.Vella/J.McGonagle
Reg: ACFA (pending)
Birthdate: 1/9/96

Eyes: gold

|QGC Jacat Yo Mouma of Boomin
  ACFA
  Red & White
  O/E
  Vella/McGonagle

|GC Kiddlyn's First Offender of Jacat
  SBT 090590 019 (TICA)
  Red Tabby & White
  O/E
  Linda Donaldson

|GC Kiddlyn's First Offender of Jacat
  SBT 090590 019 (TICA)
  Red Tabby & White
  O/E

|CH Takashi's Takeneko of Kiddlyn
  6690-502711 (CFA)

|CH Kiddlyn's Kiichigo
  6649-564872 (CFA)

|Jacat Protective Order--|
| JBTB031300-8931-15956-2 (ACFA)
| Black & White
| Blue
| C. Vella & J. McGonagle
| C. Vella & J. McGonagle

|CH Nekomo It's A Felony of Jacat
  SBT 080889 015 (TICA)
  Black & White Van
  Green
  Allen Scruggs/Douglas M

|GC Churippu of Yamatsneko
  6660-493392 (CFA)
  Black & White Van
  O/E

|CH Takashi Kairoku of Nekosong
  6660-375298 (CFA)

|Akumaizer's Utsukushii Neko
  6649-421062 (CFA)

|SGC Bassetti's Genji of Katzelein
  6662-429274 (CFA)

|MGC Takashi's Murasaki of Katzelein
  6649-539638

|MIGC Nekomo Roku Shini----|
  6661-459657 (CFA)
  Black & White

|GC, NW Nekomo Hirohito, DM
  6660-359275 (CFA)

|GC Nekomo Kande, DM
  6649-348838 (CFA)

|CH Kiddlyn's Kazari of Shishi
  6662-411856 (CFA)

|CH Takashi's Aoi Onna No Ko
  6691-410201 (CFA)

|DCH Jacat For The Purposes Of
  SBT 012293 009 (TICA)
  Red Cl. Tabby & White
  Blue
  C.Vella/J.McGonagle
  C.Vella/J.McGonagle

|TGC Katzelein's Eml/Out On Parole Of Jacat
  SBT 050889 001 (TICA)
  Red Tabby & White
  O/E
  James Reardon

|CH Takashi's Takeneko of Jacat
  6690-502711 (CFA)
  Brown Tabby & White
  O/E

|GC Kiddlyn's Massaka-Sama
  6660-447912 (CFA)

|GC Kiddlyn's Karada Karai
  6649-453601 (CFA)

|CH Kiddlyn's Kiichigo----|
  6649-564872 (CFA)
  Mi-Ke Van

|GC Bassetti's Saisho, DM
  6662-213616 (CFA)

|GC Bassetti's Kaminari Ga Ochita
  6649-202040 (CFA)

|SGC Bassetti's Genji of Jacat
  6662-429274 (CFA)
  Red & White Van
  O/E

|TGC Katzelein's Eml/Out On Parole Of Jacat
  SBT 050889 001 (TICA)
  Red Tabby & White
  O/E

|MGC Takashi's Murasaki of Katzelein
  6649-539638
  Mi-Ke Van
  Green

|Takashi's Akai Hansha No Chichi
  6662-308420 (CFA)

|Takashi Bunny Neko
  6649-333775 (CFA)

Jacat Breaking The Close
ACFA (pending)

This is Blizzard's pedigree. His name is on the far left (Jacat Breaking The Close). The next column lists his parents, the next his grandparents, and so on.

and many dedicated breeders to make certain these breeds still exist today. When you admire a beautiful Chartreux or Norwegian Forest Cat, two breeds that were virtually extinct for a period of time, you have many breeders to thank that you are able to see that beautiful cat.

In addition to the natural breeds, many dedicated breeders have worked very hard to make certain that distinguishing physical variations that randomly occur naturally in cats are perpetuated. When you wonder how the curly coat of the Devon Rex or the curled ears of the American Curl are maintained in that particular breed, once again you must thank dedicated breeders who worked for years to make certain those very special characteristics exist in a pedigreed cat.

This perpetuation of the many beautiful breeds of cats is why the cat fancy was formed and has grown. The various associations in the fancy register cats and kittens and license clubs. The clubs, in turn, sponsor shows where cats are exhibited and compete for titles and annual awards. In addition to these purposes, the associations provide information on various breeds, support research into feline veterinary medical issues and support legislative activities aimed at preserving our ability to breed cats. Supporting the fancy is as much a part of breeding pedigreed cats as is the ability to deliver healthy kittens.

WHAT IT TAKES TO BE A BREEDER

If you are dedicated to the breeding of pedigreed cats, you will want to be a responsible breeder. This means you will, more than likely, spend more money on the care of your cats than you will recoup by selling kittens. This is not always the case, but it is not uncommon.

In any case, you should never go into breeding if you are doing so in order to make money. The acquisition costs of necessary equipment are high. The cost of maintaining a breeding colony of cats is also high. Raising kittens until they are old enough to leave your cattery can be expensive, too. All these costs are just for breeding a litter of kittens with normal veterinary care. If you have a queen who needs a cesarean section or a litter that develops an upper respiratory infection, these additional and unexpected costs can add up quickly.

A wall of rosettes is a sign of a successful cat show career and a responsible breeder.

When you are a breeder, you must exhibit your cats at cat shows. In order to get a cat of the quality you will want, your contract with that cat's breeder may require you to exhibit the cat until it earns a title. If this is not a requirement, you will want to do so anyway, as you will want your breeding cats to be titled. If you are not willing to exhibit your cats, you should not even consider breeding pedigreed cats. Responsible breeders buy from other responsible breeders, and responsible breeders are also exhibitors.

Breeding pedigreed cats takes time as well as money. If your schedule does not permit you to exhibit at cat shows, which are held on the weekends, or keeps you away from your cattery for most of the 24 hours in a day, you should reconsider breeding. Cats take time to care for, and kittens take more time. Naturally, you will want to be in attendance when your queen delivers to make certain she can get the care she needs. Even though most queens deliver their kittens at night when you are usually home, you must be fresh and rested in order to help the delivery. If you are tired, you might well make a mistake that could result in tragedy for the queen, for the kittens and for you.

As a breeder, you will necessarily have several cats. It is your responsibility to take care of all these cats in a professional and humane manner. When you use cages, they should be easy to clean, large enough for exercise and equipped with litter boxes, food and water dishes, and toys to entertain the cats.

Your cattery area itself must be kept spotlessly clean and free of odors. A good cattery does not smell. Taking care of a cattery is time-consuming. Litter boxes have to be disinfected and deodorized daily. Food must be fresh. If you let your cats feed freely from a communal bowl of dry cat food, this must be replenished regularly. Water must be changed several times a day.

When you have newborn kittens, the queen must be let out of the cage to exercise. The kittens must be weighed and checked every day. As the kittens grow older, they must be weaned and socialized.

As a breeder, you must be willing to spend time learning about a range of subjects, including:

- genetics
- feline veterinary medicine
- animal husbandry as it relates to cats
- animal rights activists and their agenda as it applies to owning and breeding cats
- legal issues as they apply to cats and catteries
- the registering associations of the cat fancy and their rules
- how to prepare your cats for shows and how to exhibit them
- emergency veterinary care
- appropriate and healthy breeding techniques

This means you must have the time and dedication to keep up with these important topics, and you must have a library of reference books that are useful for you. (We have listed some for you in the Appendix.)

You must also have time to spend with people. Many of your peers will now be other breeders and exhibitors, and your conversations will deal with cats and breeding. No matter which breed you have chosen, other responsible breeders will be your best friends and your best resource because they know what you are talking about and they may have had to face similar situations.

You will also want one of these breeders to be your mentor. Mentoring is *critical* in the cat fancy. It is the only successful way to start. Many breeders will not sell whole (unneutered) cats for breeding to a new breeder, but this usually changes when you mention that you have a mentor who has been a responsible breeder for many years and who is respected in the fancy.

Trust your mentor to help you through the process of exhibiting and breeding cats. This does not mean you should do whatever your mentor tells you to do, especially when it comes to something like feeding a raw meat diet or breeding a daughter back to her father. Since your mentor has been breeding pedigreed cats for many years, he or she may well have fallen into some bad habits. However, your mentor's years of activity in the fancy will help you as you find your way.

One of the worst things you can be called in the fancy is a "newbie." This is a person who is new to the fancy, who does not have a mentor, and who does not seem to know what they are doing. This attitude toward newcomers does have some validity. Even to this day, when it is becoming more and more difficult to obtain a whole breeding cat from an established breeder,

A responsible breeder ends up with a wide-ranging library.

there are still incidences of new breeders getting in over their heads, making mistakes and then not knowing what to do.

The most common mistake new breeders make is to decide that it is cruel to confine their stud cats, so they let them run loose. This results in unplanned litters and, if the male sprays, in a malodorous, unhealthy environment for the cats as well as for the

> FIRST, DO NO HARM.

breeder who lives with these cats. Ultimately, many of these people just give up and try to place the cats they have because they are so overwhelmed. These are people who may not have realized that breeding pedigreed cats is a commitment not just for today when you begin, but for every year of the life of every cat you keep in your home.

As part of your job as a responsible breeder of pedigreed cats, it will eventually be up to you to help the newcomers to the fancy. As you gain experience, be certain you pass that experience along. When it comes your time to be a mentor and to help someone who is new to breeding, be certain you are the best mentor you can be. As each of us retires from breeding, it is nice to know that we have helped to start someone who will take our place and breed pedigreed cats in the same manner and with the same attitude we had when we were breeding. It is this dynamic that keeps the cat fancy alive and vital. This same dynamic protects, preserves and promotes each and every beautiful breed that exists today and that will continue to exist tomorrow.

CAT REGISTRIES

Unfortunately, just as breeders are not perfect, neither is the cat fancy as a whole. While there are three major national cat registering bodies in the United States, other registries spring up from time to time for one reason or another and then either stay small or eventually die. When a registry dies, people may be harmed because they spent time and money to support this registry, only to have it fail to establish itself.

Just as registries come and go, breeds will be "discovered" or "created," and then some of these will cease to exist. More importantly, when a breed ceases to exist, cats may have been harmed. Too many people in the fancy have no qualms about experimenting on cats. To them, cats are no more important than farm animals. These "breeders" will break the law, especially when it comes to keeping wild cats. Some will go so far as to stake out a female domestic or pedigreed cat so that she can be mounted and bred by a wild cat. Some "breeders" will continue to breed to a severe genetic anomaly without knowing whether or not there will be health consequences of this experimental breeding. Many cats have died in pain. Many more will. This is the part of the fancy to stay away from, and these are the people to avoid. There are good breeders. There are good registries, but you are going to have to find them.

When checking into national registering bodies, find the most conservative one and one with which you are comfortable. Make certain this registry doesn't make it easy for a new breed to be accepted for Championship exhibition. Make certain the registry does not jump to accept wild-blooded cats into the show hall. Make certain that when the breeders on the breed committee have decided what the standard for the breed should be, the registry listens to them. If your breed does not allow you to breed your pedigreed cat to a pedigreed cat of a different breed, make certain the registry does not have a way to get around this important prohibition.

In short, be knowledgeable and very careful. Do not get involved in breeding domestic to wild cats. Never experiment with cats. If the health and happiness of the cat is not of paramount importance to you, do not even consider breeding pedigreed cats.

You know you are a cat breeder when . . .

- Your cat owns more personal grooming supplies than you do.

- Grooming routines are considered as secret as nuclear detonation codes.

- You plan your wedding date around your region's show schedule.

- You need a calculator to reconcile your checkbook, but you can instantly figure possible grand points to ten decimal places in your head.

- You can remember show dates for the next six months, but you can't remember what is on your personal calendar for the next day.

- The fanciest drapes in your house are for your cat's show cage.

- Your cat has two special blow dryers, but yours is broken.

- You have a pouch and a drawer full of special cat combs, but your own brush is somewhere under a litter box so you have to borrow a cat comb for yourself.

Adapted from *101 Ways to Know You're a Cat Fancier.*

CHAPTER TWO

Your Breed and Your Cattery

LEARNING AND MORE LEARNING

Breeding pedigreed cats is not an easy thing to do. The problems usually do not arise during the actual mating, delivery and care of the kittens, but at the beginning when you first begin to acquire, house and care for your breeding cats. Problems continue to surface as you add cats to your cattery, and they always arise as you decide which cats should be bred to one another.

The most important attribute of a successful breeder of pedigreed cats is that breeder's ability to continually learn about breeding, genetics and cat care. More and more research is being done on health issues affecting pedigreed cats. More and more drugs are being tested and approved for pedigreed cats used in breeding programs. If you don't keep up with what is current, you may miss vital information that will affect your cattery, your cats and you.

The number of cats being kept as pets is now greater than the number of dogs being kept as pets. This has created an increased interest in all aspects of cat care, and the cat-related industries have responded in various ways. Cat food companies have increased their selections as well as their output. New kinds of cat litter are on the market.

Research into the health of cats is at an all-time high, with new vaccines being introduced, new testing procedures tried and found valuable, and new illnesses and conditions of cats recognized and treatments found for them. Veterinary schools are teaching their students more about the health of cats.

The genetics of pedigreed cats is being more closely studied than ever. Because of that, changes are being considered, especially in Europe, that may result in restrictions on the breeding of certain breeds. The driving concern is that breeding may be perpetuating certain characteristics that cause some degree of harm to the offspring of these matings. "Harm" is currently being defined as everything from painful arthritis to deafness.

As a breeder of pedigreed cats, you must keep up with all these new developments.

You must also be sure your veterinarian does. In fact, before you even begin to register your cattery or acquire your breeding cats, you must select a veterinarian with whom you can establish a relationship and work closely. You will find that your veterinarian is the most important person in your cattery. To help you in this process, we have discussed how to select a veterinarian and how to work with him or her in Chapter Eight.

SELECTING A BREED

Most breeders select a breed because they go to cat shows, watch a particular breed in the show ring, see it being handled by its owner at the benching cage, and just fall in love with the breed. This is one of the very best ways to start when you are selecting a breed. But this is just the beginning. As a prospective breeder, you have to find out all you can about that particular breed. If you start without detailed knowledge, you will almost certainly run into difficulties along the way.

There are some breeds that are extremely difficult to breed because they harbor lethal genes. There are three types of lethal genes:

- The classical lethal gene causes kittens to die before they are born.

- The teratological lethal gene causes monstrous defects in kittens, which are either stillborn or die shortly after birth.

- The delayed lethal gene causes kittens to appear normal at birth, but they eventually die due to the lethal affliction they carry.

In addition, genetic anomalies (which are not the same as lethal genes) are found in some breeds of cats. Some of these anomalies, such as the short and kinked tail that typifies the Japanese Bobtail, are perfectly harmless. Other anomalies may ultimately cause pain and death to the cat.

Some of these genetic problems, such as blindness or spina bifida, show up immediately. Others, such as progressive retinal atrophy or patellar luxation, may not manifest themselves for years. In either case, you must be very careful to watch for them and react if and when they are found. If they show up later, a responsible breeder will not only stop breeding the cats that produce the fault, but will seek to "shut down the line." That means stopping all breedings from cats that are descended from those carrying the genetic problem. A careful breeding program, therefore, not only seeks to prevent bringing in cats with such traits, but also affirmatively works to eliminate them if they show up.

If you are unwilling to work with breeds that carry lethal genes or that have genetic anomalies, stay away from those breeds where these genes are commonly found.

You must also find out which associations register your breed and recognize it for Championship status. If you want to show your cat in the ACFA because these are

The Legal Tangle

To help you understand just how complex breeding feral bloodlines can get, let's look at a few of the federal, state and local legal issues involved in using wild animals in breeding programs.

Wild animals on the endangered species list can be bought, sold, bred and kept only under very strict conditions, and then only by organizations that are licensed to do so, such as zoos. These licenses are not granted for breeders to generate new cat breeds to show.

Depending on state law, most domestic cats must have a rabies shot. If a domestic cat bites someone, it can be isolated to ensure that it is rabies free. An exotic or wild animal can, at the discretion of a public health officer, be put down immediately. A cat with more than 10 percent feral blood can be treated as a wild animal, and thus be put down if it bites someone; the owner has no right to a hearing.

States have the right to control the traffic in exotic animals, including requiring that exhibitions of exotic animals, such as circuses and fairs, obtain special licenses and undergo special inspections. Showing a mixed wild-domestic cat in some states is illegal without that license (and without humane society on-site inspections).

States have the right to outlaw the ownership of wild-domestic hybrid animals (as some have done with wolf-dogs). These laws may already apply to wild-domestic crosses in cats, as well.

Local governments, through zoning and public health laws, can prohibit housing in residential areas any animals except domestic pets. Under these laws, an animal with a wild heritage might be ineligible to be classed as a pet, regardless of its disposition.

Veterinary care issues also come into play when you use wild animals in breeding programs. The American Veterinary Medical Association (AVMA) is on record that it "strongly opposes the keeping of wild carnivorous species of animals as pets and believes that all commercial traffic of these animals for such purposes should be prohibited."

the shows that are most convenient for you, but only TICA registers the breed, you have a problem. Not every association recognizes every breed.

Even if you go to a cat show to see the various breeds, not every cat in the show hall is necessarily able to be shown in the Championship class. Some breeds you see at cat shows are just there to help attract a crowd. Others may be on their way to recognition but may not be eligible to compete for Championship status.

Breeds that are new to the fancy or new colors within an already recognized breed must be exhibited in shows for a period of time before they are accepted for Championship status, and acceptance is not automatic.

New breeds undergo scrupulous examination by the boards of directors of the various cat associations. The genetics of the breed are examined, as are the offspring resulting from the new breed's breeding program. The cats produced must meet the standard for the new breed, and the kittens must be healthy. This is a long process, so while you are busy asking questions about the breed you are interested in, be sure to find out which registries recognize and allow Championship competition in this breed.

Additionally, make certain the breed you want to work with is not in the process of being decertified by some of the European cat registries, if for no other reason than that it will limit the market for your cats. Our market for cats is everywhere around the world, and we buy from breeders all over the world. If you are involved with a breed where the market is limited, not only will you be unable to sell to breeders in other countries, but you will also be unable to buy from abroad.

Some of the lines of the most popular breeds in the United States can be traced directly to other countries. In order to bring certain qualities into your breeding line of cats, you may want to acquire one of these foreign cats. If you fall in love with a breed that can no longer be bred outside the United States, you will not be able to acquire the cats you want to continue the qualities you seek or to expand the genetic diversity of your cattery.

Likewise, if a new breed is currently being perfected, it may have somewhat complicated genetics. You may have to maintain a cattery with the new breed, plus other breeds or randomly bred cats needed to produce the breed you desire. This can make for a house filled with cats, only some of whom can be sold as your breed. For example, someone who wants a pet-quality American Curl may not care about the proper coat texture, but they do want their cat to have curled ears. But some pet-quality American Curls are pet quality because their ears *don't* curl. That makes it more difficult to sell them.

Randomly Bred Cats

In addition, there is an ethical issue involved in using randomly bred cats in breeding programs. While pregnancy is a natural and normal function, it is always a risk for any cat. When we breed our pedigreed cats, we are doing so to

Defining Wild

Words like *feral* and *wild* are often used interchangeably to describe various types of animals, so it's important to be clear about what they mean. You can see how imprecise these terms are.

Wild usually describes an animal that is found naturally only in a wild state, is descended from wild animals and is bred in captivity only to propagate the wild breed.

Feral usually means the same as wild, but is also applied to animals that are born in the wild and live there, even if their heritage can be traced to domesticated animals.

Exotic usually describes an animal that was either once wild but is now sufficiently domesticated to be kept in homes (such as a pot-bellied pig); a wild animal that has been bred with a domestic animal and that can be kept as a pet with an appropriate license (such as a wolf-dog); or any animal that is odd, such as a miniature cat, whether or not it is of any recognized breed. Unfortunately, in the context of the cat fancy, the term *exotic* is also used as a part of the title of several strictly domestic breeds.

Hybrid usually means a cross between two types of animals, but in the context of wild animals it also may mean a cross between a wild animal and a domestic one.

Domestic animals are those that have historically been domesticated and are regarded as safe to be kept in a home environment. For veterinarians, the distinction between a domestic and a non-domestic animal is that a domestic animal has less than 10 percent feral blood. While that is not a strictly scientific term, it works out to mean that any animal with none or just one wild parent five generations back is considered domestic; anything else is not.

What About Blizzard?

You may have noticed that Blizzard, who is featured in this book, had his mother walk away from him. We raised him by hand. However, we found that he did not grow as quickly as he should have. Our veterinarian's examination disclosed what had evidently triggered Jasmine's reaction—a heart murmur in the kitten. We had Blizzard altered as soon as we could, even though that murmur is no longer present.

This is one of the elements of a responsible breeding program. You accept responsibility for all births, even when they do not advance your own program.

maintain that particular breed, to perfect it, and even to keep it from becoming extinct. So we are willing to expose our beautiful cats to the risks of supervised pregnancy and delivery.

However, those of us in the cat fancy care about every cat, including cats who live in stray populations and have to fend for themselves. Because we care about all cats, fanciers subscribe to the humane trapping, testing, vaccinating, altering and releasing of stray cats. To take these cats out of their habitat and use them in a pedigreed breeding program is not compatible with the idea of caring for all cats.

In addition, the vast majority of animal shelters in this country do not release their cats without an agreement to alter the cat. To violate this agreement is unethical.

If you really want to use randomly bred cats in your breeding program, you can always buy unaltered pet cats from a pet store or from a newspaper advertisement, but this also has ethical implications. When you buy such a cat, you are encouraging those people who breed pet cats to continue to do so. With the pet overpopulation problem in this country, to encourage the breeding of non-pedigreed cats is unethical for the breeder of pedigreed cats.

Feral Breeds

As a prospective breeder, you must also determine whether or not you want to work with a breed that contains any *feral blood*, that is, cats only recently descended from a wild animal. These cats may be more difficult to care for if they exhibit feral traits. They may be difficult to handle, and they may even revert to cannibalism after they deliver a litter. You may have to tranquilize a queen of feral blood in order to prevent this cannibalism. If breeders believe (as we do) that when a queen walks away from a kitten, perhaps she knows more about the kitten than we do, then why would you be willing to step in when the feral queen may be feeling that the kittens are "wrong" and therefore should be destroyed? Sometimes nature knows better than we do.

There are also many legal issues you will have to deal with if you decide to pursue a breed that is a feral mix. These legal and related issues involved in dealing with the cats in these programs are complex and often contradictory. Your authors strongly recommend staying away from any involvement with any breed that has (or claims to have) any feral blood in its heritage.

When you go to cat shows, you might very well see some of these feral-blooded cats being exhibited and sold. You may also hear from these breeders that the cats are, in fact, completely socialized and will not cause any problem. No matter what you hear, run away from these breeders and

> **WARNING!**
>
> THERE IS NO WAY TO CALCULATE PRECISELY HOW "FERAL" A CAT WITH A WILD ANCESTRY IS. BECAUSE OF THE WAY THE LAWS OF GENETICS PLAY OUT, IT IS POSSIBLE THAT A CAT FIVE GENERATIONS REMOVED FROM A WILD CAT WILL HAVE NO FERAL GENETIC MATERIAL IN ITS MAKE-UP, BUT IT IS ALSO POSSIBLE TO HAVE AS MUCH AS 50 PERCENT FERAL GENETIC MATERIAL. CONSIDER THAT PROBLEM WHEN YOU THINK OF SELLING A GENTLE-LOOKING PET KITTEN DESCENDED FROM FERAL STOCK.

these feral-blooded cats as fast as you can! If you like the look of a particular feral breed, you can find a similar look in a domestic, pedigreed cat that does not have any wild blood.

These breeders are, in many cases, breaking the law, and if you go into one of these breeds you could be breaking the law also. If a cat registry is irresponsible enough to encourage the breeding of these cats, exhibit your cats somewhere else. Just because a registry exists and sponsors shows in your area does not mean it is a registry you will want to be involved with. There are irresponsible registries, just as there are irresponsible breeders.

Ten Ways to Spot a Fad Breed

1. The breeders talk more about how much money they get for kittens than how healthy the kittens are.

2. Cat publications classify their ads under "experimental" or "exotic" breeds.

3. Advertisements use words and phrases such as "investment," "rare," "newest," "legal in most states" or "breeders wanted."

4. Written materials on the breed appear overly defensive, such as stressing how tame the cats are.

5. None of the advertisements for the cats tell you where they are (or can be) registered and shown.

6. Breeders and advertisements make claims unrelated to the cats and their dispositions, such as being "hypoallergenic."

7. Breeders tell you more about which celebrities own the breed than why you should own one.

8. The cats are sold through a catalog.

9. The breeder also breeds other "exotic" animals, such as miniature horses.

10. After you have gone to several cat shows, you *still* have not seen one exhibited.

Fad Breeds

Unfortunately, there are fads with animals just like there are fads with anything else. For some reason, and no one quite knows why, a particular breed of cat will catch the fancy of the public for awhile. Owning a cat of this breed becomes fashionable, and we suddenly have a fad breed. People then decide they *must* have a cat of this particular breed solely because it is popular.

Unfortunately, where there is such a market, there will always be people who will make certain the market has what it wants—now. So when a breed becomes a fad, you will find more and more people who will decide to get into it in order to make some quick money. When that fad wanes and the next fad takes its place, these breeders will get out of the breed immediately. This is because they can no longer sell their kittens as easily as they could in the past, or they will have to settle for getting less money for the kittens.

No matter how attractive the current fad breed is, stay away from it. Here's why:

- Some fad breeds may contain a degree of feral blood. As noted previously, that adds a whole spectrum of problems based on the laws in your state and the veterinarians you may want to work with.

- Some fad breeds may very possibly contain genetic problems we do not understand, and the beautiful little kitten you hold in your hand may very well be facing a future filled with pain due to genetic defects.

- Other fad breeds are extremely difficult to breed, or have to be bred with household pets, which can be considered irresponsible behavior by a professional breeder of pedigreed cats.

While most of the cats you see being exhibited today at cat shows were not accepted for Championship status when the cat fancy was first established in the United States, you will find that the majority of the fad breeds never achieve Championship status in more than one association. Some of the fad breeds have finally had to end active breeding altogether because of the defective kittens that were produced.

There are more than three dozen breeds accepted by more than one association in the cat fancy. With this many, there is no reason to get involved in breeding the cat that just happens to be this year's fad.

LEARNING THE GENETICS OF YOUR BREED

At first glance, genetics can be a very intimidating subject. However, if you know absolutely nothing about genetics, you will not be able to deal knowledgeably with your breed or your own breeding program.

- If you are breeding a breed with more than one acceptable color (and this is the case with most breeds), you will not be able to deal with the distinctions of color genetics.

- You will not be able to handle a situation of having a stud cat who produces 80 percent male kittens if you do not know that the sex of the kittens is determined by the male of the species.

- You will not be able to work toward the perfection of your breed if you do not realize what colors are sex linked, or what traits are dominant and what traits are recessive. This varies breed by breed, and you will have to completely understand the genetics of your chosen breed in order to have a successful breeding program.

- You will also be unable to eliminate abnormalities if you do not know which ones are inherited. No responsible breeder will breed a cat who carries traits such as hip dysplasia or cleft palate.

You must learn the genetics of your breed in order to do justice to the cats you are breeding. If you choose a specific breed because you like the way that breed looks and because you want to make certain this breed continues into the future, you must breed correctly to accomplish these ends. If you like the gentle dip in the nose of a Ragdoll, you will want to avoid using for breeding a Ragdoll with a straight nose. When you are breeding Persians or Himalayans, you will want to avoid having a cat with a crooked mouth pass this trait on to its progeny.

In addition, you will want to breed according to the registration rules of the association where you exhibit. Entire registries have been formed after arguments over genetics. Registries in the cat fancy are considered either *phenotypical* or *genotypical*. In a phenotypical registry, cats are classified for judging based on their appearance. In this case, you may breed a Persian cat to an Exotic Shorthair cat. Out of the resulting litter, the longhair kittens may be exhibited as Persians and the shorthair kittens may be exhibited as Exotic Shorthairs.

IMPORTANT!

INBREEDING MAXIMIZES THE NEGATIVE QUALITIES OF THE CAT AS WELL AS THE POSITIVE QUALITIES.

In a genotypical registry, you may breed your Exotic Shorthair cat only to other Exotic Shorthair cats. If you end up with a kitten with long hair that looks like a Persian, this cat is a pet, since Shorthair cats are, by definition, shorthaired. You may not show it as a Persian, because its parents were not Persians.

If you breed Oriental Shorthair cats and you have a beautiful, top show-quality pointed kitten in the litter, you will not be able to show this cat in the CFA, except as an AOV (Any Other Variant). An AOV cat cannot earn a CFA title. However, if you exhibit in ACFA or TICA, you can exhibit this cat in the Championship class. Breeders would describe this difference as being due to the fact that TICA and ACFA are basically phenotypical registries, while CFA is basically a genotypical registry.

In some breeds, you will be working with genes that are difficult to control. Examples of this problem are the Birman and the Ragdoll. These cats get their unique markings from controlling the gene that causes the whiteness in the coat, which is called *white spotting factor* or the *white spotting gene*. This gene is also found in other breeds, such as the Japanese Bobtail, but in these breeds there is no need to control the white spotting factor. So if you choose to work with a cat whose pattern is affected by the white spotting gene, you must understand this gene completely.

Breeding toward perfection means more than just producing cats that are show quality. It also means *not* breeding cats again who have produced deformed kittens. Breeding pedigreed cats is an ongoing commitment to the controlled reproduction of healthy cats who meet and carry forward the standard for your breed. No breed, no matter how healthy the breed may be as a whole, is free from genetic abnormalities.

Your Genetics Bookshelf

One of the easiest ways to begin your study of general genetics is to get a good, basic text on animal genetics. These are available in libraries. After you have studied a basic book, you can move on to a book of cat breeds that features a section on genetics. In addition, most of the cat care books you will want for your library will have a general section on genetics.

From there, move on to a book specifically on the genetics of pedigreed cats. The book most breeders rely on is *Genetics for Cat Breeders* by the geneticist Roy Robinson. You must have an understanding of basic genetics in order to read this book.

To learn about the specific genetics of the breed you have selected, you will want to speak with other knowledgeable, experienced breeders. Not only will they know the genetics of the breed, they will also know which specific lines, when bred with other specific lines, will produce the health and quality you desire.

Breeders of breeds which carry lethal traits have, in many cases, traced back through their pedigrees and will be able to advise you about combinations of matings or even which cats carry the genes for specific malformations.

In addition to talking to breeders, you can ask them for the address of the breed society's publication. These newsletters are invaluable sources of information on the genetics and health problems of specific breeds. This will help you to avoid problems as you begin your breeding program.

The Value of Genetic Diversity

Unfortunately, you will sometimes hear breeders talking about a particular cat who is the product of a mother-to-son or father-to-daughter breeding and who, for all intents and purposes, looks like a perfect example of the breed. Inbreeding does, in fact, produce cats of excellent type who carry the traits that we all desire in the kittens we produce. However, inbreeding is ultimately destructive and must be avoided at all costs if you are going to continue to have a viable cattery and a long-term breeding program.

Problems Resulting from Inbreeding

- Smaller than average litter sizes.
- Increase in the number of stillborn kittens.
- Increase in the number (and percentage) of kittens born with abnormalities.
- Decline in average birth weight.
- Small, thin or depressed kittens.
- Poor growth patterns and rates.
- Smaller than normal size adults.
- Problems with reproductive performance in males.
- Problems with reabsorption of kittens in queens.
- Partial or total sterility in either or both sexes.

While inbreeding can maximize the good qualities of the cats being used, it also maximizes the bad qualities. While genes that cause bad type or ill effects may be found in every cat, their number may be small. When inbreeding is practiced, this small number of genes is used again and again, resulting in more prevalent manifestations of these genes and in-breeding depression, a decline in vigor in a group of cats (see the Glossary for more on this problem).

In addition, inbreeding can lead to several problems in both the pet kittens you will want to sell and the show-quality kittens you will want to keep for your breeding program. Kittens that are sold are expected by their new owners to have a normal life span, which is long for a cat, with minimal health problems. Inbreeding can shorten life spans and cause constant health problems because inbred kittens tend to be smaller and have compromised immune systems.

The show-quality cats you planned to keep to breed can have sterility or fertility problems when inbreeding is practiced. If you do nothing else when you develop your breeding program, make the decision that you will never, under any circumstances, inbreed, and never violate that decision.

Establishing a Breeding Program

While you might see pedigreed cats for sale in pet stores, you do not want to buy these cats. You have no real idea where they come from or how they were raised. The people who sell to pet stores are not respected members of the cat fancy. These people are usually the breeders who are breeding cats in volume to make a quick profit.

In order to get the cat you want, you will be buying from an established, responsible breeder of the breed you want to get involved in. You can easily find these breeders through advertisements in the various cat magazines (see the listing in the Appendix) and by going to the cat shows. However, getting a breeder to sell you a kitten that you can breed is not going to be as easy as buying a pet kitten. Breeders are extremely cautious about selling whole (intact) cats from their cattery. That's because your cats will come out of a line they established, and they have a reputation to protect. In addition, they want to make sure all their cats will be treated with the care, love and respect they deserve.

Choose the lines and the kittens you want. Check the pedigrees carefully, making certain you do not buy a kitten from a line that is already inbred. This is also the time to find a mentor who can guide you through the process of formulating a breeding program. No one can begin responsible breeding without a clear breeding plan. You should determine, from going to the cat shows and by looking at pictures of the various lines that are prominent in your breed, which catteries can provide the "look" you think best meets the standard of perfection for the breed. What is the standard of perfection? It depends on who you ask. Find out under which associations you will be exhibiting your cats, then contact these associations and buy copies of their official Standards of Perfection. Then watch the judges at the shows as they judge the cats of the breed that you are interested in. See how the judges interpret the standard and which cats they give their Final awards to. Form a clear picture in your mind of what the perfect cat should look like. Then, and only then, should you approach breeders and find the ones who are willing to spend time helping you formulate your breeding plans and who will discuss various pedigrees with you. This is not something you can rush into, so take your time.

WHAT ARE CAT REGISTRIES?

The cat fancy in the United States is made up of three large national registries: ACFA, CFA and TICA. These national associations register cats and litters and maintain these records in a data bank. They also sanction cat shows, train and license cat show judges and award titles to the cats who have earned them. They sponsor awards at the end of the cat show season recognizing the best adult cats, kittens and altered cats of that show year. They recognize the beauty of the non-pedigreed or pet-quality pedigreed household pet.

They also produce publications with articles of interest and yearbooks featuring the cats that were exhibited during the previous show season. In addition, they may have programs that enable you to have your cattery inspected and approved by the association, and they all work toward educating the general public on cat care and responsible cat ownership. They may also have legislative action groups that assist breeders and municipalities where restrictive breeding ordinances are being considered.

As you can see, the cat fancy is critical to breeders, and it is our responsibility to support the associations as they go about their work.

Sanctioning cat shows is one of the important aspects of the registries' work for the pedigreed cat breeder. We show our cats in competition with other cats in order to earn titles for our cats. These titles are critical on our pedigrees, as they are an independent verification of the success of our breeding program. When we sell a cat to another breeder, it will be important to show how many titles we have achieved for our cats.

Of course, these titles must be earned in an association where the title means something. There are some very small regional (or even state level) registries that hold shows but get an extremely small number of entries. The titles you may earn for your cats in these associations will not be of interest to breeders who show their cats in the larger national associations such as ACFA, CFA and TICA, since so few cats are judged in these small associations' shows. In fact, you may even be viewed with disdain by those breeders who have their cats judged in the larger competitive fields of the national associations. You may be viewed as a breeder of inferior-quality cats who must go to small associations in order to obtain any title at all.

In addition, some small associations have been known to compromise their show rules and even their health rules in order to save money when they are putting on a cat show. Compromises on the rules, made just to get more entries, can be considered amateurish by exhibitors in other associations. Compromises on health rules can expose your cat to a contagious or infectious disease which, in turn, can spread throughout your entire cattery.

In order to help you choose the associations where you want to show, go to shows as a spectator. Ask questions of the exhibitors. Ask questions of those in the club who are putting on the show. Ask what disinfectant is being used by the judge before they examine each cat. Write the name of it down and check when you get home to make certain that it is, in fact, a disinfectant that provides protection against fungus, bacteria and viruses.

Watch how the judges handle the cats that they are judging. Are they gentle while still maintaining control over the cat? Will they call the owner up to handle a cat that is snappish, rather than trying to prove they can handle each and every cat? Do they appear to know the standards of the breeds they are judging? Is the show running smoothly? Is there tension in the show hall, which can make the cats nervous? Are the judges or the members of the club yelling at each other and disrupting the show? Is the lighting the same for every ring? Is the hall climate controlled and is the environment pleasing? Do you think you would be comfortable spending your weekend at a show in this association? Would your cat be comfortable?

REGISTERING YOUR CATTERY

Once you have decided you will be showing pedigreed cats, whether or not you have decided to breed them, you should apply for a cattery name. Without a name on file with the cat registry in which you are showing, your cat will be shown without your cattery name. While that does not mean that you cannot claim titles, such as Championships or even year-end awards, the cattery name is like your brand name. That is, over time, you want to build a sense of recognition among the breeders and exhibitors of your breed that you show and breed good cats. So start early.

Where Should You Register?

Before you register a cattery, you should think carefully about where you want to register it. Consider the following issues:

- In which association(s) do you intend to show your cat(s)?

- Where are your foundation cats likely to be registered?

- When you breed, in which associations are your potential buyers likely to be showing? Will they be buying show-quality altered cats only, or will they be seeking to buy cats for *their* breeding programs?

In general, it is a wise idea to make sure you have as much flexibility as possible. The time to make sure of that is at the beginning. For example, since your authors have been showing cats, at least two regional U.S. registries have gone out of business and two others (regional or state-level) have been created.

Some catteries routinely protect themselves by registering their cattery name in *all* active registries. While this is somewhat cumbersome and expensive at the beginning, it does provide your cattery with at least two important benefits:

- The cattery protects its name, so that it cannot be used by anyone else.

- The cattery is able to register its litters and kittens *with the cattery name affixed* in each of these registries. Even experienced breeders sometimes forget that no association will accept as a prefix (or suffix) any cattery name that is not registered with it.

If you do not want to do this, make sure you register your cattery with each association where you expect to show and with each association where you expect to be selling kittens. If these choices do not include at least one of the national associations (ACFA, CFA and TICA), you should consider registering in at least one of these as well. The reason is that each of these can serve as a kind of clearinghouse for you. That is, you can usually arrange to register a cat (or kitten) from any one of the national groups with most of the smaller associations. The same is *not* true in reverse (see Chapter Ten).

We recommend that you seriously consider registering your cattery in all three of the national registries, as well as in any regional or state-level associations where you expect to show or which appear to be good markets for your kittens. The goal here is to preserve your right to a unique name, because registering your cattery name with one registry does not protect it everywhere. In fact, the opposite is true. If, for example, we registered the cattery name *Myname* with TICA, that

Designating Ownership

If you are the only owner of a cat, you will list your name only on all litter and cat registrations. If you have one or more co-owners of a cat, things can get more complex. While any co-owner can show a cat (and sign the show entry form), and any co-owner can file to claim a cat's titles, there can be problems when registering kittens and transferring ownership. And that can turn on something as simple as whether you used the word *and* or *or* when you first listed the co-owners.

While no registry has a formal limit on the number of co-owners a cat can have, the computerized record-keeping of the registries imposes a de facto limit on the number that can be shown on paperwork. That means in CFA, for example, the owners' names are limited to a total of 30 spaces on paperwork.

There are four ways in which co-ownership can first be established. Co-owners can be listed as "C. Smith and J. Brown," "C. Smith or J. Brown," "C. Smith & J. Brown" or "C. Smith/ J. Brown." A slight change in the connectors can have a significant effect on the rules about paperwork.

The table below outlines who has to sign a litter registration form for a litter out of a queen that is co-owned. As you can see, one little word can make a big difference.

REGISTRY CO-OWNERSHIP CONNECTOR			
	AND	&	/	OR
ACFA	both	both	only one	only one
CFA	only one	only one	only one	only one
TICA	both	both	only one	only one

name is recognized only with TICA. You could register *Myname* with CFA as well, but your friend could do the same with ACFA. Then your cats could be shown as *Myname* cats at TICA and CFA shows, while your friend's could be shown as *Myname* at ACFA shows. In practice, this rarely happens, but it is easier to prevent problems now than to try and straighten them out later.

One other consideration: If you will be registering with several registries, check and see if they all require renewals. Not all registries require regular renewals, but some, such as CFA, do. Take that into consideration when you are deciding about registration, as the fees for initial registration range from $15 to $50, and renewals are $10.

How to Register

The first thing you want to do is to get the current official form from each registry you want to register with. The addresses of the national registries are in the Appendix.

Next, decide who will be an owner of this cattery. What are the issues here?

- The co-owner of the cattery is automatically a co-owner of every cat owned by the cattery.

- Every litter registration from the cattery will have to be signed by at least one owner of the cats involved in the breeding. However, a registry may require *every* co-owner of the cattery to sign litter registrations (for specifics, see the chart on the previous page).

- It takes the signature of *every* co-owner of the cattery to add another co-owner.

- Joint ownership of the cattery and its cats is one way of handling the transfer of ownership and care of your cats if you should become very ill or die (see Chapters Three and Ten for more).

Then, you have to select a cattery name. Remember, *once a cattery name has been approved by a registry, it cannot be changed.* In fact, it is a good idea to be ready with several backup names, because if the name you choose is identical to a name already registered, you cannot use it (even if the other cattery has not been active for years).

Make sure you understand what kinds of rules and restrictions each registry places on cattery names. The rules are summarized in the chart below, but be sure to get the complete rules from the registries you plan to work with.

RULES FOR CATTERY NAMES			
	ACFA	CFA	TICA
Maximum number of characters (including spaces)	15	12	15
Can you use an apostrophe?	yes	yes, but not as a possessive	no
What other non-letter characters are not allowed?	all other characters	none	spaces, hyphens, marks such as #
Can you use the name of a breed?	no	no	yes
Are there any other major prohibitions?	no abbreviations or variations of existing cattery names	no titles (e.g. Princess, Earl) or words used "extensively" in naming cats (e.g. Ming, Pyewacket)	no abbreviations or different spellings of the same word

As you can see, it can get pretty complicated. Here are some points to remember:

- When counting the length of a cattery name, you have to include all spaces and characters, such as dashes and hyphens (if they are allowed).

- Consider making up a word that means something to you, instead of using the name of someone or something that is very common.

The easier it is to think of, the more likely it is already registered. For example, we selected *Jacat* as our cattery name instead of combining our names (VellaMcGonagle). Jacat is only five letters, while our names are 14 letters, which is too long for CFA. Jacat stands for JApanese CATs (we breed Japanese Bobtails) as well as John And Carolyn's cATs.

- Keep the name you want as short as possible. Remember, when you add a cattery name of, say, six letters to an existing cat's name, you are actually adding nine characters ("of" plus a space plus the name). If the cattery's name is long (or the name of the cat is long), you may find you do not have room for your cattery's name on the cat's registration papers. In that case, the cattery will be left off all paperwork.

- Do not look at existing names for guidance on what you can and cannot do in a cattery name. Over the years the registries have modified their rules, so some things allowed in the past are no longer allowed in new cattery names.

- If you will be involved in joint ownership with another breeder/ exhibitor on a regular basis, consider getting a separate cattery name for the cats under that arrangement.

- If you will be registering with more than one registry (now or in the future), select a name that meets the *most restrictive* standards (no more than 12 characters, no apostrophe, and do not use a breed name).

After you have settled on a name, call the registry to see if that name is available. Some of them may be able to tell you this over the telephone, although they do not have to. But even if you are told that name is available, it is only available *then* and for *that registry*. It may not be available for another registry, and if you wait too long, it may not even be available for the registry you called.

Fill out the application completely and clearly. The way the registry reads the name you supplied is the way it will be issued. Make sure you understand all of the instructions. If you do not, call the registry office before you send in the application. We have included the applications of the major registries to show you what the forms look like.

APPLICATION TO REGISTER A CATTERY NAME

I wish to register my cattery name with ACFA. I understand the fee for registration is a <u>one time</u> charge only and the name approved will be for my exclusive use or for the use of those additionally named as co-owners. Registration fee enclosed:

Registration Fee:

ACFA Member – $45.00   **Non-ACFA Member – $30.00**

Rules Pertaining to Cattery Name Registration:

1. A cattery name [characters and spaces combined] may not exceed 15 letters and spaces.

2. Abbreviations or variations of registered cattery names are not permitted.

3. Registered cattery names may be added to a cat's name as: [1] a prefix, if the cat is bred by the owner of the cattery name, or [2] as a suffix if the cat is owned, but not bred, by the owner of the cattery name.

4. The prefix cattery name denoting the breeder of the cat may <u>never</u> be removed. However, the suffix cattery name may be removed and replaced with a new owner's cattery name when the ownership of the cat is transferred.

5. The owner of a cattery name may add additional names as co-owners of the cattery name upon written notification to ACFA, surrendering the original registration certificate and upon payment of the appropriate fee [same fee as transfer of cattery name].

6. Ownership of a cattery name may be transferred by written notification to ACFA by the registered owner, surrendering of the original registration certificate and payment of the transfer fee.

Cattery Name Registration Information:

Cattery Name to be Registered:
Note: Applicant <u>must</u> provide three [3] name choices. Please list in your order of preference. If your first choice is already in use, then your second or third choice will be used.

Cattery Name – First Choice: _____

Cattery Name – Second Choice: _____

Cattery Name – Third Choice: _____

Name of Owner of Cattery: _____

Name[s] of Co-Owners: _____

Owner's Address of Record:

Street Address: _____

City/State/Zip: _____

Note: Unless otherwise stated <u>either</u> the owner, or co-owner, may sign for the cattery. Both signature <u>will</u> <u>not</u> be required.

Owner's Signature _____   Date _____

Revised 1995

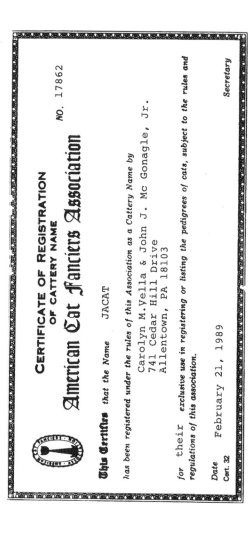

CERTIFICATE OF REGISTRATION
OF CATTERY NAME

American Cat Fanciers Association

NO. 17862

This Certifies that the Name   JACAT

has been registered under the rules of this Association as a Cattery Name by

Carolyn M. Vella & John J. Mc Gonagle, Jr.
741 Cedar Hill Drive
Allentown, PA 18103

for their exclusive use in registering or listing the pedigrees of cats, subject to the rules and regulations of this association.

Date   February 21, 1989
Cert. 32

Secretary

This certificate shows that our cattery is registered with ACFA.

APPLICATION/RENEWAL
MEMBERSHIP AND/OR CATTERY

☐ Life Membership $1,000
☐ Additional Life Breed Section . . . .$ 100
☐ Regular Membership (New/Renewal) . . . . $ 25
☐ Family Membership-NO TICA TREND-(Voting: One per Regular Membership)(US/Canada/Mexico ONLY) . . . . . . $ 10
☐ Family Membership-NO TICA TREND-(Non-Voting, Add'l Family, Junior, etc.) (US/Canada/Mexico ONLY) . . . . . $ 10
☐ International Membership-Outside US and Canada (NO FAMILY MEMBERSHIP) US Funds ONLY . . . . $ 30
☐ Each Additional Breed Section . . . . $ 5
☐ Cattery Registration (ONE-TIME FEE) . . . . $ 50
☐ TICA TREND - First Class (Life/Regular Members ONLY) . . . . $ 8

Please type or print legibly one character per box:

Last Name |_|_|_|_|_|_|_|_|_|_|_|_|_|_|_|_|_|_|_| First Name |_|_|_|_|_|_|_|_|_|_|_|_|_|_|_|_|_|_|_|

Family Membership
Last Name |_|_|_|_|_|_|_|_|_|_|_|_|_|_|_|_|_|_|_| Family Membership
First Name |_|_|_|_|_|_|_|_|_|_|_|_|_|_|_|_|_|_|_|

Address |_|_|_|_|_|_|_|_|_|_|_|_|_|_|_|_|_|_|_|_|_|_|

City |_|_|_|_|_|_|_|_|_|_|_|_|_|_|_|_|_|_|_|_| State |_|_|_|_|_|_|_|_|_|_|_|_|_|_|

Zip |_|_|_|_|_|_|_|_|_|_| Phone |_|_|_|_|_|_|_|_|_|_|_|_|_|_|

Cattery Name |_|_|_|_|_|_|_|_|_|_|_|_|_|_|_|_| (SEE INSTRUCTIONS ON REVERSE)

Your membership automatically entitles you to be listed in one breed section at no extra charge. You may be listed in more than one breed section. Additional breed sections are $5 per year, per person. Please CHECK below all breed sections to which you wish to belong.

AB-Abyssinian	BU-Burmese	JB-Japanese Bobtail	OL-Oriental Longhair	SE-Serengeti
BB-American Bobtail	SP-California Spangled	JL-Japanese Bobtail LH	OS-Oriental Shorthair	SG-Singapura
BH-Am Bobtail SH	CX-Chartreux	KT-Korat	PS-Persian	SN-Snowshoe
AC-American Curl SH	CR-Cornish Rex	LP-LaPerm	PB-Pixiebob	SO-Somali
AL-American Curl	CU-Chausie	MC-Maine Coon	RD-Ragdoll	SX-Sphynx
AS-American Shorthair	CY-Cymric	MX-Manx	RB-Russian Blue	ST-Sterling
AW-American Wirehair	DR-Devon Rex	MK-Munchkin	SF-Scottish Fold	TO-Tonkinese
BA-Balinese	EM-Egyptian Mau	ML-Munchkin Longhair	SS-Scottish Fold LH	TA-Turkish Angora
BG-Bengal	ES-Exotic Shorthair	NB-Nebelung	SR-Selkirk Rex	TV-Turkish Van
BI-Birman	HB-Havana	NF-Norwegian Forest	SL-Selkirk Rex Longhair	Other:_____
BO-Bombay	HI-Himalayan	OC-Ocicat	SI-Siamese	_____
BS-British Shorthair	HH-Household Pet	OA-Ojos Azules	SB-Siberian	_____

☐ **I would like to join a TICA Club!**   ☐ **I would like to organize a TICA Club!**

Membership fees are due May 1st of each year.   *WE ACCEPT AMERICAN EXPRESS, VISA, MASTERCARD OR DINER'S CLUB*
FEES MUST BE REMITTED IN U.S. FUNDS ONLY

Card Number |_|_|_|_|_|_|_|_|_|_|_|_|_|_|_|_|_| Mo.   Yr.
Expiration Date |_|_| |_|_|

Signature _____

Send this application with appropriate fees (no cash please) to
THE INTERNATIONAL CAT ASSOCIATION
P.O. BOX 2684, HARLINGEN, TEXAS 78551
210/428-8046

FORM A-1010 (05/01/95)

THE CAT FANCIERS' ASSOCIATION, INC.
Worlds' Largest Registry of Pedigreed Cats
CATTERY NAME REGISTRATION APPLICATION
Effective January, 1991

REGISTRATION & RENEWAL POLICY

1. The Cat Fanciers' Association, Inc. will initially register a cattery name for a period of five years. The registration fee is $50.00.
2. Upon expiration of the initial five year period and any subsequent renewal period, a breeder may apply for a five year extension of the registration. There will be no limit on the number of extensions allowed, but not more than one extension will be permitted per renewal. The renewal fee is $10.00 per five year period.
3. It is the breeder's (registrant's) responsibility to apply for a renewal of the cattery name registration. CFA will send notice (maximum of two) of the impending expiration, but failure on the part of the registrant to receive these notices will not be the basis for any future claims which may arise due to the reissuance of the cattery name to some other party.
4. Each five year renewal period starts at the expiration of the prior paid period. Fees for renewals are payable from the expiration of the prior paid period. For example, if a cattery name registration period expires March 31, 1988 and the breeder renews it on December 1, 1988, the effective renewal date is April 1, 1988 and the renewal period will expire March 31, 1993.
5. The use by the registrant of the cattery name either as a prefix or suffix will not be allowed after the expiration date. Upon renewal of a cattery registration, the cattery name may be added to the names of cats which were individually registered after the expiration and prior to the renewal date. The applicable fee(s) for corrected registration and/or addition of cattery suffixes will apply.
6. For cattery names issued **on or after January 1, 1988** — Anytime after a cattery name is registered, a breeder(s) other than the original applicant(s) may be added to the registration upon submission of a new cattery application signed by ALL current registered owners of the cattery. Payment of the fee in effect for an initial cattery registration will apply. The registration period will extend for five years from the date of re-registration. For cattery names issued **before January 1, 1988**, a breeder(s) other than the original applicant(s) may be added to the registration upon submission of a letter signed by all current registered owners of the cattery. Payment of the fee in effect for an initial cattery registration will apply, however, the cattery will not be subject to renewal rules.

RULES GOVERNING THE ACCEPTABILITY OF A CATTERY NAME.

7. Existing cattery names will not be duplicated.

8. A cattery name cannot exceed twelve (12) characters, including dashes, hyphens and blanks. No other punctuation is permitted.
9. A given name — Marie, Frank, John, for example — cannot be used.
10. Titles such as Princess, Earl, or Madam cannot be used.
11. The cattery name cannot be the name of a recognized breed.
12. Words or names that have been used extensively in naming individual cats, such as "Ming" or "Pyewacket" cannot be used.
13. Cattery names, once registered, cannot be changed. Should you wish to use a different cattery name in the future, it will be necessary to reapply for a new/additional cattery name. A breeder may have more than one (1) registered cattery name.

PLEASE NOTE:

14. The cattery name will be registered in all capital letters.
15. Unique or manufactured words are most likely to be approved, as such names are most likely to conform to the above rules and less likely to conflict with names already registered.
16. Second, third, or fourth name choices **WILL BE USED ONLY** if first or preceding choice is not available.
17. Enter **ONLY THOSE ADDITIONAL NAME CHOICES THAT YOU ARE READY TO ACCEPT AS YOUR CATTERY NAME** if we are not able to register your first preference.
18. You are not required to enter second, third or fourth name choices, however failure to do so may cause delay if your only choice is unacceptable due to a conflict with existing cattery names (see #7 above). You may attach a separate list if you wish us to consider more than four choices.

USE OF CATTERY NAMES

19. Prefix — when a cattery name is registered with CFA, cats bred by the owner(s) of the name shall carry the cattery name as a prefix.
20. Suffix Addition/Deletion — a new owner of record may add his cattery name as a suffix (preceded by "of") when the cat name will not then exceed the limit of 35 spaces. Any existing suffix will be deleted upon the addition of the new owner's cattery name.

Complete the section below and return the WHITE AND YELLOW COPIES of the form to CFA with a fee of $50.00. Keep the PINK copy for your reference and do not detach at lines below.

CATTERY NAME APPLICATION

PLEASE PRINT OR TYPE — Cattery names not to exceed twelve (12) characters, including dashes, hyphens and blanks.

List your first, second, third, and fourth choice for your cattery name. DO **NOT** enter a word which you are not willing to accept as your cattery name.

1ST CHOICE

2ND CHOICE

3RD CHOICE

4TH CHOICE

The person(s) to be listed as owner(s) of this cattery is(are):

Name (First)   (Middle)   (Last)

Address

City   State/Province   Zip/Postal Code

Signature:_____ Breeder #:_____

If cattery has more than one owner, please complete below:

Name (First)   (Middle)   (Last)

Signature:_____ Breeder #:_____

Name (First)   (Middle)   (Last)

Signature:_____ Breeder #:_____

2063-10/92   The Cat Fanciers' Association, Inc. • 1805 Atlantic Avenue • PO Box 1005 • Manasquan, New Jersey 08736-0805 • 908-528-9797

Do not provide a second or third alternate name on your application unless you are ready to accept each of them as your cattery's name. If your first choice is declined, contact the registry and see what changes you can make in your first choice to get it accepted.

Allow enough time for the registry to process your application. Do not wait until the last minute to apply for a cattery name.

USING YOUR CATTERY NAME

Once your cattery name has been approved, you can use it. What does that mean?

- All new litters for which you are the breeder (that is, you own the queen) will carry your cattery name as a prefix when they have been properly registered. That prefix is permanent.

- Any cat you buy from another breeder can have your cattery name added at the end as a suffix. Your name is added following *of,* so the kitten you bought from *Breeder* cattery will be *Breeder [Cat's Name] of Your cattery.*

- A suffix (but not a prefix) can be removed or changed, but only *after* you have applied to the registry to do this. That usually happens when you sell a cat you have previously purchased.

- You can add a new owner to the cattery name, but you have to apply to each registry to do it, and that application must be signed by every registered owner of the cattery.

YOU KNOW YOU ARE A CAT BREEDER WHEN . . .

- Your cat has accumulated frequent flier miles.

- Your show luggage consists of one small overnight bag for you and an entire fleet of Samsonite for your cat.

- You always describe distances from city to city in terms of hours.

- The speed dial numbers on your telephone are all show entry clerks.

- Your show attire consists of T-shirts and sweats, but your cat has velvet cage curtains.

- Saying, "See you in Atlanta" (or some other city) carries volumes of information.

- "Going on campaign" doesn't mean for political office.

Adapted from *101 Ways to Know You're a Cat Fancier*.

CHAPTER THREE

Acquiring Your Foundation Cats

THE IMPORTANCE OF TITLED CATS IN YOUR PEDIGREES

If you are going to become a responsible, professional breeder of pedigreed cats, you will also become an exhibitor of pedigreed cats. Unless you are willing to become an exhibitor, you will not be able to buy a pedigreed cat from another responsible breeder. In addition, exhibiting your cats is part of the obligation of being a breeder. Responsible breeders promote the cat fancy and take an active part in its important work.

Whether or not you particularly want to show cats, it is a requirement for you if you want to be respected as a breeder. Those who breed cats but don't exhibit are not highly regarded in the fancy. They are seen as irresponsible even if they have a legitimate reason why they cannot show their cats. Once you go into the show environment and begin to make friends, you will realize how important this aspect of breeding pedigreed cats actually is. This is the time when breeders get together. We discuss all aspects of breeding and raising kittens while we are in the show hall. This is where we socialize and where we learn. You will make friends in the show hall and will be able to discuss any problems or concerns you have with others who have the experience to help.

BUYING YOUR FOUNDATION CATS

Now that you have decided which breed you want to work with, you must contact breeders and talk with them. Many breeders are reluctant to sell whole, breeding cats to anyone who is new to the fancy. They may be concerned about how their cats will be cared for, they may question your knowledge, or they may want to restrict the lines they have produced.

The best way to approach a breeder when you want to buy a cat for breeding is with a resume in hand. The resume should explain what experience you have had in the fancy, what you plan for your breeding program and why you want this particular breed. You also should include a letter of recommendation from your veterinarian. Expect to spend time discussing your desires with various breeders and listening to what they expect of you. When you have reached an agreement with a breeder, expect to wait for the kitten of your choice.

As you continue to expand your cattery, keep your resume up-to-date. You should add any titles your cat may have achieved, as well as any national, regional or breed placements. Include any special awards your cat may have won in your breed society, along with pictures of your litters and your cattery itself.

Sometimes you will find you are interested in obtaining a cat or kitten from a breeder who lives across the country from you. The only way you may have of seeing this kitten is by the pictures the breeder sends to you. This is not a good way to buy a kitten, because all you see is the surface. In judging pedigreed cats, a full three-quarters of the judging is done by feeling the cat. Color is critical only in breeds such as the Somali and Abyssinian, where the breeders have put much emphasis on the bands of ticking on the coat, or in the

While being groomed by his owner Gail Dolan for another ring appearance, Red Somali Hemingway admires the rosette he won.

Russian Blue, Korat and Chartreux, where the color must be clean, clear and without darker or lighter bands of color. While color is a factor in the other breeds, and eye color is critical in some breeds such as the Siamese, Oriental and Himalayan, it does not reach the same level of importance as other structural factors. Since you will be exhibiting your kitten, you will want to feel the kitten and judge for yourself. Obviously, a picture is not a good substitute for having the kitten in your hands.

HOW TO JUDGE A KITTEN

If it is at all possible, arrange to see the kitten and handle her. If this is not possible, make certain the breeder understands, by putting it in writing, that if you decide the kitten is not of the quality you want, you can return the kitten to the breeder.

When you handle a kitten you are considering buying, let your hands guide you. The first thing you will feel as you pick up the kitten is her weight and her boning. If you are interested in buying one of the bigger-boned cats, such as a Maine Coon or a Persian, feel the bones carefully. While the bones in one of the larger breeds will be large, bones that are porous will make the kitten feel extremely light. This condition, called feather boning, will be very harmful to the cat when it is older, because these very light bones cannot provide the proper framework the cat needs for its body size. As an adult, the cat may be unbalanced.

If you are buying a slender-bodied cat such as an Oriental Shorthair or a Siamese, the boning of the cat will feel fine and light. However, if the bones are too fragile, the cat will look as if it cannot stand upright.

If you are interested in breeding a large-boned breed, such as the Maine Coon, you should have the cat checked to make certain he does not have hip dysplasia. Even though this problem can occur in any breed, it tends to be more common in the larger breeds. Hip dysplasia occurs when the head of the leg bone (the femur) does not fit properly into the hip socket. Specifically, the cat may not have the musculature to keep the end of the femur from rotating out of the hip socket. When this happens, the cat can experience minor chipping or fractures of this bone. The cat can become crippled and can be in great pain.

In order to make certain that the propensity toward hip dysplasia is not passed on to future generations, breeders do not breed any cat who has hip dysplasia.

SHOULD YOU BREED THIS CAT?

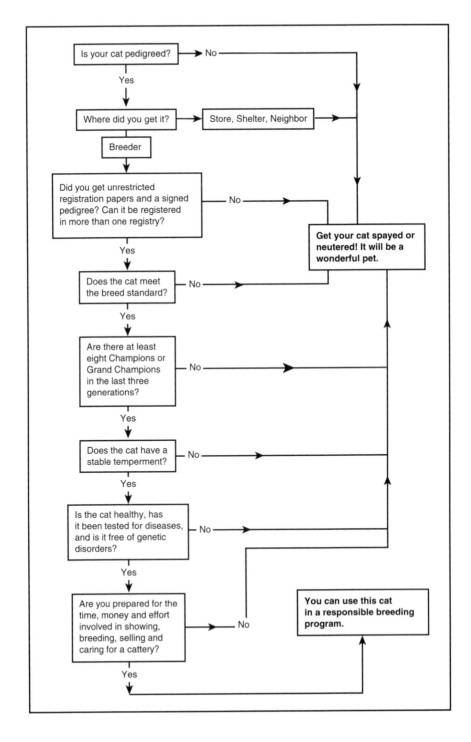

Is your cat pedigreed? → No

Yes ↓

Where did you get it? → Store, Shelter, Neighbor

Breeder ↓

Did you get unrestricted registration papers and a signed pedigree? Can it be registered in more than one registry? — No →

Yes ↓

Get your cat spayed or neutered! It will be a wonderful pet.

Does the cat meet the breed standard? — No →

Yes ↓

Are there at least eight Champions or Grand Champions in the last three generations? — No →

Yes ↓

Does the cat have a stable temperment? — No →

Yes ↓

Is the cat healthy, has it been tested for diseases, and is it free of genetic disorders? — No →

Yes ↓

Are you prepared for the time, money and effort involved in showing, breeding, selling and caring for a cattery? → No →

You can use this cat in a responsible breeding program.

Yes ↓

The Orthopedic Foundation for Animals (OFA) evaluates the X-rays of cats for orthopedic problems. OFA's address is 2300 Nifong Boulevard, Columbia, MO 65201 (314-442-0418). You can X-ray a kitten as young as six months of age to check for hip dysplasia, but the best results are not found until the cat is one year old.

You can have your cat X-rayed at your veterinarian's office and then have the X-rays sent to OFA for evaluation. You will receive an evaluation that states the cat's hips are Excellent, Good, Fair or Poor. The OFA recommends that no cats whose X-rays are graded as poor be used for breeding.

The OFA currently charges $25 for each evaluation, but discounts this rate for the evaluation of siblings.

The OFA also keeps statistics on hip dysplasia by breed. For example, 19.6 percent of Maine Coons evaluated by the OFA were in the Poor category. However, when looking at testing statistics always bear in mind that the breeds suspected of having a problem are generally the ones taken to the veterinarian for evaluation. The more cats of a breed that are evaluated, the more problems will be found.

In addition to the boning, look carefully at the jaw. The jaw on every breed of cat should be good and firm, neither weak and receding nor overshot. Improper alignment can cause problems later in life. Regardless of breed, cats with jaw problems should not be bred.

The Registry Question, Again

The rules governing the registration of cats in each registry vary not only from registry to registry but also over time. For that reason, it is best to find out whether or not a kitten you are seeking to buy is registerable *before* you buy the kitten.

Let's assume that you are ready to buy a kitten from a breeder for your program. That kitten's litter is already registered in registry A. That means the kitten can be registered there as well. However, it may be important to you that this kitten be registered and then shown in registry B (and that your kittens can be registered there, too). Before you bring home that kitten (and fall in love with it), make sure it can be registered in registry B. The easiest and fastest way to do this is to have the breeder register the kitten before you buy it. If the breeder does this and anything unforeseen happens, you are protected—as long as you have made the purchase conditional on the completion of registration in registry B.

There is an additional cost for this registration, and the breeder may ask you to pay it. Remember, you would have to pay for it when you do it anyway.

Jaw problems in kittens:

- Upper Jaw Pronounced: The upper teeth are in front of the lower teeth due to either a weak jaw or an extension of the upper jaw.

- Lower Jaw Pronounced: The lower teeth are in front of the upper teeth, causing a Bulldog-like appearance.

- Wry Jaw: The jaws do not align properly, with upper teeth to one side of the lower teeth. This is the most deleterious of the jaw problems.

Remember at all times that you are looking at a kitten, and kittens can change daily. The ears that look too tall on a kitten may turn out to be a perfect height on a cat. However, very tall ears on a kitten that is supposed to have very short ears, such as an Exotic Shorthair, are an indication that the kitten may have tall ears as an adult, and this will be considered a fault when the cat is being judged. Likewise, ears that are set too low on the head of a Maine Coon will not likely turn into perfect ears. You will have to rely on the kitten's breeder to give you his or her best evaluation of how the kitten will look as an adult, particularly when it comes to the coat and the body of the kitten.

Being able to see the parents of the kitten will also help you make your own determination. While it happens often enough that two top show-quality cats will produce many pet-quality kittens, remember that you are just starting your cattery and need to establish yourself. You do this by obtaining only top-quality kittens, exhibiting them and breeding the best male you can obtain to the best female you can obtain. Only later in your breeding program may you comfortably fit into your cattery a queen of less than show quality just because you need a specific line for outcrossing.

Understanding a Breeder's Contract

When you are ready to buy your first cat (or your second or third), you will be presented with a contract from the breeder. First, realize that the existence of the contract does not mean the breeder does not trust you. On the contrary, contracts are a very good way to make sure a good relationship does not deteriorate into a bad one because the parties to a sale did not clearly understand what was involved.

Increasingly, you will see contracts for a number of reasons:

- Breed societies require that all their members' cats be sold with a contract.

- If a state "lemon law" applies to the sale (see Chapter Eleven), the breeder *must* have a contract.

- Breeders find that having a contract clears up problems *before* they happen.

Contracts will be discussed in some detail in Chapter Eleven. At this point, as the buyer of a cat or kitten, make sure you understand several key concepts.

- There is no such thing as a "standard" contract.

- If you do not understand something in the contract, have the breeder explain it and rewrite it, if necessary.

- If there is something you want, such as the paperwork to register your new cat in another registry, make sure it is written into the contract.

- If the contract does not allow you to do something you want, such as breed the cat, do *not* buy the cat and plan to ignore that restriction. Either get the item changed or get another cat.

As a new breeder, you may find that an established breeder will raise some issues with you that might not be raised with a more experienced breeder. For example:

- If you have not bred cats before, the breeder may want you to buy and show an altered cat first, before selling you a whole cat.

- If you are inexperienced, the breeder may offer to co-own the cat so that he or she can guide (and control) both the exhibition and breeding of the cat. You may want to have the contract allow you to become the sole owner after a certain period of time.

- The breeder may want to take a kitten from a future breeding (called a *cat back*) and may, in fact, require that your first breeding be to a cat in his or her cattery.

- The breeder may want the right to control what cats or lines this cat is bred to. If so, make sure you understand exactly what this means and that you will be able to breed your cat.

Realize that the contract reflects not only the breeder's experience and restrictions imposed by breed societies and registries, but also the fact that this breeder does not know you. In fact, most responsible breeders are reluctant to sell to new breeders, knowing full well the maturity needed to manage a cattery. Their approach to selling whole males and females will reflect that caution and care for their breed, as well as their desire to start only responsible breeders.

Acquiring Your Foundation Queens

You should start by deciding how many females you can easily house and accommodate. Since you will want to start small with your breeding program and see what level of quality is produced by mating a cat from one line to a cat from another line, and since you will want to use the kittens you produce in your breeding program, you may want to start with three or four queens from different lines. These cats should be as unrelated as possible. This is an easy thing to do when you are breeding Persians, Himalayans or Maine Coons, but may be more difficult when you are specializing in a less populous breed such as Japanese Bobtails or Chartreux.

There are reasons why you would want to start with this number of queens. If you start with just one male and one female, you will have only kittens that should not be bred to one another, or to their parents. You will then be forced to acquire another cat, rather than having the luxury of a long search for just the right cat to add to your breeding program.

On the other hand, unless you start with only proven queens you run the risk that one of the queens you have acquired will be unable to breed, or may abort or reabsorb her kittens. If every one of your queens is able to breed, you may end up with a litter that is made up of only pet-quality kittens. When you begin your program, you want to try to cover as many contingencies as possible. While you will not be able to plan for everything, you should do the best you can.

Blood Typing Your Females

There are two distinct blood types among pedigreed cats, and current research suggests there may be a third. The occurrence of these types, designated as Type A and Type B, vary from breed to breed.

There are two problems connected with the disparity in blood types. The first, which affects all cats, is the fatal reaction that occurs when a cat of one blood type is infused with blood of the other type.

The second problem directly affects the pedigreed cat breeder. When a Type B queen delivers kittens with Type A blood, some of these kittens may be affected by neonatal erythrolysis, a condition in which the red blood cells of the kitten are destroyed by the maternal antibodies that gain access to the kitten through the queen's colostrum. The kittens then weaken and die. At least, that has always been the traditional view of the problem. But current research seems to show a different mechanism at work. Maternal antibodies are produced throughout the entire lactation period. But kittens with Type A blood born to a Type B queen may be unable to absorb these antibodies during the critical period of the first 16 hours. Because of their compromised immune systems, the kittens weaken and die.

In either case, we do know that Type A kittens nursing on Type B queens may die for what appears to be absolutely no reason at all. The kittens may, at first, appear to be perfectly healthy and active. By the time you notice the signs of neonatal erythrolysis, it may be too late to save the affected kittens. Some symptoms the alert breeder will notice include kittens that are no longer nursing, weakness, lassitude and general failure to thrive. Other signs include dark urine and jaundice. Clinical signs can include anemia. These symptoms may be followed by the sudden death of the kitten.

If you are breeding a Type B queen, you should assume that all resulting kittens may be affected by neonatal erthrolysis if they are permitted to nurse on the queen. You can deal with this problem by making certain you have a Type A queen who is still actively lactating and is willing to accept the newborn kittens herself.

If this is not possible, you will have to supplement the newborn litter for at least the first 16 hours of the kittens' lives. During that time you cannot let them nurse on the Type B queen at all. However, you can use

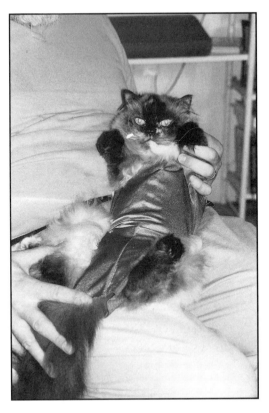

Gaiety models the garment used on Type B queens who want to have their newborn kittens with them during the first 16 hours of their life. This garment enables the queen to cuddle her kittens while it prevents them from nursing on her.

a "body stocking," custom made for the queen, that enables her to cuddle and wash the babies without having them be able to nurse. This body stocking is a simple garment, similar to a cat bathing suit, and is easily made by the breeder. Be certain the stocking covers the nipples completely and will not ride up or creep down.

Fortunately, you can easily deal with this disparity of blood types, but it is critical to know the blood types of all of your cats, especially your queens. Once, all blood typing of cats was done through the University of Pennsylvania School of Veterinary Medicine. After a while, private laboratories began to do the work as well. Now you can buy a system that enables you to do this yourself with newborn kittens. If you know that your queen is Type B, you can use the home system to type the placental blood of each baby as it is born. After the cord is cut, obtain a drop of blood and type it following the instructions exactly. In this way you will know which kittens are Type B and can be kept with the queen and which are Type A and must be hand-raised for the early critical period or transferred to a lactating queen who is Type A.

While this may sound convenient, it can be more difficult than it sounds. Sometimes kittens are born in rapid succession. When this happens, you may cut a cord and obtain a sample of blood, only to put it aside to assist in the delivery of another kitten. If this continues for two or three kittens, you may mix up the samples. You may also be assisting at a delivery in the early hours of the morning when you are tired. As you can imagine, you may easily misread the tests if you are tired. While there is always an error rate in any kind of lab test, the rate of error in instances such as this can be much higher than the normal error rate of veterinary laboratories.

In addition to the practical aspects of home-typing kittens, you are missing the opportunity to be of help to other breeders of pedigreed cats. The value of a central data bank containing blood types by breed is critical to many aspects of research on the health and welfare of pedigreed cats.

If you choose not to deal with the problem of differing blood types at all, make certain you always breed Type A queens to Type A males and Type B queens to Type B males.

BLOOD TYPES IN SELECTED BREEDS	
0 to 5 percent Type B	Siamese, Russian Blue, Tonkinese, Ocicat, Oriental Shorthair, American Shorthair, Burmese, Maine Coon, Manx
10 to 20 percent Type B	Norwegian Forest Cat, Himalayan, Persian, Sphynx, Abyssinian, Scottish Fold, Persian, Japanese Bobtail, Birman, Somali
25 to 50 percent Type B	Exotic Shorthair, British Shorthair, Devon Rex, Cornish Rex

ACQUIRING YOUR FOUNDATION SIRES

Since your foundation sire will be able to continue breeding for longer than your queens, you will want him to have the very best characteristics of the breed. While your queens may vary slightly from the standard of perfection for the breed, your male should be the very best quality you can afford.

Since it is not always easy to acquire a show-quality stud male, and since you are starting with several queens, you will have the time to acquire your second male once your foundation queens are breeding. Your second male is for the kittens who will be produced by the matings between your original foundation queens and your first stud male. Your second stud male will also be able to mate with your original foundation queens, producing kittens who are then able to mate with your original stud.

Blood Typing Your Males

It is just as important to have your working males blood typed as it is your queens. Only in this way are you assured that you are breeding Type A cats together or Type B cats together. In every breed of cat, Type B blood is recessive. This should be taken into account as you map out your breeding program.

Using Outside Stud Services

You will hear some breeders talking about taking a queen to an outside service. They mean they are arranging for a breeding between a queen in their cattery and a sire in another cattery.

There are benefits to using outside stud services. Primarily, it means you don't have to house as many whole males. Also, using an outside male can give you the new, unrelated blood you may need in your breeding program. In addition, if you are using a proven outside male, you will have the opportunity to see the kittens he has produced.

Most breeders will negotiate a contract for stud service with you (see Chapter Eleven for a checklist on stud service contracts). Generally, the fee will be the price of a show-quality kitten purchased from that breeder; in turn, the owner of the stud will guarantee two live births. If your queen does not have two live kittens, you will be able to repeat the breeding with the same stud. Sometimes, instead of money, the owner of the male will ask for the pick of the litter, generally specifying which sex they need for their cattery.

The major drawback of using outside stud services is that it violates all the rules of a closed cattery. A closed cattery is one in which cats neither come into the cattery nor go out and return. With a closed cattery you can control the environment and the exposure of your cats to any outside cats, ensuring that contagious and infectious diseases, such as feline leukemia, feline infectious peritonitis and feline AIDS, do not come into your cattery. When a cat from a closed cattery is being exhibited, this cat is usually kept away from the general cattery population.

If you have a closed cattery and still want to use outside stud services, you can if you follow some isolation and testing procedures. Before your queen goes to the male's cattery, she should be tested for infectious and contagious diseases. A certificate stating that she is free of these diseases should be provided by your veterinarian, and a copy of this should accompany your queen as she goes into the cattery of the stud male. Naturally, you will want to have proof that the tests were done on the stud male. Proof should also be provided that both your cat and the stud male are current on all immunizations. The tests on both cats should be done as close as possible to the time the female will be going to the male's cattery, and both cats must be kept isolated until they are put together. Your contract must specify that your queen is to be kept isolated from all other cats in the cattery, with the exception of the one male to whom she is being bred. After mating occurs and she returns to your cattery, she must be isolated once again and retested.

If you are concerned that the owner of the outside male may have fed both cats raw meat, include a test for toxoplasmosis when the blood tests are being performed. Once the test comes back negative and she has been examined by your veterinarian, you may admit your queen back into your cattery population.

In addition to these precautions, you must also specify in your contract that your queen is free from flea and fungal infestations, and you should have the same guarantee from the owner of the male. If you want to make certain the queen is free from ringworm, you will have to isolate her for a longer period of time. Frankly, if you have a concern about the presence of fleas or fungus in the cattery your queen is visiting, perhaps she should not be sent there in the first place.

You will also have to work out how and what your queen is to be fed and how long she is to stay at the male's cattery after she is bred. If she is traveling a distance, you may not want to have her back until her pregnancy is confirmed. If the male's cattery is close to you, you might choose to take her back to your cattery after she has been bred but before her pregnancy is confirmed. However, if you take her back immediately and the pregnancy does not take, you will have to go through the entire testing and isolation procedure all over again.

LEASING CATS

Leasing cats can be an alternative to the outright ownership of cats. The person who leases a cat (the leasee) can use the cat in their breeding program as if they are the owner, but does not have the long-term responsibilities associated with ownership.

However, leasing can present some problems.

- Breeders are extremely reluctant to enter into leases with anyone other than breeders with whom they have been working for a number of years.

- For the leasee, bringing a leased cat into the cattery carries with it all of the concerns that bringing in any cat does. And the same concerns (such as testing, isolation and the like) arise when the cat is returned to its original cattery at the end of the lease.

- Leasing involves the execution of a formal written document establishing the lease, its terms and all conditions. And that means the major registries are involved, as you'll see in the chart that follows.

If you get involved in leasing a cat, you *must* have a written agreement. It should cover at least the following points (for additional subjects, review the checklists in Chapter Eleven):

- Cat's name and registration number(s).

- Names of leasor (owner) and leasee (the person who will get possession of the cat).

- When is the leased cat to be returned to the owner, and after what tests?

- Which veterinarian examines the cat, what tests must it pass, and who pays for the tests before it leaves the leasor and before it returns to the leasor?

- Who pays for shipping costs and the necessary health certificates, both at the beginning and at the end of the lease?

- Who pays what portions of expenses while the cat is away from home?

- What happens if the leased cat becomes ill—that is, who pays for expenses, who determines what treatment is needed, and what happens if the cat dies?

- Can the leased cat be shown? If so, under what conditions?

- What cat(s) may be bred to the leased cat? What cat(s) may *not* be bred to it?

- In what registries will litters be registered?

- What is the compensation for the lease: pick of the litter (by whom and when), or payments of how much? Who owns any other kittens? Can the leasee sell them?

LEASES AND THE NATIONAL REGISTRIES			
	ACFA	CFA	TICA
Does the registry office have to be notified of leases?	yes, at the time a litter is registered	no	yes
Do copies of the lease have to be filed with the registry office?	yes, in order to register a litter	yes, along with a litter application (the owner must sign the litter application)	yes
Can a leasee sign as the owner on a litter registration?	yes, with the lease agreement attached	yes	yes

YOU KNOW YOU ARE A CAT BREEDER WHEN . . .

- The necessities of life include a Tokyo cage.

- You have screen doors *inside* the house.

- Your vacuum cleaner vendor knows your first name and smiles whenever he sees your car pull into the parking lot.

- "Doing nails" doesn't mean what it used to.

- You consider scoopable litter to be one of the ten greatest inventions of the 20th century.

- You think it's normal to have a scratching post in every room of the house.

- You don't think it's strange to have flea shampoo on the edge of your kitchen sink.

- You act insulted if someone gives you a poinsettia for Christmas.

Adapted from *101 Ways to Know You're a Cat Fancier.*

CHAPTER FOUR

Housing Your Cats

When you have a small number of neutered indoor pet cats, you do not have to worry about housing them. You can permit them to run around the house and, perhaps, even let all of them sleep on the bed.

But when you have a breeding colony of cats, housing becomes an important issue that must be planned for in advance. This does not mean you cannot have some cats that run around the house and sleep on your bed. On the contrary, almost every breeder has a retired queen or stud male around the house, now happily neutered and free to be a house pet. You will also find every breeder has that one special cat they could not use in their breeding program but also could not bear to sell. You will see that cat, now altered, as a pet. Many breeders had pet cats before they started to breed, and these cats are still their pets. So as you see, breeders are also pet owners.

However, whole cats can not be permitted to run around indiscriminately. First, if the males spray, your house will eventually become unlivable. Second, you will almost certainly end up with unplanned pregnancies. And if you have more than one whole male running free, you may not even know which male sired the litter, assuming it was just one of the males and not both. Since cats are induced ovulators (the act of copulation causes the female to ovulate), a mating by one male may produce one or more kittens and a mating later with a different male will also result in kittens—born in the same litter. When this happens, you have a litter of kittens of a specific breed but the litter cannot be registered because you cannot say for sure which male is the sire. An unregistered litter, even if you know the kittens are purebred, is not a pedigreed litter. To have a pedigreed kitten, the litter must be registerable.

If you are breeding two different breeds and let the cats run loose around the house, you may well end up with a litter of kittens that is mixed—with a queen of one breed bred by a sire of the other breed. These kittens are not even purebred, much less pedigreed.

When these things happen, you are being irresponsible and are not breeding for the long-term good of the breed. You are producing non-pedigreed pets, and this is not the goal and the purpose of pedigreed cat breeders.

There are many options when it comes to housing your breeding cats. Any of these options will permit your cats to live a happy life, but one that is controlled.

CAGING OPTIONS

While the pedigreed kitten you start your program with is still young, you must begin to consider your housing options for the short term and for the long term as well. For example, a young cat can be confined at various times in order to get him used to the idea of being caged. To start, you might consider putting the kitten in his cage with a treat. You can even feed him his meals in the cage. In this way, he associates the cage with good things and the transition becomes an easy one for him to make.

Once cats get used to the idea that the cage is where they stay for certain hours of the day and night, they accept it completely. In fact, when they are ready to be returned to the cage after they have been let out for their exercise time, many cats will just come up to the cage on their own. Cats are very much creatures of habit, and they will very quickly get used to what time they are to be caged, what time they are out for exercise, and what time they are to be returned to the cage.

The Ideal Cage

Minimum size: 30 cubic feet.

Maximum number of cats per 30 cubic feet: one, weighing four pounds or less.

All caging must take into account the size of the breed being housed.

The bottoms of the cages should be flat and *not* wire mesh.

All cages must be clean and in good repair.
Adapted from the CFA Approved Cattery Environment Inspection Form.

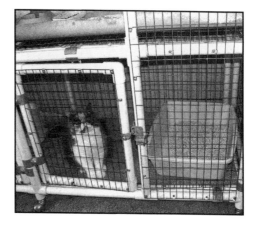

These portable cages are easily cleaned and provide a safe and comfortable environment for your cats.

There are many caging options that will fit into your own home. The basic tenets of caging for your cats are to be certain your cats have enough room to live comfortably while they are caged; that they are allowed out of their cage for adequate exercise; that their cages are easy to clean, disinfect, deodorize and maintain; and that they are easy for you when you are working with your cats or cleaning the cages. If you will be applying for certification in one of the association-sponsored cattery programs (described at the end of this chapter), you will want to start acquiring your caging early, so that your cattery meets the guidelines that will eventually be applied.

There are many styles and types of cages available. Once you have decided where you will be housing your whole males, pregnant and lactating queens with their litters, and other cats, you will be able to decide which types of cages you want to buy.

Some cages, such as those made of PVC plastic, can be purchased as individual pieces that you then put together the way you want, so that you essentially build a cage to your own specifications. These cages are lightweight and very easy to take apart and take

outside for cleaning. The easiest way to clean these cages is to use a hose with a garden sprayer attached to it that is filled with your disinfectant and deodorizer. You can use a small scrub brush to clean the rims or even use an old toothbrush for this. These cages are also easy to clean in the cattery using your disinfectant and deodorizer mixture in a spray bottle.

This floor-to-ceiling cage is built into the cattery and provides a very roomy environment for your working males.

Other cages have a coated wire cage top with a wooden bottom covered with vinyl floor tile, or with a Plexiglas bottom. The wire tops on these cages are easy to take apart and clean, but they are heavy and so are the floors of these cages.

Galvanized wire cages such as the ones you see in show halls are very handy for individual cats under certain circumstances. These cages are also easy to clean. But the bottom platforms are usually made of unpainted, lightweight wood, and this is not easy to clean or disinfect. However, this can be remedied by painting the wood with polyurethane paint, which is readily available in a hardware store or home repair center. When the paint is dry, you have a sturdy surface that is easy to clean. Placing a beach towel or bath sheet on the bottom of cages like these will make the surface warmer for your cat, and it is also easy to clean just by washing the towel in the washing machine.

If you have a section of your house that you can devote to the cattery alone, you will be able to build caging directly onto the wall surfaces. You will then be able to control the sizes of the cages by having them go from floor to ceiling and be as wide

---

Checklist for an Ideal Cattery

❏ Is there a source of fresh air by doors, windows or vents?

❏ Is the facility heated and/or cooled to a safe temperature?

❏ Is there an absence of odor?

❏ Is there an absence of moisture condensation?

❏ Is there an ample supply of artificial or natural light?

❏ Is the overall appearance clean?

❏ Are food and water bowls present and clean?

❏ Is there fresh water and fresh food?

❏ Is the food stored in a sanitary manner?

❏ Is the bedding clean?

❏ Are there sufficient clean litter boxes for the number of cats?

❏ Is there an absence of hazardous materials?

❏ Are the wall outlet plugs covered?

Adapted from the CFA Approved Cattery Environment Inspection Form.

---

as you want. Caging like this is very easy to clean, as all you have to do is to walk inside with a vacuum cleaner or a mop.

There are also some lovely custom-made cages that you can purchase from vendors at cat shows or build yourself. Just remember that any cages you have must be as easy to clean as they are pretty.

OUTFITTING YOUR CAGES

All your cages must be roomy enough to contain a litter box, food and water dishes and a bed for your cat as well as room for your cat to walk around. You should make certain the litter box area is separated from the food and water dishes. With some wire cages, you can hang the food and water dishes on the sides of the cage. You can also do this with the PVC cages by using special hangers that are made for these cages.

Cages that are walk-in size or are floor-to-ceiling cages can also contain a cat tree so your cat can jump, climb, scratch his nails and generally get some exercise. Putting them in the cage is a very good idea. Make certain you have some toys in your cage for your cat to play with. Many toys, such as balls and catnip mice, are easily contained within the cage and can not be pushed out of the bars if you buy the larger sizes.

Housing Working Males

Many breeders keep their working males (whole males used for breeding) in a room of their own and then move them into a special area when they are breeding a queen. If you are not able to provide this kind of environment for your males, you will have to cage them as comfortably as possible. Walk-in cages or floor-to-ceiling cages are ideal for working males.

With some breeds, whole males do not have problems living together. In other situations, housing more than one whole male together is just asking for spraying contests. Some males, in defending what they view as their own territory, will actually attack the other male to try to assert dominance and control. If you are going to try to house two whole males together, get them used to each other when they are young. If one whole

---

What is Cruelty in Housing?

Cats residing in the cattery facility shall be treated humanely and without neglect.

Catteries shall not allow a cat to be deprived of necessary sustenance.

Catteries shall not allow a cat to be deprived of clean water.

Catteries shall not allow a cat to be deprived of clean quarters.

Catteries shall not allow a cat to be deprived of protection from weather.

Catteries shall not allow a cat to be beaten.

Catteries shall not allow a cat to be mutilated.

Catteries shall not allow a cat to be cruelly treated.

Catteries shall not allow, through neglect, any situation to exist or persist that would cause a cat to be in distress at any time.

Adapted from the Cat Fanciers' Association.

Stud pants enable a male who sprays to be out of his cage for exercise without the danger of unwanted spraying.

male is already working and the second is a kitten, try to get them used to each other while the kitten is still young and sexually immature. By doing this, the older working male does not view the kitten as a threat to his domain and may very well settle down with him and accept him as part of his territory.

Dealing with a Spraying Male

A major difficulty in dealing with whole males is that they can spray. When a male cat sprays, he backs up to a spot and urinates in a stream. The urine of a working male becomes extremely pungent. This odor is unmistakable, and you certainly do not want him to spray indiscriminately. Fortunately, not all whole males spray. Unfortunately, some whole males spray all the time, even when they are caged. A good cattery deodorizer will be able to get rid of this smell.

HINT!

ROOM SPRAYERS THAT RUN ON BATTERIES, CONTAIN A CANISTER OF DEODORIZER AND SPRAY EVERY 20 MINUTES OR SO, ARE A GOOD WAY TO KEEP ODORS DOWN IN A CATTERY. PLACE THESE IN THE AREAS WHERE YOU KEEP YOUR LITTER BOXES AND NEAR YOUR STUD MALE'S ROOM OR CAGE. BE CAREFUL THAT THEY CANNOT SPRAY A CAT IN THE FACE.

Checklist for Cattery Cats

❑   Do the cats have good skin and coat condition?

❑   Are the cats well groomed and is the coat free from mats or knots?

❑   Do the cats have the proper weight for their size?

❑   Are there any ill cats, and if so, are they under the care of a veterinarian?

❑   Are the cats observed daily?

❑   Are there parasites present?

❑   Are the cats clean?

Adapted from the CFA Approved Cattery Environment Inspection Form.

When you have your whole male out of his cage for exercise, you can put a garment on him that is known as stud pants. Stud pants are just underwear for male cats. They go around the legs, cover the genital area and are usually fastened with Velcro strips. In the crotch area, you place a part of a thin feminine napkin in case the male sprays in his stud pants. When they are removed, you discard the pad. The pants are then easily laundered in the washing machine with a deodorizer. For some males, spraying into the pad is not comfortable and they will avoid spraying while wearing the stud pants.

An alternative to stud pants is to use disposable baby diapers on your stud male (if he is large enough). They serve the same purpose.

No matter what you use, make certain the fit is snug enough so the pants do not fall off or can get pulled off by your male or by another cat. Try getting your male used to stud pants as a young kitten, before he is sexually mature. It will take several days for your male to get used to these garments. At the beginning, the male will flop around and act as if he is unable to walk. Keep the pants or diaper on him for a little while and gradually increase the time he wears these pants or diapers. Despite what it may look like when you first attempt to get your male used to stud pants, he will eventually grow accustomed to the feeling of wearing the pants and will be able to run and jump as he normally does.

If your working male sprays in his cage, you can drape the cage with sheets or disposable diapers so the spray is absorbed by these items before it gets on the floor, carpet or walls. Some males will choose a particular spot where they will always spray, so you can confine your precautions to that area. If your male sprays all over, you will have to make certain the cage is draped as much as possible. If you have a male who sprays in his cage, you may have to change these hangings several times each day to make certain your entire cattery does not smell like male urine. Unfortunately, shower curtains do not seem to work—the urine just streams down them into a puddle instead of being absorbed.

Fortunately, once a male has been neutered, his urine smell will gradually return to normal and he should stop spraying. If he does not stop spraying within a few months, your veterinarian can treat him with tranquilizers or hormones to stop this behavior.

> **HINT!**
>
> WHEN USING A CAGE TO CON-
> FINE A FEMALE IN SEASON AND
> A WORKING MALE TOGETHER
> FOR A BREEDING, MAKE CER-
> TAIN THE MALE WILL HAVE A
> FLOOR SURFACE WHERE HE
> CAN GET SOME TRACTION. IF
> THE SURFACE IS TOO SLICK, HE
> WON'T BE ABLE TO GET PROPER
> FOOTING AND WILL BE UNABLE
> TO BREED THE QUEEN.

HOUSING A PREGNANT QUEEN

For most of her pregnancy, your queen should continue to carry on her normal routine. Let her run and exercise as she did when she was not pregnant. A couple of days before your queen is due, you will want to place her in the cage where she will deliver her kittens. This is for her safety. Professional, responsible breeders of pedigreed cats do not permit their queens to just deliver their kittens wherever they choose.

If your queen is permitted to roam the house when she is due to deliver, she may find an excellent hiding place and have her kittens where you will not be able to find her. Then, if something goes wrong, you will not

A cattery should be well equipped and have everything within easy reach.

be able to help her. If she finds a really good hiding place, or a place too small for you to get to her, you will have no idea of what is happening. If you permit your queen to run loose, having her kittens anywhere she chooses to have them, you may lose the kittens or even lose your queen if something goes wrong.

A queening cage should be a comfortable place for your queen. Instead of a bed, you will want to cage her with her birthing box so she can get used to it. Make certain her water dish is kept hanging on the side of the cage or is a shallow dish with a small amount of water that you can refill frequently. You want to handle the water this way for the time she has small kittens. If she gets restless or wants to move the kittens around, you do not want her to drop them in a dish of water so full that the baby will drown.

You also want to make certain her litter box is always kept clean, as some queens try to have their kittens in the litter box. This may sound like an appropriate place, but you do not want your queen to get excreta in her birth canal or in the mouth of a newborn kitten.

In addition to making your queen comfortable, you will also want to make certain you are comfortable, since you will be with your queen when she is in labor and when she delivers. Be sure you have a chair to sit on, because labor and delivery can last for several hours.

Also make sure the equipment you will need for the delivery is easily accessible, as you do not want to have to go looking for something you need right away. The equipment you will need for the delivery can be kept in a plastic, lidded box under the queen's cage. Plastic is the best for this because it can be easily cleaned.

You will also want to be able to reach comfortably into the cage. You should have adequate light, and the temperature of the room should be comfortable for both of you. You should be able to shut off your queening areas from the rest of the cattery, as you do not want some of your other cats to decide they want to get involved with the birthing process. Since queens usually deliver at night, you might want to try to have the queening cage in your bedroom or as close to your bedroom as possible. If your queen's room is a distance away, you might consider using a baby monitor to monitor the room when your queen is due to deliver. When she is in labor, you might be able to hear her nesting in her birthing box or moving around in her queening cage.

Once your queen has delivered, you will be able to let her out of the cage for exercise, so you want to be sure the cage is safe for the kittens when they are without their mother.

HOUSING KITTENS

It is surprising how very early the smallest kittens will try—and succeed—to get out of the birthing box and explore their world. For this reason, the bars of the cage where your newborn kittens will begin their lives should be close enough together so that the kittens cannot stick their heads through the bars and get stuck. If you feel this may be a problem, you can cover part of the cage from the inside. The easiest way to do this is by buying a roll of the padding that is used in a human baby's crib to protect the baby from hurting himself on the bars of the crib. You can attach this padding to the inside of the cage using clothespins.

You should be able to close off the area where the kittens are housed, if need be, even after they are delivered. Sometimes one of your other cats may be so curious that she will stick her paws through the cage bars to try to touch the kittens. While this is not necessarily an aggressive act, the cat may accidentally claw the kitten as she tries to pull it close to her.

When the queen is out of the cage to exercise, the baby cage should be kept closed. You may think it is more convenient to keep it open so she can come back when she wants to, but there are other issues. For example, some cats will try to steal the kittens of a queen. This is not meant to be harmful behavior, but the cat who is trying to take the kittens can inadvertently harm them. Also, if the birthing queen returns to find her kittens missing, she can become extremely agitated.

Common Poisonous Houseplants

Keep these houseplants out of reach of any of your cats or kittens. They are considered toxic.

Amaryllis	Holly
Avocado	Hyacinth
Azalea	Lily-of-the-Valley
Balsam	Mistletoe
Bird of Paradise	Peony
Cactus	Poinsettia
Caladium	Poppy
Chrysanthemum	Sweetpea
Elephant Ear	Tobacco
Eunonymus	Tulip

Cat-Proofing

Once the kittens have opened their eyes and you feel they are old enough, you will want to let them explore a larger and larger area. In order to keep the kittens, as well as your other cats, safe, you will want to go through your cattery and cat-proof everywhere a kitten might go.

One of the easiest ways to do this is to crawl on the floor and look at things from a cat's eye view. You should be looking for small nooks and narrow areas where cats can hide and not be found. You also want to make sure that any small objects they might try to swallow and may choke on are eliminated. Watch for loose cloth they can pull. Make sure that all electrical outlets are covered.

Some adult cats are notorious kitten thieves. They do not harm the kittens; they just want to adopt them for a little while. If you have a cat like this, watch her closely when the kittens are out of their cage. Some of the greatest kitten thieves can be male cats, so do not suspect only the females if you find one kitten being snatched. If you do have a kitten thief, you may find that they tend to take the kittens to the same "safe" place each time.

Once you are sure their area is safe, let the kittens out to explore and sit back and enjoy these beautiful, delightful little kittens as they find out about the world.

CATTERY INSPECTION AND CERTIFICATION PROGRAMS

A cattery inspection and certification program is a program sponsored by a cat registry that allows a cattery to advertise that it has passed an inspection. At present, two of the national cat registries, CFA and TICA, have cattery inspection programs. The older one is CFA's. Over time, other registries may initiate similar programs.

Why Should You Participate?

Participating in one of the cattery inspection programs has several benefits for you.

- It forces you to look at your cattery's overall management annually.

- It brings your veterinarian to the cattery, not only to conduct the inspection but also to help you by suggesting changes you can make in its operation or layout.

- Once you pass an inspection, you can advertise that your cattery has been certified. Some breeders

Checklist for a Safe Cattery Environment

❑ Are there working smoke detectors in the cattery?

❑ Are there working carbon monoxide detectors in the cattery?

❑ Are enough carriers readily available in case all cats must be removed to a safe place?

❑ Are all poisons kept secure and away from the cats?

❑ Is the telephone number of the National Animal Poison Control Center readily available?

❑ Are all drugs kept secure and away from the cats?

❑ Is there an emergency kit readily available?

❑ Is there a working fire extinguisher available?

❑ In case something happens while you are away, does someone (the police department, your insurance agent, a neighbor) know how many cats you have?

believe this gives them a competitive advantage, particularly in selling pet-quality kittens to people unfamiliar with the reputations of many catteries.

Inspection Is Not a License

It must be stressed that cattery inspection and certification is not the same as, or a substitute for, a kennel license. While it is not often used by cat breeders, catteries can (and do) receive a license from the U.S. Department of Agriculture as a "kennel" (the only term they have to describe this type of facility). That program, which is beyond the scope of this book, involves coordination with state officials, including state licensing.

Under the kennel licensing program, the cattery has a scheduled inspection and is also subject to unannounced inspections by the licensing authorities. That inspection covers not only the physical facilities (as do the registry programs), but also involves a review of health records, immunization records and the like.

One of the benefits of a USDA kennel license is that it exempts the kennel from local government licensing and inspection procedures. Given the frequency with which such initiatives are merely disguised efforts by the animal rights movement to put responsible breeders out of business, it is not surprising to find that some catteries have sought refuge under the USDA program to avoid punitive local initiatives.

Who Conducts the Inspection?

In both the CFA and TICA programs, the inspection is conducted by a licensed veterinarian, with both the veterinarian's inspection fee and the registry's certification fees (about $20) being paid by you, the breeder. Under the TICA program, the veterinarian must be a small animal veterinarian.

To initiate the inspection, you arrange for a veterinarian to visit your cattery. That means the veterinarian is the regular veterinarian for your cattery, although this is not specifically required by the programs. On arriving, your veterinarian is given a copy of the inspection form, which you must obtain from the national office of the association. The veterinarian must complete this form during the inspection and then sign it.

Under the CFA program, the veterinarian mails this evaluation (and the inspection fee) directly to the office. Under TICA's program, you return it (and the fee) to the TICA office. In each case, the veterinarian also keeps a copy of the inspection report for his or her records.

Your veterinarian will check that all your cats are receiving nutritous food served in a clean, sanitary environment.

What Does the Veterinarian Look At?

The benchmark here is the CFA program, since it was the first. The TICA program is somewhat similar, with a few significant differences. However, these programs can change at any time, and it is important for you to get a copy of the registry's most recent guidelines and requirements before your cattery is inspected.

Caging: Your veterinarian establishes whether or not the cats are caged, the sizes of cages you have and whether that space is adequate. He or she must also examine the cages' state of repair and cleanliness.

In the TICA program, breeding males and females, as well as near-term pregnant and nursing queens and kittens, must be segregated.

The Cats: The veterinarian is required to examine all of the cats to make sure they have good skin and coat condition, and must check to see that all cats are well groomed, without matted fur, and of proper weight for their type. The veterinarian must also make sure there is either an absence of parasites or an acceptable treatment program in process. Finally, the veterinarian must establish that *all* cats receive proper veterinary care when needed and are observed daily by a responsible person.

In the case of TICA, the veterinarian must also establish that the cats appear to be content and well-socialized and that all kittens are isolated from the cattery colony for their first six weeks.

Facilities and ventilation: Your veterinarian checks for adequate fresh air, makes sure heat and cooling is proper, makes sure odor and condensation are not present, and checks for the amount and uniform distribution of light.

Under the TICA program, you must have smoke detectors and fire extinguishers in the cattery; and an isolation area must be used for new, incoming, show or ill cats. There must also be an isolated birthing area.

Sanitation: Your veterinarian checks the overall appearance of any areas where cats are kept or allowed to roam, including a check for the absence of odor. The veterinarian checks for clean litter boxes and the absence of dust, dirt, dried food and fecal matter, and makes sure there is sufficient clean fresh water, food and bedding.

In the case of the TICA program, the veterinarian must also establish that used litter is being disposed of in a sanitary manner. In addition, the veterinarian must establish that all medications and vaccines are stored properly and that all chemicals, cleaning agents and toxic plants are inaccessible to cats.

> ## WARNING!
>
> NOT ALL VETERINARIANS ARE WILLING TO SIGN THE TICA FORM, SINCE IT DEALS WITH ACTIONS THE BREEDER MUST TAKE IN THE FUTURE WHEN THE VETERINARIAN IS NOT ON THE PREMISES, SUCH AS ISOLATING CATS WHO ARE BEING ACTIVELY EXHIBITED. SINCE YOUR VETERINARIAN CANNOT POSSIBLY MONITOR WHAT YOU DO EVERY DAY, MANY FEEL THAT THEY CANNOT PROPERLY STATE THAT YOU ARE, IN FACT, DOING WHAT THE PROGRAM REQUIRES. THEY TAKE THE POSITION THAT THEY CAN ONLY CERTIFY WHAT THEY SEE— WHICH IS YOUR FACILITIES AND THE CONDITION THEY ARE IN. IN ADDITION, SOME VETERINARIANS DISAGREE WITH THE ISOLATION PROTOCOLS IMPLICIT IN THE TICA PROGRAM, AND FOR THAT REASON MAY ALSO DECLINE TO PARTICIPATE. THEY HAVE THE RIGHT TO REFUSE TO SIGN THE TICA FORM, EVEN THOUGH YOUR CATTERY MAY BE AN EXCELLENT ONE.

Food: Your veterinarian checks on the amount, nutritional value and proper storage of all food.

Other: Your veterinarian checks that each cat has adequate space, checks that there is a sufficient number of litter boxes, examines for overall cleanliness and for the absence of hazardous materials, open flames or uncovered wall sockets.

In the TICA program, your sales contracts must require that all pet/companion kittens are to be altered.

In the CFA program the inspecting veterinarian must, in writing, explain all items he or she has rated as "unacceptable" or "below minimum standard." TICA's rules permit the veterinarian to make written comments, but don't require it.

When the veterinarian's written report is received by the registry, it is scored. The breeder is notified of the results by mail. That notice advises the breeder if the cattery has passed the inspection. If the cattery passed, the notice states what designation the cattery can then use in its advertising. The available designations are as follows (higher first):

- CFA: CFA Approved Cattery of Excellence
  CFA Approved Cattery

- TICA: TICA Outstanding Cattery
  TICA Cattery of Merit

Only after receiving this approval notice is the breeder permitted to use these designations in their advertising, and then only for one year. Catteries must be reinspected annually to keep their certification current. The designation cannot be used if the cattery does not have a current inspection certificate.

If buying a kitten from an inspected cattery is important to you, you should also check with CFA or TICA to be sure the designation has not expired or has not been withdrawn by the association.

Is One Program Better?

Very few catteries will participate in more than one inspection program. While both inspections can be done at the same time, it still involves paying two fees each year for certification.

Cattery of Excellence is a designation you can display proudly.

The choice of which program to use usually depends on one or more of several considerations:

- Active affiliation: The registry with which you and your cattery are most closely involved is likely to be the one whose program you will consider using.

- Market for your kittens: If most of your buyers (or potential buyers) are in one part of the country and that area is dominated by shows from one association, you may want to use that association's program.

- Difference in the focus of the two programs: The CFA program is aimed at the physical nature of the facilities and the condition of the cats and kittens. The TICA program, on the other hand, includes within it requirements for how the cattery is managed, such as isolation policies and contents of contracts. In addition, the breeder must be a current TICA member and agree to subscribe to TICA's "voluntary code of ethics."

Why Don't All Catteries Have Inspection Certificates?

What does certification actually mean? The language on the CFA certificate puts it well:

> "The approval relates to the physical conditions of the cattery at the time of inspection by an independent, licensed veterinarian. It is not intended to nor does it guarantee the physical condition or health of any cat or kitten housed in said cattery or owned by the breeder, nor is it an endorsement of the breeder."

There are a few legitimate reasons why catteries may not have or may not be able to get approval under an inspection program. If a cattery is not registered with either TICA or CFA, it cannot participate in that registry's inspection program. However, most active U.S. catteries are registered with at least one of these two national registries.

In a few parts of the country it is virtually impossible to arrange for a veterinarian to make a house call, which is absolutely necessary in order to have the cattery inspected. This is most often true in some urban areas.

Finally, some breeders do not want to go to the extra expense required to have their cattery formally inspected and to pay the fee to the association for their certification.

> ### Key Elements of Cattery Health Care
>
> A cattery should promptly provide medical care to any cat in distress and/or any cat exhibiting signs of severe illness.
>
> Cats should be observed daily and diseased cats should be promptly provided with medical care.
>
> A vaccination program, under the advice of a veterinarian, is highly recommended.
>
> Cats should be kept clean, free of severe coat mats and generally groomed sufficiently to maintain a healthy condition.
>
> *Adapted from The Cat Fanciers' Association.*

But the biggest and most important reason may be that the cattery cannot pass an inspection.

Is There Any Enforcement Mechanism?

As a matter of policy, neither TICA nor CFA will intervene in private disputes between the catteries registered with them and buyers of their cats or kittens. This policy has been extended to the cattery inspection programs as well. That means the only sanctions that can be imposed on an inspected cattery are withdrawal of its certification or disciplinary action by the association against the cattery *if* the certificate was obtained by fraud. In neither case will the enforcement be swift, nor will it likely settle a breeder-buyer dispute.

YOU KNOW YOU ARE A CAT BREEDER WHEN . . .

- You can't help going into a fit of giggles when you see a stud finder in the local hardware store.

- You have your best stud neutered and only half-jokingly discuss having his equipment bronzed.

- Your child has learned the basic facts of life: that there are four sexes—male, female, neuter, and spay; and which ones are allowed in with which others and at what times.

- When your own hair mats, your first thought is to shave it off.

- You remember people by their cattery names instead of their own names.

- You see the veterinarian more than all your own doctors combined.

- You grill the vet who is treating your cat, but you barely say two words to your own doctor at your check-ups.

Adapted from *101 Ways to Know You're a Cat Fancier.*

CHAPTER FIVE

The Mating Process

SIGNS YOUR QUEEN IS IN SEASON

Female cats go into season several times each year. It is when they are in season that they are receptive to being bred. A cat's normal seasonal cycle will last anywhere from seven to ten days. While each cat is individual and has her own cycle, a female generally has her first season around the age of seven to nine months.

As a very general rule, long-haired cats go into their first season later than short-haired cats, and younger cats cycle more frequently and with more regularity than older cats.

The first season of any female may be light and may go unnoticed by the breeder. This is generally called a baby heat. However, if you have a whole male running free with your whole female kitten, she may not go unnoticed by him. He may very well breed this young kitten, resulting in an unplanned pregnancy.

While there are some traditional signs that indicate your queen is in season, cats are individuals and will vary in the way they show they are ready to be bred. Most queens

---

HINT!

FOR BEST RESULTS, YOUR QUEEN SHOULD BE APPROXIMATELY EIGHT TO FOURTEEN MONTHS OLD BEFORE HER FIRST MATING.

---

will roll around on the floor and periodically assume a position where they lengthen their body, carry their tail to one side and knead their paws on the ground as if they are inviting mounting by a male. Cats who are vocal may call loudly, and even those breeds that are not so vocal may become much more talkative when they are in season. However, some cats are quite silent, exhibiting virtually no signs of their readiness at all.

With some cats, you must get to know them very well in order to determine when they are in season. If you know your cat well, you will be able to pick up the very subtle signs she exhibits. Perhaps she becomes much more friendly to you, nuzzling and purring more frequently, or she may just roll on the floor under your feet. All these signs are subtle indications that she is ready to be bred.

When Pregnancy Is Not Desired

Sometimes your queen will be in a really strong season (also called *heat*) at a time when she is not able to be bred. Perhaps she is resting between litters or perhaps at the time she would be due to deliver her kittens, you will not be able to be there to assist her. In these cases, you can either confine her until her season is over or you can induce a false pregnancy.

Generally, confinement until the season is over is easier. However, inducing false pregnancy may be preferred in some situations. For example, if your queen cycles quite often (such as every two or three weeks), a false pregnancy might be something to consider. In most cases, when you induce a false pregnancy the queen will stop cycling for the average duration of a true pregnancy—more than 60 days.

> **HINT!**
>
> BREEDERS REPORT THAT WAIT-
> ING MORE THAN ONE YEAR
> BETWEEN MATINGS SEEMS TO
> RESULT IN MORE DIFFICULTY
> GOING INTO A STRONG LABOR
> AND, THEREFORE, A HIGHER
> RATE OF CESAREAN SECTIONS.

One method of inducing a false pregnancy is by using a slender but strong glass rod, such as a thermometer, to stimulate ovulation. Soak a glass rod in rubbing alcohol for half an hour to clean it of all bacteria. Be certain you completely rinse all the alcohol off the rod with warm tap water, because alcohol will sting the mucous membranes of the vagina. Then insert the rod into the vagina of your queen and move it very gently a short distance into and out of the vagina. Your queen will react as if she had been bred.

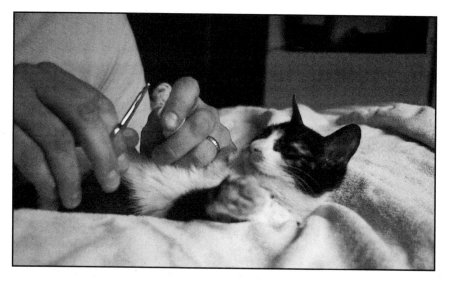

Make certain you clip the claws of both the queen and her mate before putting them together.

The second way to induce a false pregnancy is to use either a vasectomized or a castrated male who still has the ability to mount a female cat and to penetrate (but not impregnate) a queen in heat. You can have a male cat vasectomized, but this is generally done only at veterinary hospitals. A few males who have been castrated still retain the ability to mount and penetrate, so these males can also be useful in your cattery to take queens out of heat. (With either a vasectomized or a castrated male, you will want to wait for awhile after the surgery to make certain they are no longer fertile.) These males are called "teaser toms" and are highly valued for their ability to mate but not impregnate queens.

You must be careful not to use either method of inducing false pregnancy too often.

> **WARNING!**
>
> THERE IS CURRENTLY NO SAFE METHOD OF ORAL CONTRACEPTIVE FOR USE IN CATS AVAILABLE IN THE UNITED STATES. SOME CONTRACEPTIVE PILLS ARE BEING USED IN EUROPE, BUT THIS FORMULATION IS NOT THE SAME AS THE ONE AVAILABLE TO VETERINARIANS IN THE UNITED STATES. ALL ORAL CONTRACEPTIVES AVAILABLE HERE HAVE LONG-TERM SIDE EFFECTS AND SHOULD NOT BE USED IN CATS.

Remember that all you are doing is fooling your queen's body into thinking it is pregnant. This false pregnancy is still a stress, though, since the queen's body, including her endocrine system, starts acting as if she is really pregnant. Her metabolism changes, allowing her to build up body weight; her body gets ready to make milk and, in some cases, may even produce milk at the end of the "pregnancy." The rare queen may even go into a mild labor at the right time. False pregnancy also can result in a uterine infection if it is done too often.

WARNING!

WAIT SIX MONTHS BEFORE YOUR QUEEN IS BRED AGAIN AFTER A MISCARRIAGE.

A breeding male grasps the neck of the female during mating in order to maintain the control he needs.

Mating

Once you establish that your queen is in season, you should put her together with the mate you have chosen for her. The female should be brought to her mate, rather than the other way around. If a male is transported to an area he doesn't know, he will spend too much time examining his new environment to pay enough attention to his mate.

It is critical in breeding pedigreed cats that the mating take place under controlled conditions. The breeding area should be somewhat confined, with a floor that provides good traction for the cats. It should be a secure area with no access for any other males. You should provide a shelf or a cat tree so the male has some place to go if the queen turns on him and attempts to scratch him after breeding.

The breeding area should be easily accessible to you. While you will want to be sure to document that a mating has occurred, you might not necessarily want to spend all your time observing the entire mating process, as it can go on for hours or days.

Many times, especially if the queen is in a very strong season, mating will occur rather rapidly. With a queen who is extremely receptive and a male who is experienced, up to four matings have been known to occur within the first hour after the pair was put together. This is unusual, however.

> **HINT!**
>
> IF YOUR QUEEN HAS THREE UNSUCCESSFUL MATINGS WITH THE SAME MALE, TRY A DIFFERENT MALE.

Some males will take their time, and you may see the sire "talking" to the queen and preening himself, rubbing against her and washing her. This can be a very interesting courtship ritual and can go on for hours, but eventually, mating will occur. During mating, the male mounts the female, grabbing her neck in his teeth in order to control his position and limit her movement.

After penetration and ejaculation, the male will generally jump away, as the withdrawal of his barbed penis may cause the queen some discomfort. (You must provide an area for him to leap away, as the queen will sometimes attempt to scratch him.) At this point the queen usually gives a loud cry, known as the mating cry, and you may be able to document a mating if you are able to hear what is going on. If you witness the mating, you may feel that it appears rather dramatic or even brutal.

After the male has withdrawn from the queen, she will usually roll around on the ground for awhile and wash herself vigorously.

Once you establish that mating is occurring, check the cats frequently. Pay special attention to the neck of the queen, as some trauma may occur to this area. Also, be certain that both cats have adequate food, water and litter if you are leaving them together for awhile. If the queen stops showing signs of being in season, you may separate the cats. Most breeders, however, will leave the cats together until they hear a set number of matings over a set number of days. For example, you may decide to leave the cats together for three days and confirm three matings on each of those days.

Cats are one of the very few mammals that are induced ovulators. This means the act of mating stimulates the female to release eggs so that they can be fertilized; fertilization usually occurs approximately 24 hours after mating. Induced ovulators can be made pregnant at each intercourse with the male. If your males are not controlled and if two different males are able to breed your queen while she is in season, then she can become pregnant by both of the males. Needless to say, this is not a proper breeding practice.

HINT!

FOR BEST RESULTS, YOUR MALE SHOULD BE EIGHT MONTHS TO ONE YEAR OLD BEFORE HE STARTS BREEDING.

While your pair should mate several times while the queen is in season, you will not know which of the matings resulted in a pregnancy. For this reason, you must be *very careful* about recording the dates when the matings took place. This will be your key to determining your queen's due date—the day on which she should have her kittens.

While pregnancy may not occur at the first mating, you will find that if your counting is consistent every time you breed a cat, you will have a fairly good idea of your queen's due date. If you have had to leave your cats together for several days without supervision, check your queen daily for any roughness on the back of her neck. Mark this on your calendar as evidence of breeding.

With the new ultrasound machines that are used by veterinarians, you will be able to establish a fairly close estimate of your queen's due date during her pregnancy checks.

The Reluctant Sire

While you do not want your male to be overly aggressive and injure your queen, you also do not want a male to be so reluctant that mating never occurs. There are many reasons for reluctance on the part of males:

- Your potential sire may just be too young to breed. Male cats mature slightly later than female cats, and many males will begin to show signs of sexual maturity before they are actually sexually mature. In this instance, the best thing to do is just to wait until your male gets a bit older.

- Some males are reluctant because they do not know the queen being confined with them. In this case, the courting ritual can last until the queen is out of season.

- Some males who are normally confined may feel a new cat is an unwelcome addition to their area, even if she is a queen in season. Male cats become extremely acclimated to a set routine, and anything that changes this routine may be viewed with great reluctance and displeasure.

- Some males just seem not to respond to one particular female.

Many times, all that is necessary to change a male cat's reluctance is time and patience. However, if your male never breeds a female even though he has been put together with different, proven queens, take him to your veterinarian for a thorough check-up. If necessary, your veterinarian may draw blood and have it checked to make certain the male has adequate levels of hormones. If he does not and you still want to use him for breeding, discuss with your veterinarian the possibility of hormone supplements.

> ### HINT!
>
> PUT A FIRST-TIME MALE WITH A PROVEN FEMALE. THE EXPERIENCED QUEEN WILL MAKE HER INTERESTS KNOWN TO HIM AND HE MAY BE BETTER ABLE TO BREED HER.
>
> THE REVERSE IS ALSO TRUE: A VIRGIN (UNBRED) QUEEN IS BEST TAKEN TO AN EXPERIENCED WORKING MALE.

The Reluctant Queen

Queens may be reluctant in two very different ways. The first problem is the queen who just does not seem to come into season. This may be due to inadequate light in the cattery and can be easily remedied by adding lights, especially those that approximate the natural light spectrum. This also happens in winter. Cats in the wild tend to come into season in the late winter or early spring, when the days lengthen. So your reluctant queen may very well begin to cycle as soon as spring arrives.

Reluctance in queens may also occur when stud males are kept in a completely separate room. If the queen cannot smell the males, she may not go into season. You might consider cleaning the litter boxes your queens use with a dilute solution of chlorine bleach. The lingering odor of the bleach, while not perceptible to you, may stimulate the queen because it is somewhat similar to the scent made by an intact male.

Some queens, even though they are in season, may not permit a male to approach them. There are several reasons why this may happen. The first is that she may not feel comfortable with the new environment of the breeding area or breeding cage, and wants to get to know the new area first. Avoid this problem by having your queen visit the breeding area, without a male, several times so she gets to know it.

Your queen may also feel uncomfortable with the male cat she is put in with, if she does not know him. This may be remedied by having the two cats live with each other to let the female get used to the male. After awhile he is no longer an unknown cat, and when she goes into season, she may very well let him approach her for breeding.

If you do not want to have your queen living in the same cage as your male, let her live in a cage next to him or in the same room as his cage. This way she gets to know him and he becomes a familiar cat in the cattery. Of course, with your male in stud pants having the freedom to run loose in the cattery at certain times, he will be a member of the colony and all the cats will know him.

In other situations, your queen may not have adequate hormone levels to become pregnant or to maintain a pregnancy. Your veterinarian can help determine this and can usually remedy the situation by administering hormone therapy.

If you have a queen who continually exhibits signs of being in season but is a reluctant breeder, you might want to make certain she is actually going into season. To determine this, take her to your veterinarian while she is exhibiting seasonal behavior and have your veterinarian take a vaginal smear. Examination of the cells in this smear will reveal whether your queen is truly in a seasonal cycle.

There are, of course, medical reasons why queens do not cycle. One common problem is ovarian cysts. This can be diagnosed by your veterinarian using sophisticated ultrasound equipment. If your veterinarian does not find evidence of cysts while viewing the abdomen using ultrasound, ask that he or she also view the side area of the queen. An ovarian cyst may be more easily viewed from the side of the body.

Your queen may also have a problem of inadequate hormones. This can be diagnosed by blood testing. At day 25 of a queen's pregnancy, the hormone progesterone, which is normally produced by the ovaries, begins to be produced by the placenta. Progesterone helps to make certain the pregnancy goes to term. If this hormone is not produced efficiently by the placenta, the pregnancy can be lost through a spontaneous abortion or by having the fetuses re-absorbed by the queen. If you find this is your problem, ask your veterinarian about supplemental hormone therapy.

DIFFICULTIES IN BREEDING

You will not usually find too many physical difficulties with breeding. The one that seems most apparent is differences in size. While the majority of males in every breed are larger than the females, this size difference can be quite obvious in certain breeds of pedigreed cats. If your male is much larger than your female, he may have some problem mounting her, holding her neck and completing penetration, simply because he is so much longer.

Some breeders will assist a breeding by holding the queen down in position so the male can breed her. This may well work, but it is *not* recommended. If your queen is being bred against her will, she might very well panic, especially when the male withdraws his penis and she feels pain. In her panic, she may turn not only on the male, but also on the breeder who is holding her down. You can get injured this way, and if she is frustrated at not being able to get to you, your queen may go after the male in a very aggressive manner and harm him. In addition, there is the matter of ethics. If we really care as much about our cats as we claim we do, it is not ethical for us to participate in what is the feline equivalent of rape.

We start our breeding program with several queens to protect our program from all those small difficulties that inevitably arise. If one of our

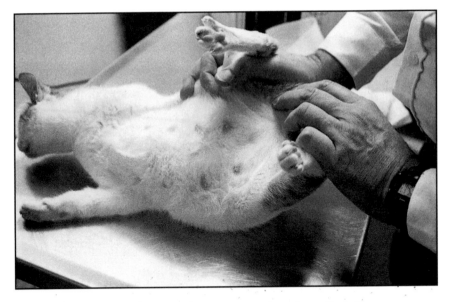

Jasmine, 55 days pregnant, exhibits pink, prominent nipples and a swollen belly.

queens does not become a breeder, then it may be a problem but hardly an insurmountable one. We can always acquire a new queen. Force and intentionally inflicting pain have absolutely no place in a cattery.

Pedigreed cats are a precious gift, and while we are breeders, we also have a responsibility to our cats to protect them from harm and pain. If your attitude toward pedigreed cats is not consistent with the concepts of care, love and protection for them, you should not be breeding at all.

Breeders of pedigreed cats are dealing with nature, and we all know that nature is not always pretty, nor is it cooperative. There is only so far you should be willing to go and still call yourself a responsible breeder. Our concern is ultimately for the cats we own and not for a litter of

---

IMPORTANT!

AFTER YOUR QUEEN HAS BEEN BRED, YOU MUST TREAT HER AS IF SHE IS PREGNANT, EVEN BEFORE YOU KNOW FOR CERTAIN. NEVER GIVE A POSSIBLY PREGNANT QUEEN ANYTHING STRONGER THAN REGULAR FOOD AND WATER, AND IF YOUR QUEEN MUST SEE YOUR VETERINARIAN FOR ANY REASON, ALWAYS TELL HIM OR HER THAT YOUR CAT HAS BEEN BRED.

kittens that may or may not be born some time in the distant future. Until artificial insemination is readily available and the resulting litters are accepted by the cat registries, you will just have to face the difficulties that can occur when breeding pedigreed cats and realize that everything will not always go just as you planned.

SIGNS OF PREGNANCY

After you have witnessed your queen being bred, watch very closely for signs of pregnancy. Most breeders look for the nipples to become more apparent and to turn a reddish hue. This is known as *pinking up*. However, many queens do not pink up until late in their pregnancy and some don't pink up until they deliver their kittens.

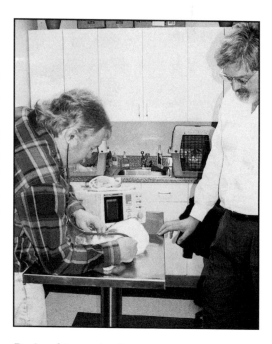

The first sign of pregnancy may be a change in behavior. Most queens will become extremely affectionate when they are pregnant; they purr, knead their paws and rub themselves on their owners.

Dr. Stanglein examines Jasmine.

Some queens will even roll on the ground as if they are in season again.

A clinical diagnosis of pregnancy can be made by palpation between 15 and 20 days and by X-ray at 45 days. Your veterinarian can confirm a pregnancy much earlier than this using ultrasound, but how early depends on how sensitive the ultrasound machine is and how skilled the veterinarian is in interpreting its readings.

There are many different methods of counting the days from the time the queen was bred until her due date. One way is to count the number of days of gestation from the day of the first verified mating. A queen's gestation can range from 58 to 71 days. This will vary not only from breed to breed, but also from line to line within a breed and even from cat to cat in a particular line.

As a general rule, a queen who delivers her kittens at 67 days the first time will generally deliver at 67 days, or a day later, each time she is pregnant. If you count her days the same way after mating for each pregnancy, you will have a fairly good idea of her due date with every delivery.

WHEN TO ADD NEW CATS TO YOUR PROGRAM

Adding new cats to your cattery is important when you find you are facing a situation where you will begin inbreeding unless you add new cats. It may also become necessary when a female you had planned on for your breeding program just does not breed good-quality kittens, or does not breed at all. You can also have a queen who does well when she is pregnant but is just not a good mother. While you can always move her kittens onto another wet queen, you will have to do this every time she is bred or you will end up hand-raising her entire litter.

> **IMPORTANT!**
>
> A PREGNANCY THAT RESULTS IN STILLBORN KITTENS STILL MUST COUNT AS A PREGNANCY.

You can generally keep your working males at stud for several years. As they get older, the number of sperm cells produced in their ejaculate may decrease, but that may be the only difference between a younger male and an older male. The fact that working males can breed for several years is one of the reasons you want them to be as close in conformation to the standard of perfection as possible.

You will want to constantly study the standard of perfection for your breed, as well as check the cats of your breed very carefully in the show hall, to make certain that your male does, in fact, still conform to the standards as closely as he did when he was first used as a working male. Over time, certain refinements occur naturally in many breeds, so that your first show-quality cat may be slightly different in appearance from the cats who are currently winning at the shows.

If your older male does not seem to be producing kittens anymore, make sure he has tried to impregnate various queens. If he has had various queens and none of them became pregnant, have him checked by your veterinarian.

Whole females should not be bred for more than five to six years, assuming they have had no difficulty with their pregnancies, deliveries or the care of their kittens. You will know when your queen is no longer viable for breeding. Older queens tend to have more difficult labors and deliveries. When your queen is at risk from being pregnant and delivering kittens, she should be spayed.

You know you are a cat breeder when . . .

- When you hear "queen," you don't think of Elizabeth.

- You say, "Thanks for the offer of a free trip to Hawaii, but I have a litter due that weekend."

- You refer to your uncle or aunt as your father's littermate.

- You are constantly on the lookout for a better spray bottle.

- Your rapid dial phone has your vet at the #1 slot.

- You comb your cat's hair more often than your own.

- The spouse with the fewest cats in their lap must answer the door or phone.

Adapted from *101 Ways to Know You're a Cat Fancier.*

CHAPTER SIX

Pregnancy and Delivery

While you will want to be very careful with your pregnant queen, pregnancy is normal and natural and your queen should not be treated much differently from your other cats. However, you will want to watch her very carefully and monitor her food and exercise. She will need prenatal care and will have to be prepared for her delivery in the birthing box.

FEEDING THE PREGNANT QUEEN

If you regularly feed a nutritionally balanced diet, you really do not need to change foods just because your queen is pregnant. But you will want to make certain your queen is eating her food. At the beginning of the pregnancy some queens experience some stomach upset, akin to morning sickness in women, but this is rare. If it does occur, it usually passes quickly.

> **HINT!**
>
> MAKE SURE YOUR QUEEN HAS ACCESS TO FRESH, CLEAN WATER AT ALL TIMES.

As your queen goes further in her pregnancy, she may experience some constipation. If you want, you can add some foods with laxative properties to her diet. One of the most common, and easiest to use, is canned pumpkin. It mixes easily with cat food and adds very little additional flavor. Most cats actually enjoy pumpkin. But make sure you use plain pumpkin and not pumpkin pie mix, which has unwanted additives such as sugar.

If you feel your queen is gaining too much weight or you want to add some extra bulk to her diet, you can replace a small portion of her regular wet diet with green beans or other cooked or canned vegetables.

No Raw Meat

Feeding a raw meat diet is never recommended for any cat of any age. The argument bas been made that in the wild a cat eats raw meat, so there is nothing wrong with feeding a domestic cat the same way. However, remember that free roaming cats eat the entire animal they kill, and not just the meat. Typically, cats eat vegetarian animals, such as mice, and also eat the contents of the mouse's stomach, which contains some of the vegetation the mouse has been eating. In addition, it eats the mouse immediately after it kills it, so the mouse is fresher than anything you could buy in a supermarket. Also, frankly, little research has been done on the health of free roaming colonies of cats. We do not know how many die due to illnesses or poisons that may be found in their diet.

We do know that raw meat is not an adequate diet for pedigreed cats from a nutritional point of view, and would have to be supplemented. Cat foods these days, both canned and dry, are of excellent quality and are formulated to be nutritionally complete, so there is no reason to feed any cat raw meat. You may hear breeders discuss how raw meat helps good, strong bones to develop in cats. This is not true. Good boning comes from breeding strong-boned cats to other strong-boned cats. It does not come from diet.

We also know that feeding a raw meat diet exposes your cat to contaminants, bacteria and parasitic diseases that may be present in the meat. And we know that feeding a raw meat diet can expose your cat to toxoplasmosis, a protozoan infection. Cats can often carry this protozoa without exhibiting any symptoms of illness, but they transmit the infection to their unborn kittens, and prenatal infection can cause abortion, stillbirths and unexplained deaths of newborns. Kittens may exhibit encephalitis, liver problems or pneumonia.

> **WARNING!**
>
> THE STRONGEST "MEDICATION" YOU SHOULD GIVE A PREGNANT QUEEN ON YOUR OWN IS WATER.

Toxoplasmosis can also lead to various other problems, including cardiomyopathy, which is impaired function of the heart muscle. Cardiomyopathy is a condition, not a specific disease, and many things can cause it. Sometimes it's a genetic problem, and a cat with inherited cardiomyopathy should be eliminated from your breeding program. Unfortunately, not all veterinarians will do a blood test for toxoplasmosis when cardiomyopathy is discovered in a breeding cat, and an entire line may be eliminated from a breeding program unnecessarily because cardiomyopathy is discovered without the underlying causal agent, toxoplasmosis, being found. This is unusual, but it does happen.

> ### HINT!
>
> FIRST, DO NO HARM. IF YOU HAVE ANY DOUBT AT ALL ABOUT THE EFFECTS OF A PREPARATION ON THE HEALTH OF YOUR CAT OR HER DEVELOPING KITTENS, DO NOT USE IT.

It is not necessary to supplement the diet of a pregnant queen as long as she is eating a balanced diet. Dry cat food will provide all the calcium she needs, so you will want to give her some dry food. Make sure both the canned food and the dry food you feed your queen are high quality and say on the label that they are nutritionally complete for all stages of your cat's life.

Pregnancy is not a time to use any drugs on your pregnant queen. If she becomes ill, you should follow the advice of your veterinarian and use only the medications he or she prescribes. But even then, you should make certain your veterinarian knows your queen is pregnant if she has shown any signs at all of pregnancy. If she has been bred but you do not know whether or not she is pregnant, tell your veterinarian when she was bred.

Non-Prescription Products

Be extremely careful about treating your queen with over-the-counter medications or even herbal or homeopathic remedies. While you will want to take care of any problems in a very natural way, too many breeders make mistakes using herbal and homeopathic remedies. They have a tendency to extrapolate a dosage for their cat based upon a given human dosage. It is very easy to over-medicate your cat this way. Even though you are dealing with natural remedies or herbs, these are effective medicines and, as such, can adversely affect your pregnant cat.

In addition, we do not know what, if any, effect some of these remedies may have on the developing kittens. There are some natural remedies that are safely used during pregnancy, such as red raspberry, but even this should not be overdone.

ULTRASOUND AND X-RAYS

Owners of pregnant queens have used X-rays for many years to see exactly how many kittens their queen is expecting. This procedure is painless and harmless. By knowing the number of kittens that are due, you are prepared when you help your queen with her delivery. You will know that if only two kittens are delivered but three were seen on the X-ray, something is wrong and you will have to call your veterinarian.

X-rays also show any dead or disintegrated fetus. If there is, your veterinarian may recommend immediate action, such as a cesarean section or termination of the pregnancy, since the dead matter in the body poses a threat of infection. If the pregnancy does go to term, you must make sure this material has been delivered. If it remains in the body, your queen can "go septic," that is, quickly develop a deadly internal infection.

The X-rays can also show whether there is a great disparity in size among the fetuses. If there is, you should prepare for:

- A difficult delivery, possibly requiring a cesarean section, if the larger fetus is too large.

- Delivery of a dead kitten, if the smaller kitten is not thriving in the womb.

- A problem newborn, if the smaller fetus is undersized at birth.

X-rays can be taken any time after the 45th day of pregnancy, but it is usually better to have them done closer to the time your queen is due to deliver. Any earlier may damage the fetuses.

Ultrasound is the latest development that breeders have to help us deal with a queen's pregnancy. It is critical to have a veterinarian who knows how to do ultrasound on pregnant queens for the readings to be of any use. While it is important that the machine itself is the best available in terms of technology, it is even more important that your veterinarian has had training in how to read the results. If you've ever seen an ultrasound photo of an unborn baby, you know it really looks like a grayish blob. Skilled eyes are needed to interpret the information that blob presents. If your veterinarian does not know how to read what is on the ultrasound screen, the ultrasound is not going to do you or your queen much good.

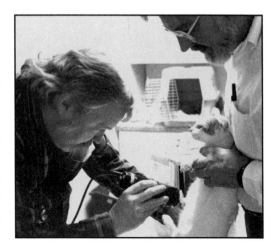

Dr. Stanglein shaves Jasmine's belly to maximize the effectiveness of the ultrasound.

Ultrasound costs more than an X-ray. In fact, it can be quite expensive depending upon where you live and your veterinarian's fee schedule. You can use ultrasound relatively early—at about 30 days—to confirm whether your queen is pregnant, but this may not be the best way for you to use this expensive tool.

Using a portable ultrasound machine, Dr. Stanglein begins the procedure . . .

The very best use of ultrasound is near the end of your queen's term. Near the end of pregnancy, your veterinarian can see the heartbeats of the kittens and count the rate. If the rate is still high, the kittens are not yet ready to be born.

Ultrasound can also be used with overdue queens, again to count the heart rate of the kittens. If your queen is

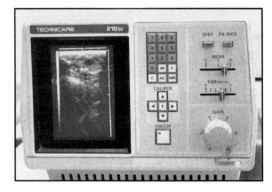

. . . and ultrasound reveals that Jasmine has one healthy vesicle showing the rapid heartbeat of her kitten.

Delivery Equipment Checklist

❏ Birthing box with layers of towels or diapers on the bottom for your queen to deliver her kittens. A layer of white towels or cloth diapers are easily removed from underneath the queen and, being white, you can easily see the blood and discharge.

❏ Small flashlight to illuminate the birth canal so you can check your queen's progress.

❏ Bulb syringe to suction the newborn kittens. These can be found in the drugstore. They are used to clean the ears of human infants.

❏ Small scissors in case you need to cut the umbilical cord.

❏ Clamp or dental floss in case there appears to be too much blood after the cord is cut. A clamp, or hemostat, can be purchased through veterinary supply catalogues. They may be in the grooming section, labeled as "hair pullers."

❏ Iodine to dab on the cut end of the cord of the newborn kitten to prevent bacterial infections. Iodine can also be used to mark the babies for identification.

❏ Thin rubber gloves in case you need to put a finger inside the birth canal to help rotate a kitten.

❏ K-Y Jelly to facilitate your entry in case your fingers must enter the birth canal.

❏ Sterile 4x4 gauze pads to dab the area of the birth canal during labor and delivery.

❏ Clean washcloths to hold the kittens if you must deliver a breech birth. These are also useful if you want to rub and warm the babies.

❏ Covered trash can for disposal of the waste and the placentas.

❏ Small plastic bag to hold a dead baby that you want to take to your veterinarian for a necropsy.

overdue by 48 hours, is not showing any signs of labor and the heart rate of the kittens is dropping, then your veterinarian may decide to do a cesarean section to ensure the kittens are delivered while they are still alive. You might also find out that the heart rates are still high and your queen just needs a little more time to deliver normally.

REABSORBED LITTERS

Occasionally a queen, usually one who is pregnant for the first time, will become pregnant but then the kittens will be reabsorbed, so there is not a delivery. If you breed your queen a couple of times and she always shows signs of pregnancy but the pregnancy just seems to disappear, you may be dealing with reabsorption. To confirm this, you can have an ultrasound done relatively early, for example at 30 days, to confirm her pregnancy. If your queen then seems to no longer be pregnant, the test can be performed again to see whether or not the kittens are still there.

Reabsorbed litters that happen time after time can

be extremely frustrating, but there is really not very much you can do about it. Your veterinarian can administer hormones to help your queen maintain her pregnancy, and this may work. However, you may be dealing with a much more basic problem. Perhaps your queen is unable to maintain a pregnancy at all. This is not uncommon when a queen is too highly inbred or the stud is too closely related to her. You can try using a different male to see if that will remedy the situation. If it doesn't, you may have to resign yourself to getting no kittens out

> ## Delivery Equipment Checklist
>
> *(continued)*
>
> ❑ Box with a covered heating pad on the bottom to place the kittens out of the queen's way when she is in active labor with another kitten.
>
> ❑ Postage scale to weigh the newborn kittens.
>
> ❑ Pad and pencil to record the time of birth, kitten's weight and whether or not the placenta was also delivered.
>
> ❑ Telephone in case of emergency, since you will not want to leave your queen.
>
> ❑ Your veterinarian's telephone number and beeper number (put them on your speed dialer if you have one).
>
> ❑ Stethoscope to check the newborn kitten's heartbeat.
>
> ❑ Alcohol to clean the equipment.

of this particular queen. This is one of the reasons you should never rely on a single queen for your breeding program. It is also one of the reasons you should avoid inbreeding.

PLANNING FOR THE BIG MOMENT

Pregnancy and the subsequent delivery of kittens are very natural and normal activities, so most queens are quite capable of handling their delivery by themselves. However, things can and do go wrong, so if you are not there to assist the queen you may lose kittens. In extreme cases, you may even lose your queen. Because this is always a possibility, you should plan to be with your queen while she is in labor and when she is delivering her kittens.

Equipment for Delivery

Some equipment is necessary when you are helping your queen. Even with a completely natural and routine delivery, you will find that some queens act as though it is the breeder's job to deliver the kittens! As soon as the kitten has been delivered, some queens seem to feel it is up to the breeder to tear the sac and cut the cord. Other queens will do everything themselves. Since you don't know how your queen will act at her first delivery, you should be ready to help all you can.

Signs of Labor

There are a number of external signs that your queen's period of labor is near. The body temperature of a queen in the first stage of labor should drop. However, some queens maintain their body temperature until the time they deliver, at which point, of course, you have no need to check their temperature. In addition, when the queen is within a day or two of being ready to deliver, she may not be too cooperative if you do try to take her temperature.

At approximately two weeks before the onset of labor, you should be able to obtain milk from the nipples if you press around them. However, some queens will remain dry until they have delivered, or until the nursing action of the baby helps produce the milk.

Jasmine's birthing cage is ready for her.

Other signs of labor will vary with each queen, and over time you will recognize when *your* queen is beginning active labor. Generally, your queen will have a period of restlessness where she will try to nest. This usually consists of rearranging the towels in her birthing box. After this period of restlessness, she will settle down as she begins contractions. You will be able to feel the contractions when you rest your hand on her abdomen or on her side.

As the kittens are ready to be delivered, you queen may squat so that gravity can help with the delivery. If your queen wants to deliver her kittens in a squatting position, let her do so. Your job as a breeder is to help make your queen comfortable, to watch for any signs that something is going wrong and to care for the kittens after they are born.

You must learn to work with your queen so you can help her as much as possible while not getting in her way or giving in to her if she would rather have her kittens under the bed or in some place other than her birthing cage. If your queen prefers to have her kittens in a dark environment, then darken the environment. You can turn down the lights with a dimmer switch, place lamps in the far side of the room or cover her cage with a sheet. You will need enough light to be able to see what is going on, but that is all. You can make certain you have enough light by using an adjustable floor lamp near the cage.

HELPING THE QUEEN IN LABOR

The old rule of breeding was to leave the queen completely alone, checking on her occasionally. Unfortunately, breeders found many kittens were lost this way. Even worse, many queens died trying to deliver their kittens because there was no one there to help them. Now, the responsible breeder is present at all times in case they are needed.

In most cases, your queen will do everything that has to be done to deliver the kittens.

HINT!

WHEN YOUR QUEEN BEGINS LABOR, GO OVER THE DELIVERY PROCEDURE IN YOUR MIND. THIS WILL HELP TO REASSURE YOU SO YOU CAN CONCENTRATE ON HELPING YOUR NEW MOMMY.

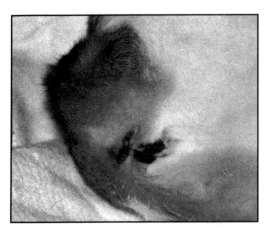

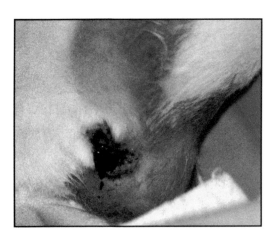

Jasmine's labor progresses.

Your job is to help the queen stay calm while she is in labor by petting her and reassuring her that you are there. First-time queens may be nervous, and speaking to them in a calming voice is very beneficial.

Most of the time, the queen will push out her kittens by herself and may only need some assistance in the case of a breech birth. However, with many breeds the queens want someone to help them during or after the birth. You must monitor the situation and administer as much help as you feel your queen wants and needs.

When you see the kitten's head emerge, the rest of the kitten should just slide out, because the head is the biggest part of the newborn and, therefore, the most difficult part for the queen to deliver.

Breech Birth Kittens

Many queens require some assistance from the breeder to deliver a breech birth kitten—that is, a kitten that does not present itself head first. This is especially true of first-time queens, since the

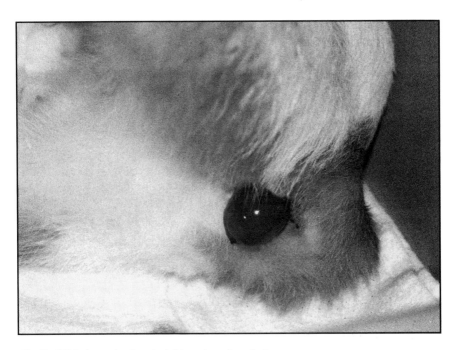

The "bubble" shows that Jasmine's kitten is ready to be born.

birth canal has never been used and is not as flexible as in an experienced queen.

When you see the feet of the kitten emerging, or if you can see the little white claws when you see the emerging sac, be ready to assist the queen. Once the body has been delivered, watch carefully at the next contraction. Sometimes, the contraction alone will be enough for the head of the kitten to deliver through the birth canal. If it is not, take your hand, covered with a thin, clean washcloth, and support the kitten's body. At the next contraction, very carefully maintain downward pressure on the kitten, easing your finger under the head of the kitten. *Be extremely careful that you never pull the body of the kitten while the head is still in the birth canal, as this can cause injury.* All you want to do is assist the queen along with her contractions.

Releasing Kittens from the Sac

Most kittens are still in a sac when they are born; this sac must be broken. If you look carefully, you may be able to see the little kitten moving

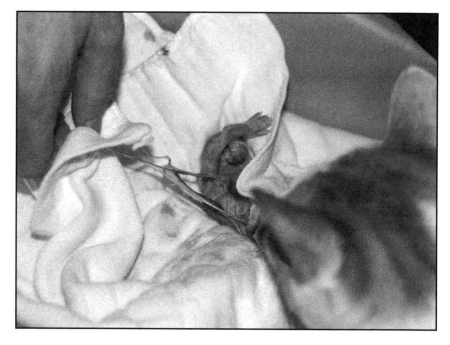

Be ready to assist the queen if she fails to cut the cord.

in this sac, clawing at it. Some kittens may even break the sac themselves, but usually the queen will do this with her teeth. If she does not, you must gently do so.

You do this by carefully tearing it apart with your fingers. There is no immediate rush to do this. Since your queen may have just had a large contraction to enable her to expel this kitten, wait for a couple of minutes and let her break the sac if she will. If it becomes apparent that she is not going to break the sac, then do it for her and place the kitten next to her so she can wash it and cut the cord.

Cutting and Caring for the Cord

Some queens may release the kitten from the sac but then not cut the cord attaching the kitten to the placenta. Again, there is not an immediate rush to cut the cord, but if it becomes obvious that the queen is not going to do this, you will have to do it for her.

When you cut the cord, you will want to be very careful that you do not pull on it. Pulling the cord has been known to cause an umbilical hernia. While this is easy for your veterinarian to repair, it will require surgery at a later date, so you will want to avoid this problem.

Carefully cut the cord with a scissors about one and a half to two inches from the body of the kitten. Once you have cut the cord, put iodine on the end of it to prevent bacteria from going through the cord into the kitten's body. You will see some bleeding from the cord—this is normal. Even if the queen has cut the cord herself, you should put iodine on the cord to prevent bacterial infection. If you prefer, you can tie off the end of the cord with dental floss, but this is not really necessary. The bleeding from the torn or cut end of the cord will stop on its own very quickly. If it doesn't, clamp or tie the end to prevent further bleeding.

At this point, the queen may eat the expelled placenta. This is perfectly normal. If the queen does not eat it, take the placenta out of the birthing box and dispose of it. You might want to limit the number of placentas your queen eats, as eating

---

HINT!

MAKE VERY SURE THAT IN YOUR NOTES ON THE DELIVERY YOU NOT ONLY LIST "KITTEN DELIVERED" BUT ALSO "PLACENTA DELIVERED" FOR EACH KITTEN.

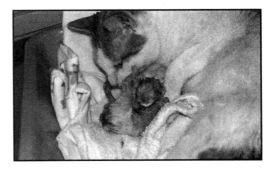

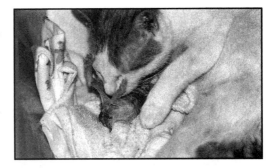

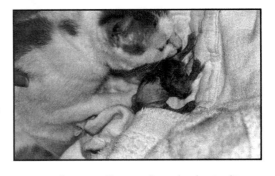

Jasmine takes care of her new kitten by cleaning him completely.

Birthing Records

In keeping the records of births, you will want to note the following:

- Name of queen and stud male.

- Date(s) of mating.

- Dates of X-ray and ultrasound, and the results of both.

- Any problems that occurred during pregnancy, including any medications given to the queen.

- Time of the onset of labor.

- Time each kitten was born.

- Special note if the birth was a breech.

- When each placenta was delivered.

- Weight of each kitten.

- Sex of each kitten.

- Any deformities that may exist.

- Color of kitten or how you marked each kitten to identify it.

These records should be kept with the permanent records of the queen. When this queen is bred again, review this record to remind yourself of exactly what happened with her pregnancy and delivery.

too many placentas may give her diarrhea.

Usually the queen will now completely clean the kitten. This washing not only cleans the kitten but helps to stimulate it to begin to breathe. The kitten may or may not cry, but if it does not, that does not necessarily indicate something is wrong. If you see the kitten wriggling around and the queen caring for it, the kitten is probably just fine. If she stops caring for him, she is probably having another contraction. You can feel her abdomen to make sure this is what is happening.

Many breeders will take the kitten at this point and use the bulb syringe to suction any fluid out of the kitten's mouth. Do this very gently, as the kitten is small and the bulb syringe can really cause more suction than you may expect. Remember, you are just trying to clear out remaining mucus.

Delivering Late Placentas

As the kittens are delivered, the attached placentas can be delivered either at the same time or shortly after the kitten itself has emerged. It is critical to make certain you have a placenta delivered for every delivered kitten. Retained placentas can cause problems that may ultimately lead to dangerous uterine infections for your queen.

If you are missing a placenta after all kittens have been delivered, your veterinarian may prescribe oxytocin to stimulate further contractions, which will cause this placenta to be delivered. If Pitocin (oxytocin) is administered to your queen, you must watch her carefully for the side effects of this drug. Pitocin can cause abdominal pain due to the uterine contractions it stimulates, and this can make your queen exhibit signs of pain or behave abnormally. It can also cause pupil dilation, so you will want to make certain the delivery cage area is darkened.

The biggest side effect of this drug, however, is hypocalcemia, a sudden decrease in calcium in the body. While hypocalcemia can occur after birth when there are many kittens nursing or if the queen's diet was low in calcium, it can be dramatic with the use of Pitocin. If your veterinarian has given your queen a shot of Pitocin, you might want to add oral calcium to her diet and watch her carefully.

> **WARNING!**
>
> NEVER ADMINISTER PITOCIN OR OXYTOCIN UNLESS THE QUEEN IS UNDER THE DIRECT SUPERVISION OF YOUR VETERINARIAN. THESE DRUGS CAN CAUSE THE UTERUS TO RUPTURE AND YOU MAY LOSE YOUR QUEEN AS WELL AS HER KITTENS. THESE DRUGS ARE FOR VETERINARY USE ONLY!

> **WARNING!**
>
> UNDER NO CIRCUMSTANCES SHOULD YOU EVER ATTEMPT TO "PUT DOWN" A DEFORMED KITTEN AT HOME. THERE IS NO KNOWN WAY FOR A KITTEN TO BE PUT DOWN IN A HUMANE MANNER BY THE BREEDER. WHEN EUTHANASIA IS BEING CONSIDERED, THIS MUST BE DONE BY YOUR VETERINARIAN, WHO HAS HUMANE METHODS AVAILABLE.

Checking for Defects and Deformities

Congenital defects are not very common in pedigreed cats, but they do occasionally occur. If you are working with a breed that has some common deformities, you will know about this before you start breeding and will know what to look for.

Major Complications of Pregnancy

ABORTION

Clinical Signs: Since cats are so fastidious, you may not notice if a pregnancy has been aborted other than seeing that a queen did not appear to become pregnant or, if pregnant, that her pregnancy did not continue to a delivery.

Treatment: None is necessary unless the queen begins to hemorrhage, at which point she should be taken immediately to your veterinarian.

UTERINE INERTIA (LABOR FAILS TO PROGRESS)

Clinical Signs: In primary inertia, labor stops before any kittens are delivered. In secondary inertia, labor stops after one or more kittens have been delivered.

Treatment: In the cattery, to prevent secondary inertia administer a calcium supplement every 30 minutes during labor. The easiest way to do this is to give your queen half a Tums antacid pill every half hour during labor.

Primary inertia requires veterinary treatment. A veterinarian may administer oxytocin/Pitocin if, in his or her opinion, doing so will not rupture the uterus or harm the queen in any other way. These ecbolic drugs should never, under any circumstances, be administered by a breeder unless it is under a veterinarian's supervision.

UTERINE RUPTURE (COMPLETE TEAR OF THE UTERUS)

Clinical Signs: Vomiting, depression, anorexia, abdominal pain.

Treatment: Your veterinarian should perform a prompt exploratory laparotomy with the goal of saving the queen as a breeding animal. If this is not possible, she may have to be spayed in order to save her life.

Except in this instance, you may breed for many years without ever seeing evidence of a congenital abnormality in a newborn kitten. Still, after the kittens are cleaned by your queen, you want to examine each one carefully for deformities. Most deformities will be very obvious, especially missing limbs or digits.

Any very deformed kitten should be removed from the queen and put aside until the entire delivery process has been completed and the queen has settled down. At that time, the deformed kitten should be taken to your veterinarian. Frankly, if a kitten is grossly deformed and yet born alive, by the time your queen finishes her delivery the kitten may well have died on its own.

You will have to open the mouth of the kitten in order to see any evidence of cleft palate. If you see an opening in the top of the mouth, separate this kitten as it will have to be tube fed to prevent choking until this deformity can be surgically corrected by your veterinarian.

Some deformities may not be apparent for a while. Since

your kittens will not be released to their new homes until they are at least four months old, and since you will be watching them carefully as they grow, you should be able to pick up any evidence of these defects before you decide whether to sell any particular kitten.

WHEN SOMETHING IS WRONG

There will be times when you will not be able to deal with the birth of kittens without the help of your veterinarian. Once your queen has established a delivery pattern, you should be careful to note any changes in this pattern. For example, if a queen who normally delivers on the 67th day after heavy labor of one hour suddenly fails to deliver until the 69th day and is in labor for two hours, she is telling you that the birth is not quite as easy as it had been.

(continued)

UTERINE TORSION (ROTATION/TWISTING OF THE HORN OF THE UTERUS)

Clinical Signs: Pain when the abdomen is palpated. Diagnosis may be confirmed by an X-ray.
Treatment: Your veterinarian should perform a prompt laparotomy with the goal of removing the horn on the affected side only. However, the queen may have to be spayed in order to save her life.

UTERINE PROLAPSE

Clinical Signs: The uterus literally turns inside out and protrudes from the opening of the vulva.
Treatment: Cover the uterus with a moist sterile dressing and seek immediate veterinary attention. If the uterus is still viable and has only been prolapsed for an hour or less, the veterinarian may attempt to replace it in the abdominal cavity manually. If the uterus is no longer viable, the veterinarian may have to spay the queen in order to save her life.

PYOMETRA (UTERINE INFECTION)

Clinical Signs: Slight anorexia, depression, occasional vomiting, vaginal discharge. Signs may go unnoticed for awhile. Pyometra may occur in a mild form, disappear and recur.
Treatment: Your veterinarian may prescribe certain drugs, along with antibiotics, to help the uterus expel the infection. If the infection is severe, has been present for too long or there are signs of complications such as severe malnutrition or kidney or liver failure, the queen may have to be spayed in order to save her life.

When you know your cat well, you will almost be able to sense when something is going wrong. Never hesitate to contact your veterinarian if you feel all is not well. While we can do many things ourselves, it is our veterinarian, our partner in the cattery, who must do the cesarean sections and other procedures, when and if they need to be done.

Unfortunately, too many breeders randomly use medications without the advice of their veterinarian. Some even give medications to pregnant queens that are known to cause problems with the kittens. This indiscriminate use of veterinary drugs is completely inappropriate and has even caused deformed and stillborn kittens. Breeders must always keep in mind that no matter how sophisticated we may become about the veterinary care of our cats, we are not veterinarians and should not use medications ourselves.

Cesarean Sections

There are times when your queen will be unable to deliver her kittens naturally and will have to undergo a cesarean section (c-section). In this procedure, your veterinarian will anesthetize your queen, make an abdominal incision, and then remove the kittens through the abdominal opening. He will suction the kittens, deliver the placentas and cut the cords. The kittens will be placed in a warm environment and kept isolated and carefully watched while the queen is being sutured. The queen will then be brought around from her anesthesia and she will be able to be with her babies.

Signs That a Cesarean Section Is Needed

- Strong contractions for more than three hours with no delivery.

- Weak contractions that never develop into the second stage of labor.

- Dark or bright red vaginal discharge with no labor.

- Strong contractions that continue for two to four hours after the delivery of the first kitten, but no more kittens are born.

The length of time it takes to perform a c-section will vary from situation to situation. Some factors affecting this will be how long the queen has been in labor and the number of kittens to be delivered. Sometimes the c-section is done because a kitten has died and cannot be delivered normally because of its position. Sometimes the queen may be experiencing uterine inertia and she just cannot expel the kittens.

While some veterinarians will permit the breeder in the operating room while a c-section is being performed, many will not. If you are allowed into the operating room, your veterinarian may ask you to assist with the newborn kittens. You might be asked to help suction the kittens, for example. Many breeders have problems dealing with this, and may have even more problems seeing their queen on the operating table. If your veterinarian asks whether or not you want to be present, be perfectly honest with yourself and with him or her. The veterinarian's patient is your cat, not you. If you become a problem in the operating room, you are harming your cat.

The care of a queen who has had a cesarean section, while it does differ from the care of the queen who has had a normal delivery, is not difficult. You must recognize that your queen may be having some discomfort from the incision, no matter how small your veterinarian was able to make it. In addition,

> # WARNING!
>
> SOME BREEDS HAVE PROBLEMS WITH CERTAIN TYPES OF ANESTHETICS. IT IS YOUR RESPONSIBILITY TO FIND OUT IF THIS IS A PROBLEM WITH YOUR BREED AND TO CONVEY THIS INFORMATION TO YOUR VETERINARIAN WHEN YOUR QUEEN IS PREGNANT AND BEFORE THE NEED FOR A CESAREAN SECTION ARISES. NEVER PERMIT A CESAREAN SECTION TO BE PERFORMED ON YOUR QUEEN WITHOUT FINDING OUT WHAT TYPE OF ANESTHESIA YOUR VETERINARIAN PREFERS TO USE. IF YOUR BREED HAS A PROBLEM WITH SOME OF THE INJECTABLE ANESTHETICS, ASK YOUR VETERINARIAN TO USE A GAS ANESTHETIC.

the kittens may stick their claws in the incision as they try to nurse. You must therefore watch the site very closely for any signs of infection. If you notice anything such as heat or redness at the incision site, oozing or evidence of foul-smelling exudate, contact your veterinarian immediately.

Other than the problems any cat may experience after a surgical procedure, your queen and her kittens should have no special needs and will require only the normal care of a queen and her litter. The queen should have milk, although the flow may not be as strong at first as if she had delivered normally.

If you were not in the delivery room or did not wait at your veterinarian's office while the c-section was being performed, your veterinarian will usually let you take the queen and her kittens home as soon as she is fully recovered from the anesthesia. You must remember that the kittens have not been weighed nor have they been sexed. You will want to do this once you have settled the queen in her cage, and make your notes on the sex and weight of the kittens.

CARE OF NEWBORN KITTENS AND THE QUEEN

Many queens, especially if they do not eat very much the day they deliver, will be extremely hungry and willing to take a short break from caring for the kittens in order to eat some food. Some queens will eat ravenously after giving birth. If you do not know how your queen is going to

react, try giving her some wet food. If she does not eat it, it can always be removed.

Once the kittens have been delivered, there is not much more for you to do. You will want to make sure the babies are nursing on the queen and that she is comfortable and happy. Newborn kittens will try to find a nipple almost immediately, but do not worry if they take a bit of time to settle down and begin nursing.

Queens can lack colostrum, the first milk, which contains antibodies that give the kittens immunity to some diseases. They may also not be able to produce

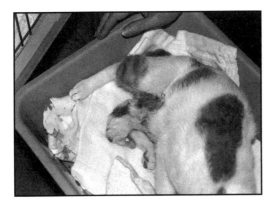

Jasmine's new baby tries to find a nipple so he can begin to nurse.

enough regular milk to properly nourish their kittens. This can be handled by the breeder with proper supplements to the kittens' diet and isolation, early vaccinations and drugs that stimulate the immune system to protect them.

There are a few causes of early kitten mortality that can be easily corrected by the breeder. Many newborn kittens die because of an inappropriate cattery environment. For example, if your cattery is not clean or some of your cats are constantly spreading upper respiratory infections or eye infections back and forth, a pregnant queen can go into labor already harboring an infection. Likewise, if your cattery is plagued with fungal infections or parasites, newborn kittens may be at risk. However, with proper husbandry techniques, these risks for kitten mortality can be eliminated.

Causes of Early Kitten Mortality

- Inappropriate environmental conditions.
- Maternal neglect or cannibalism.
- Lack of colostrum or milk and/or improper supplementation.
- Infections such as septicemia or pneumonia.
- Metabolic abnormalities or immune deficiency.
- Neonatal erythrolysis.

Source: The Robert H. Winn Foundation Report on Blood Type Incompatibility & Kitten Mortality

HINT!

SOMETIMES WHEN THE MOMMY WALKS AWAY, THERE IS A REASON.

Neonatal erytholysis, where the red blood cells of the kittens are destroyed by maternal antibodies, can be avoided by having your queens and sires blood typed. If their blood types differ, you can either avoid breeding cats of different blood types, or you can hand-raise the kittens resulting from such a breeding for their first 48 hours. (For more on blood types and breeding, see Chapter Three.)

Kittens are born with no antibodies, so the newborn kittens are very vulnerable to disease. Current research has shown that antibodies from the queen pass to the kittens for several weeks of lactation, and not just during the first 24 hours as was previously thought. However, the kittens

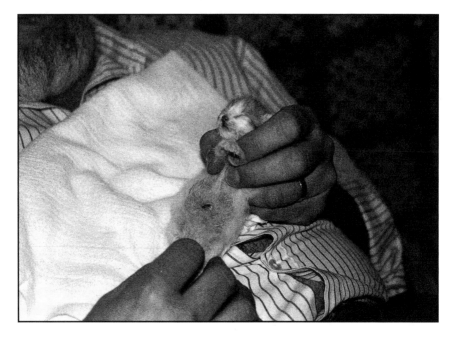

Since this baby was born during a terrible blizzard, that's what he'll be called!

are only able to absorb these antibodies during the first 16 hours of life. That is why any kittens with Type A blood should be removed from a Type B queen during this period. Since antibodies are present in the queen's milk for a few weeks, however, fostering these kittens on another lactating queen will ensure that the newborn kittens receive some maternal antibodies.

Unfortunately, even with the best of care not every pedigreed kitten that is born will live. Some kittens will be lost through abnormalities or a depressed immune system. You may lose kittens that appear perfectly normal but have a hidden abnormality that you will only be able to find on necropsy. You may also lose kittens due to severe

---

WARNING!

BE VERY CAREFUL WHEN YOU HANDLE NEWBORN KITTENS BECAUSE, LIKE HUMANS, THEIR NECK MUSCLES ARE TOO WEAK TO ENABLE THEM TO HOLD UP THEIR NECK AND HEAD ON THEIR OWN. ALWAYS BE CAREFUL TO SUPPORT THE HEAD WHEN YOU HANDLE A NEWBORN.

infections or pneumonia, no matter how much you may battle these infections. As breeders, we are dealing with nature.

Watch to make sure your queen does not reject any of the kittens. Since cannibalism is rare in pedigreed cats, you do not have to keep the litter under constant watch. Your queen may continue to have some slight, bloody discharge from the birth canal, but this is normal and will not become a problem unless there is evidence of a large amount of bright, red blood. In this case, she must be taken to your veterinarian immediately.

Some queens are very reluctant to use the litter box in the same cage with their new kittens. If this is the case, make certain your queen is released from her cage regularly in order to use her box. In any event, you will want to release her from the cage for periods of exercise. But she will probably not want to remain out of the sight of her kittens for very long. She knows she has a job to do!

Make certain the kittens are always kept warm by using a heating pad in the bottom of the birthing box, or use the bottom of a Thermocare unit as a birthing box. (A Thermocare unit is a warming unit where the temperature is controlled by heating water sealed between two walls; there's more information about it in Chapter Seven.) If you use a heating pad, make very certain the pad *never* touches the kittens and burns their delicate skin by keeping layers of diapers or towels on top of it. Also, make sure the light is not too bright in the room, even though the kittens have not opened their eyes yet.

You will want to handle the kittens every day in order to check them as well as to socialize them. Since we still do not know at what age human contact is critical to the kitten's socialization, handling them every day is the best way we can make certain the kittens will grow up to be cats who adapt well to people. Needless to say, this is the easy and enjoyable part of raising pedigreed cats.

YOU KNOW YOU ARE A CAT BREEDER WHEN . . .

- You don't bat an eye at seeing toilet paper used in home decorating.

- You maintain an altar to Bastet, and you believe that your soul will turn black if you don't venerate cats.

- You express your doubts about someone's intellect by commenting, "Three more I.Q. points and he could bark."

- There's a storm predicted and you are the one at the grocery store loading up on litter and cat food when everyone else is raiding the milk and bread shelves.

- You have half of your two-car garage filled with cat litter and food—and you own three cars and a van.

- When you have a doctor's appointment, you say you are going to the vet.

- Cat calendars are required on the walls of your office; on the first day of each month, you and your staff gather around and admire that month's cat pictures.

- *Cat Fancy, Cats* and the cat association newsletter are the first three publications you renew each year.

Adapted from *101 Ways to Know You're a Cat Fancier.*

CHAPTER SEVEN

Caring for the New Mother and Her Kittens

After the delivery, your queen will spend some time cleaning herself. She really will not need you to do anything. Most queens just want to suckle their kittens and purr. They also love to be admired and have their kittens praised, and it is now your happy job to do that. We have never met a queen with her new kittens that would not be at her happiest if you spent hours by her cage petting her, telling her what a wonderful mother she is and mentioning that these kittens are the most beautiful kittens that have ever been born.

Breeding pedigreed cats can have some very heartbreaking times. The longer you are involved with any kind of animal, the more you will see. Having helped your queen to deliver such a beautiful, healthy litter is one of the very best times you, as a breeder, will have. This is when you get a chance to sit back, relax, admire these beautiful little lives and enjoy yourself.

DIET AND EXERCISE FOR THE POSTPARTUM QUEEN

Once again, if you feed your queen a diet that is nutritionally balanced, you will not have a problem after she delivers her kittens. You will find that she eats more than usual, and you will want to make sure she has adequate canned food and has dry food available to her at all times. She will also need a constant supply of clean, fresh water.

Most queens look extremely thin after a delivery. This is partly because we've become used to them looking round. When the kittens are born, it is quite a shock to see the queen without the roundness of her pregnancy. While lactating, many of the calories your queen is taking in are being used to produce the milk to feed her kittens. Feeding her extra food at this time will not be a problem, as long as it is nutritionally balanced.

Many queens want to get out of the queening cage to use the litter box. They have a real reluctance to soil the area anywhere near their newborn kittens. If you let your queen out to exercise at regular times, you will find she will head straight for the litter box. While she is out, she will want to walk around for awhile. She probably will not be too active at this time, but the exercise she does get will help to prevent constipation and will stretch her muscles.

Queens are very patient with new kittens, and they will lie for hours in the same position while the kittens are nursing. Your queen will appreciate her time away from the kittens and will make the most of it. However, most queens do not want to be away from the kittens for too long at any one time. If your queen does seem reluctant to return to the kittens, all you have to do is pick up a kitten. As soon as the newborn kitten starts to cry, you will find your queen running back to the cage to care for the kitten.

COMPLICATIONS OF C-SECTIONS

Cesarean sections are easy and relatively routine. They are nothing to worry about, and your queen will recover rapidly and nurse her kittens just as if she had delivered vaginally. The only serious complications that exist are relatively rare. However, just as in any surgery where the muscles are cut, there will be pain. Unfortunately, veterinary medicine is just beginning to research pain relievers that can be routinely used on cats, and there are no pain relievers that can be used safely on a nursing queen at this time. But this field of veterinary medicine is changing rapidly, and soon these drugs will be discovered and will be routinely available. If your queen is in pain she may become restless, which does not facilitate the nursing process. If necessary, you can supplement the kittens for a few hours while your queen rests and recuperates. If you want to use a natural remedy to help your queen calm down, you can give her some fresh catnip or put a washcloth with catnip spray on it by her head. Avoid dry catnip, as this may find its way into her incision or into the mouths of the kittens, where they may inhale and choke on it. You may also try some of the other herbal or homeopathic remedies.

If your queen is too restless after a c-section and you are concerned about the kittens, you can remove them to a warming bed or a Thermocare unit. Then cover the cage of the queen so it is dark and let her sleep. Make certain she cannot hear the kittens if they cry, as this may further agitate her.

Be very careful when the kittens are nursing on the queen who has had a c-section. Kittens are born with sharp nails and closed eyes. They tend to feel and smell their way around the world at this stage, and while trying to nurse they may stick their claws into the surgical site. This can lead to pain for your queen as well as possible infection at the site of the surgery.

To help your queen, check her frequently to make sure the new kittens are not on the suture site. If they are, carefully move them to a new teat. Also, make sure you look at the site each day, gently clearing it and checking for any signs of infection. When the kittens' nails have firmed up (about five or more days after birth), you can *very carefully* trim their tiny claws.

CARE OF THE NEWBORN KITTENS

When it comes to the care of healthy newborn kittens, the queen does most of the work. But your job is not over, even with a healthy litter.

You must observe each kitten several times each day and weigh the kittens every other day and record their weight to assure yourself that each kitten is eating well.

Look over each kitten as you handle it. Look for small things that might indicate a problem. Is the umbilical cord drying and falling off the baby or are there signs of infection? Does there appear to be a swelling around the cord, which could indicate an umbilical hernia? If you have not been able to sex the kitten earlier, can you do so now? Are the kitten's eyes beginning to open? Is the baby breathing well or does it sound congested? You should be careful here, because some kittens will try to purr at an early age while they are still nursing. This can sound as if the kitten is congested, unless you watch it closely and learn to recognize this small sound for what it really is.

> **HINT!**
>
> ONCE THE KITTENS' EYES ARE FULLY OPEN, ADMINISTER ONE DROP IN EACH EYE OF AN EYE DROP SPECIFICALLY MADE TO TREAT HERPES INFECTIONS, AS A PREVENTIVE MEASURE.

Does the kitten feel firm when you pick him up? You can tell the general state of health of the newborn kitten by how he feels. A healthy kitten feels firm, he is squirming in your hand, searching for a teat and mewling when he doesn't find one. He is clean and active. All of these things indicate a healthy, happy newborn kitten.

Your queen will take care of feeding the kittens and washing them. She will also wash the area around the perineum, which stimulates the kittens to urinate. The queen will then lap up the urine. This is normal and does not hurt the queen. Sometimes the kittens will excrete some urine on their bedding, and this is also normal. Your queen may also be dripping a little for a few days. As long as there is not a gush of bright red blood, this is fine. If there is, get the queen to the veterinarian at once. However, because of all of this, the bedding should be changed daily and washed in a disinfectant such as bleach.

> **IMPORTANT!**
>
> FOR THE FIRST TWO WEEKS, THE TEMPERATURE OF THE NEWBORN KITTENS' BED SHOULD BE KEPT AT A CONSTANT 95 DEGREES FAHRENHEIT. THEREAFTER, IT SHOULD BE SLOWLY LOWERED TO 80 DEGREES.

Weighing the Kittens

The kittens should be weighed when they are born and this should be recorded. Since your newborn kittens will generally weigh from two to five ounces, the best scale to use while they are still young is a postal scale. This scale is meant to weigh not only ounces, but fractions of an ounce.

Blizzard stands in a small basket while being weighed on a postal scale.

Haiku, an older kitten, is more easily weighed on a baby scale.

You will want to continue to weigh the kittens every other day or so to make certain they are gaining weight. Not every kitten will gain weight at the same rate, so do not be worried if one of them seems to be gaining weight more slowly than the others. Just continue to watch that kitten to make certain he shows no signs of illness. Also, kittens may gain weight in spurts. They may weigh the same for a few days in a row and then all of a sudden gain one or two ounces.

Marking Kittens for Identification

Some breeds are born completely white and develop their color(s) as they mature. Other breeds are born in a variety of colors and patterns. Still other times, certain breedings will result in litters of all one color. When this happens, you should mark your kittens for easy identification.

It is very difficult with kittens to put something on them, such as a collar, because collars can be hazardous and because the queen will usually try to remove them when she washes the kittens. An easy alternative is to mark them using the iodine you used when you took care of the umbilical cord.

Establish a system for marking the kittens. For example, the first kitten born might have a mark of iodine on his right front paw. The second will have a mark on her left front paw. The third will be marked on his right rear paw and the fourth on her left rear paw. If you have more than four kittens, you can place a mark on the forehead, shoulder or tail. The iodine will wear off as the queen washes the kittens, so you will have to renew these marks periodically as they begin to fade.

Once you are able to identify the kittens without the mark, just let the iodine wear off. Be very certain your records are very clear about how each kitten is marked so you can accurately track weight and other important information.

Sexing the Kittens

Sometimes it is very easy to sex newborns and other times it is very difficult. Try to do it just after the kitten has been delivered (if you have the time). Hold the kitten in a position as if it were standing on its feet and gently raise the tail. Immediately under the tail you will see the anus.

Directly below the anus, you will see either a vertical slit, which desig-nates that the kitten is a girl, or you will see another opening, smaller than the anus, which indicates a boy.

However, the genital area is usually rather enlarged right after birth, due to the hormones present just before and during delivery. This can make a boy appear to have testicles, in which case he is usually easy to sex. But the swelling of the genital area can also disguise the fact that a kitten is a girl.

Don't worry if you cannot sex the kittens immediately. Just look at them every day until you are able to distinguish the sex. In this case, keep your records as "kitten number one–girl," "kitten number two–boy," kit-ten number three–sex undetermined." As you keep your daily weight records, remember to change this on your notes as soon as you have deter-mined the sex.

CARING FOR A SICK NEWBORN

Sometimes you will have a kitten that is born very weak. He may be too small to nurse from your queen, especially if he has a couple of larger lit-ter mates forcing him away from the nipples. You may find that a kitten, for some unknown reason, seems to get an upper respiratory infection very easily or just does not grow the way the other kittens do. You may even have a situation where the queen abandons the kitten, refusing to nurse him or pushing him out of the birthing box.

Sick kittens may be ill because they were exposed to feline infectious peritonitis when the queen was pregnant; feline infectious peritonitis is a virus that causes no symptoms in most of the cats who carry it, but kittens are particularly prone to develop symptoms.

Kittens can also become ill due to poor husbandry techniques. This can happen even with a kitten who has no obvious defects.

When a situation like this occurs, the responsible breeder will try to care for the kitten the best way they can. The kitten may be bottle fed if he has a sucking reflex. If he does not, he can be tube fed. If he is ill, your veterinarian will prescribe appropriate medicine. In some cases, you may have to isolate the kitten in a special environment to save his life. All these measures are appropriate in order to save the life of a kitten.

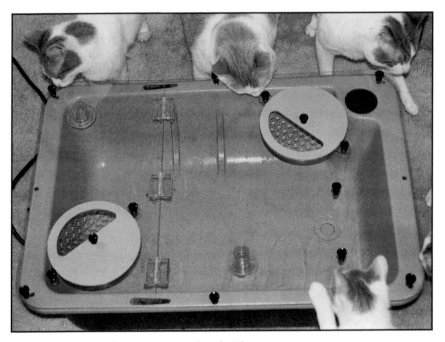

There seems to be much curiosity surrounding the Thermocare unit!

Vaporization and Nebulization

One of the first steps to take when a kitten shows evidence of an upper respiratory infection is to administer steam or nebulization. It is very easy to create a humid environment for the kitten by putting a vaporizer under the cage. Vaporizers are available at most drug stores. They are inexpensive to buy and easy to use. If you do not have a vaporizer, you can put the kitten in a cat carrier, put a towel over the top so that it hangs down and covers the side holes in the carrier, and put this carrier in the bathroom with the hot shower running and the door closed.

Nebulization, which provides a kind of medicated vapor at a constant temperature, is a more discreet method of providing a sick kitten with moisture. It is also a way you can administer drugs that are inhaled by the kitten. Nebulization requires specialized equipment. One unit that is easily available to breeders is called the Thermocare unit. This unit consists of a bottom, which is a plastic container or bed. The bed has an inner shell and an outer shell. You fill it with distilled water and plug it in. The temperature of this bed is maintained by a thermostat set on the side of the unit.

The top of the unit has a flat top or a domed top. You then plug in a separate, small air compressor and use a hose to attach this to the Thermocare unit. In this way, you can create mist, administer medications and keep the kitten at a certain temperature, all at the same time.

For young kittens, the flat top is all you will need. The domed lid is good for older cats. This unit is somewhat expensive. However, if you are able to save only one kitten with it, the cost is worth it—not to mention that you have saved the life of a pedigreed kitten.

The bottom or bed of the Thermocare unit can also be used in your birthing box to maintain the heat that is needed for the newborn kittens. The temperature of the unit can be turned down as the kittens get older.

Since it's molded plastic, this unit can be easily cleaned and disinfected. If you get a hole in the unit and it begins to leak, you can use adhesive made for aquariums to repair it.

If you are so inclined, you can make your own nebulization unit. In making your nebulizer, you will still need a source of compressed air. Air compressors are not too expensive, and if you use one you will not have to adapt it to bleed off excess pressure.

The kind of box you use is up to you. Some people use 10-gallon aquariums, plastic storage containers or carriers with plastic taped to the existing holes. You must put the air tube from the compressor into the nebulization chamber by making a hole in the chamber and then sealing around the air hose to avoid leaks. Many breeders have done this and can guide you in the design and its execution.

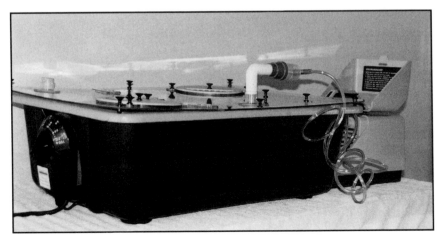

This Thermocare unit is set up with the air compressor and is ready to use.

If you choose to administer a drug in the nebulizer because the kitten is in respiratory distress and you are unable to get to your veterinarian immediately, you can use an over-the-counter anti-asthmatic such as Primatine Mist. However, these medications should never be used if the kitten may have an underlying cardiac problem.

If you do not know whether or not the kitten may have a cardiac condition, never use this drug. If the kitten appears to have a stuffy nose, you can use 0.25 ml of Neo-Synephrine nose drops, diluted to one quarter strength, in the nebulizer. As a general rule, however, only nebulize without medication until you are able to see your veterinarian and have the kitten checked.

When to Let Go

There will come a point in caring a for a very ill or extremely deformed kitten when you realize you may have to consider euthanasia. This is a very difficult decision to make. But when you see a kitten continuing to suffer despite everything you are able to do for him, euthanasia may be the only answer. While life is critical, quality of life is just as critical. Living sick is not really living. The decision to euthanize should be made in consultation with your veterinarian, who will be able to ease the passage for this kitten if it must be put down.

FEEDING PROBLEM KITTENS

There may be times when you will have to feed a single kitten, or even an entire litter, either temporarily or throughout the nursing feeding stage. Very rarely, a queen will die in the process of giving birth. If this very unusual occurrence happens, you will have to feed the entire litter. If your queen has Type B blood and was bred to a Type A male, you will have to feed the kittens for the first 16 hours. If your queen develops mastitis, an infection of the mammary glands, you must remove the kittens from her and feed them yourself.

Sometimes, for no apparent reason, a queen will reject the litter completely. Since it can and does happen, you must be prepared to bottle feed or tube feed one or all of the kittens in the litter.

Queens Without Enough Milk

Sometimes queens just do not have enough milk to feed their kittens. This is not uncommon with a first-time queen. It can also happen with queens who have unusually large litters. If a queen has had a particularly difficult labor or if she has had a cesarean section and was anesthetized, she may also have a difficult time producing milk.

Once the kittens are born and you find the queen has insufficient milk, your veterinarian may prescribe a shot of Pitocin for your queen. This can sometimes help her milk to flow much better. But not always; there may simply be times when you have to supplement one or more of the kittens, especially if the smaller ones are being forced off the queen by the other, larger kittens.

Putting Kittens on Another Wet Queen

The easiest way to feed a kitten is to put it on another queen who is lactating. Most queens gladly accept additional babies and, unless your other lactating queen has a litter that is almost too big for her to care for, will even welcome them. Cats are natural mothers for the most part. When they are nursing their kittens, they appear to be in a state of bliss.

If you feel there might be a problem with a queen and your breeding program will allow you to do so, you can breed your queens at the same time to be sure several will be lactating at about the same time. If you are breeding both a Type A queen and a Type B queen, and if you are able to do so, breed the Type A queen about a week before the Type B queen so that you can move the newborn kittens directly from the B queen onto the already-lactating A queen. Of course,

> **IMPORTANT!**
>
> WHEN YOU ARE SUPPLEMENTING A LITTER OR A SINGLE KITTEN FROM A LITTER, IT IS CRITICAL THAT THE KITTEN(S) BE WEIGHED EVERY DAY AND THE WEIGHT RECORDED.

this assumes that nature is willing to cooperate with your plans and that both queens will come into season when you want them to and that both pregnancies will go easily to term. Needless to say, this rarely happens for most breeders.

Bottle Feeding

If the kitten has a sucking reflex, the best way to feed him is using a bottle. You can check for the sucking reflex by touching your finger to the end of the kitten's mouth. If the kitten starts to suck and turn his head to get his mouth around your finger, then you can try to feed him with a bottle.

Before you make up the kitten formula, you might want to use a bottle filled with Pedialyte, a mixture of water and electrolytes made for human babies, to see how willing the kitten is to take the bottle. Make sure the Pedialyte is warm. If the kitten starts to feed from the bottle, you can move on to formula. Do not feed too much Pedialyte, as you do not want to fill the kitten's stomach or he will not eat his formula.

> **IMPORTANT!**
>
> NEVER FEED A KITTEN WHO IS COLD. THE BODY TEMPERATURE OF THE KITTEN MUST BE ABOVE 90 DEGREES BEFORE IT CAN DIGEST FOOD.

When you are feeding a kitten, you should use a commercial formula made for feeding orphaned kittens. This is the only way you will know you are meeting all of the kitten's nutritional needs. There are many homemade formulas, but you are not really able to precisely control the amount of nutrients that will be made available to the newborn by using a homemade formula. Before your queen is due to deliver, make sure you buy kitten formula and keep this and a kitten feeding bottle on hand in case you need them.

You can buy feeding bottles and kitten formula through veterinary supply catalogs or in pet supply stores. There are a variety of bottles used to feed newborn kittens, but you can always rely on the small bottles made specifically for feeding small animals. They generally come with a variety of nipples so you can use the one that fits the kitten's mouth most comfortably. These sets also come with a brush so the bottles can be washed. These bottle sets are quite inexpensive, generally costing around $2 for the set with a two-ounce bottle and $4 for the set with a four-ounce bottle. If you know you are expecting four kittens, you will have time to acquire four of these bottle sets.

While the bottles do not have to be sterile, they must be washed thoroughly after each feeding. Any formula left in the bottle may act as

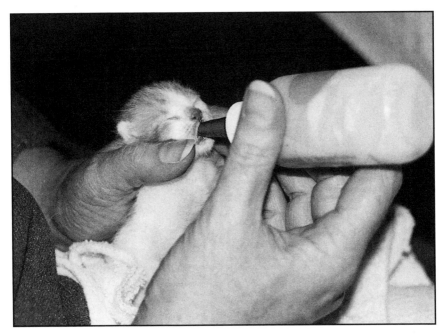

Blizzard is being fed here with a kitten feeding bottle.

a growth medium for bacteria, and these bacteria may give the kitten diarrhea.

There are several brands of milk replacement for kittens, including KMR, Kittylac and Just Born. You can buy kitten formula in two forms: liquid and powder. You can buy the liquid formula in either a small or a larger container. It costs more than the powder and has a relatively short life after you have opened it. The powder has a longer shelf life before it is reconstituted, and you can make up just as much as you need. The powder must be mixed completely with water, and sometimes this is not all that easy. If you have trouble mixing it, you can use a wire whisk or you can put the mixture into a small jar with a lid and shake it. Use cold water to mix the formula.

You do not usually mix this up in a blender because you are working with very small amounts of the product to ensure that it stays fresh. The amounts you'd need to mix up in a blender or small food processor would probably leave you with a lot of wasted formula. Also, these products are designed to be mixed by hand. A blender will add a lot of air to the formula, giving your kittens painful gas. So if you must use a blender, be sure to let the mixture settle before feeding it.

Whether you use a syringe or a bottle to supplement a kitten, the formula must be warmed.

Once you have the formula made up, you will want to heat it. Cold formula should *never* be fed to a kitten. It must always be warmed before the kitten is given the bottle. One of the easiest ways to heat the formula is to microwave water or heat it on the stove. When it is hot, put the sealed baby bottle containing the formula into the water and leave it there until it gets warm. If you have a microwave, you can heat the water in a Pyrex measuring cup and keep the bottle in this water while you prepare the kitten. By the time the kitten has eaten, the water in the cup should be cool enough to use to wash the kitten's perineal area.

When you are ready to feed the kitten, take him out of his cage and put him on your leg or a flat surface with his paws on the surface. He will feel more secure if he has traction. Then put the nipple in the kitten's mouth. You may have to open his mouth in order to do this, but generally just tickling the side of his mouth with the nipple will make the kitten open his mouth and start seeking the nipple.

Once the kitten has the nipple in his mouth, let him start eating. Keep the bottle fairly perpendicular to avoid getting air into the kitten's stomach. You might also consider rubbing the kitten's back while he is eating to help him expel any air he may have swallowed. If the kitten is reluctant to start eating or starts and then stops, rotate the nipple until he has it where he wants it. A slight change in the angle of the nipple may make it easier for the kitten to drink the formula.

> ## IMPORTANT!
>
> WHEN SUPPLEMENTING A KITTEN EITHER BY BOTTLE OR TUBE FEEDING, HIS STOMACH SHOULD JUST FEEL FULL. IT SHOULD NOT BE SWOLLEN OR OTHERWISE DISTENDED.

When the kitten is finished eating, he must have his perineal area cleaned. This is usually the queen's job. When you see the queen washing the kitten's perineal area, she is not only keeping him clean but she is also stimulating him to urinate. You can clean the kitten with a cotton ball dipped in warm water, the corner of a diaper or the end of a wash cloth. If you use something rough like a wash cloth, you may want to clean the kitten's perineal area with baby oil every now and then to soothe any irritation he may have. If you have a queen who has no milk but is taking care of the kitten, let her clean the kitten.

Tube Feeding

Tube feeding is a procedure that can intimidate the most experienced breeder of pedigreed cats. There is really no need for this. While you are, in fact, putting a tube into the kitten's stomach and running fluid into the stomach through this tube, on a small kitten the odds of the tube going into the lungs rather than the stomach are small.

Unfortunately, this is one of those procedures that you cannot really practice. You can practice giving shots into a pillow or into a stuffed animal, but tube feeding is done when you have to do it. When you do have to tube feed, you may be upset and concerned about the little kitten you have to feed, and this stress on you can make this procedure seem rather daunting. Realize that if you use the proper technique, you will do this right and you will be able to supplement the kitten that needs the food given to him in the only way the supplementation can take place.

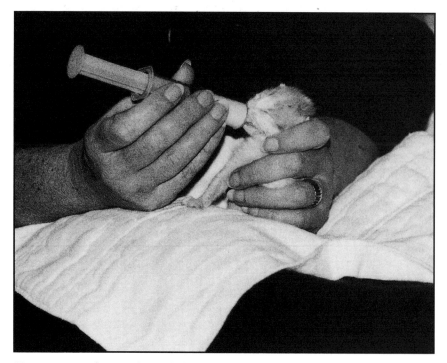

Here, a syringe is being used to feed Blizzard. The syringe can help a kitten with weaker sucking reflexes.

First, check the sucking reflex. If the kitten has a sucking reflex, he should be bottle fed. If he does not or if you have tried to bottle feed the kitten and he is not able to take the bottle at all, you should tube feed the kitten. You should always have the equipment necessary for tube feeding at hand. You will need a small catheter, generally a Number 5 French catheter, and a feeding syringe or a syringe without a needle, size 6 cc or 12 cc. You will be using the same formula you use when you bottle feed a kitten.

Find where the kitten's stomach is located. Use the last rib you feel as a guide— the stomach is at the last rib.

NOTE!

EVERY TIME YOU TUBE FEED A KITTEN, RE-CHECK THE LENGTH OF THE TUBE NEEDED FOR FEEDING. THE TUBE WILL HAVE TO BE LENGTHENED AS THE KITTEN GROWS.

(For more information on cat and kitten anatomy, see the references in the Appendix.) Hold the tube on the outside of the kitten and measure the length from his stomach to his mouth. Use a piece of adhesive tape to mark the tube on the end that accepts the syringe. This is the length of tube you will be putting into the kitten.

Place the kitten in an upright position, as this makes it easier to pass the tube. Hold his head up for him if he has a problem holding up his head on his own. Place the tube—

> **IMPORTANT!**
>
> THE AMOUNT OF FORMULA YOU USE FOR YOUR KITTEN WILL VARY BY THE BRAND YOU BUY. FOLLOW THE INSTRUCTIONS ON THE FORMULA CONTAINER.

open end first—against the roof of the kitten's mouth and pass it down the esophagus into the stomach. As you go down the throat you will be triggering the gag reflex, so do not be alarmed. However, if the kitten really struggles or continues to gag even though the tube has passed down the back of the throat, remove the tube and try again. The tube should pass easily on its own. Do not lubricate the tube with anything other than water.

Once the tube has passed to its full, marked length, it should have the open end in the kitten's stomach. You can do a simple check of this by putting the end of the tube that accepts the syringe into a glass of water. Put the end about half an inch into the water, holding the syringe end straight down so that water cannot run up the tube. If you see a stream of bubbles in the water, you may be in the lungs. If you think you are in the lungs, remove the tube and try again.

If the kitten has no problem being placed on his feet and can hold his head up, you can feed him this way, but you might feel more comfortable holding the kitten in an upright position. You can wrap him in a wash cloth if he is too active. At this point, plug your syringe, filled with warmed formula, into the end of the catheter. Depress the plunger at a slow and steady rate. The formula will be placed directly into the stomach of the kitten. He will not have to be burped after tube feeding, but should still be held and petted. This procedure may have been even more difficult on him than it was on you!

KITTEN EVALUATION FORM

You should consider using a form such as this one to track litters as they are born. Looking back over your records after the kittens have grown into adults may also help you determine if your initial evaluations of the kittens' quality was correct.

You should also use a form like this when you are considering acquiring a new kitten or cat for your program. Make notes on each cat you examine, and then you have a consistent way to compare one cat to another.

Stud

Name

Color/pattern

Eye color

Number of breedings to date

Queen

Name

Color/pattern

Eye color

Number of breedings to date

Mating

Date of first witnessed mating

Date of last witnessed mating

Kittens

Date of birth

Order in birth

Number of kittens born live

dead

Details of Kittens

	DATE & TIME OF BIRTH	CONDITION	SEX	COLOR/MARKINGS	COMMENTS
First kitten					
Second kitten					
Third kitten					

Condition at Weaning

First kitten					
Second kitten					
Third kitten					

Grading of Characteristics

	HEAD	COLOR	BODY	EAR SET	EAR HEIGHT	EYE COLOR	OTHER
First kitten							
Second kitten							
Third kitten							
At birth							

	HEAD	COLOR	BODY	EAR SET	EAR HEIGHT	EYE COLOR	OTHER
First kitten							
Second kitten							
Third kitten							
At ___ weeks							

	HEAD	COLOR	BODY	EAR SET	EAR HEIGHT	EYE COLOR	OTHER
First kitten							
Second kitten							
Third kitten							
At ___ weeks							

	HEAD	COLOR	BODY	EAR SET	EAR HEIGHT	EYE COLOR	OTHER
First kitten							
Second kitten							
Third kitten							
At ___ months							

	HEAD	COLOR	BODY	EAR SET	EAR HEIGHT	EYE COLOR	OTHER
First kitten							
Second kitten							
Third kitten							
At ___ months							

	HEAD	COLOR	BODY	EAR SET	EAR HEIGHT	EYE COLOR	OTHER
First kitten							
Second kitten							
Third kitten							
At ___ months							

YOU KNOW YOU ARE A CAT BREEDER WHEN . . .

- If you even bother with a Christmas tree, the decorations start three feet off the floor.

- Your refrigerator contains milk, some outdated eggs and some moldy cheese, and your shelves mostly have cans of tuna and boxes of instant macaroni and cheese; but your cats eat three different kinds of dry food, drink bottled water and take up most of your cupboard space with cases of every flavor of premium moist food.

- You can describe, in detail, the last medical crisis to strike one of your cats, but can't remember the last time one of your kids was sick.

- You consider finding trays of Sheba duck flavor to be a major victory.

- You have bottles of Metronidazole, Centrine and Ditrim and gentacin ophthalmic drops in the bottom of your purse at all times, but not one aspirin.

- You keep a lint roller at work to get the cat hair off your clothes before your coworkers arrive.

Adapted from *101 Ways to Know You're a Cat Fancier.*

CHAPTER EIGHT

Basic Health Care

SELECTING A VETERINARIAN

The most important component of your kitten's health care is your veterinarian. Before you even begin to register your cattery or acquire your breeding cats, you must select a veterinarian with whom you can establish a relationship and work closely. You will find that your veterinarian is the most important person in your cattery.

- You will seek his advice on every aspect of the medical care of your cats.

- He will be performing surgery on your cats and the kittens they produce.

- You will analyze his advice and follow it.

- You will be exchanging information about your breed, about cat shows, about the latest veterinary developments you become aware of, and about the techniques you use in the breeding and care of your cats.

- If you choose to have your cattery inspected, he will be out at your cattery to perform the inspection.

It may take some time to find the veterinarian you want. Some veterinarians are not interested in working with breeders. As breeders, we are very demanding. When we go to our veterinarian's office, we want to be seen immediately. We want to have the time to discuss various aspects of breeding with our veterinarian no matter how busy he might be. We tend to do much of our own veterinary care and sometimes hesitate to go to the veterinarian until the cat is quite ill. We also want the veterinarian to let us pay our bill over time. We demand house calls from our veterinarian, and we never hesitate to call our veterinarian in the middle of the night if we have a problem.

In addition, we are quite willing to argue endlessly with our veterinarian, and we expect him to do the same with us. We never take his advice without checking it out with other breeders. We insist on giving our own inoculations. We may also be practicing improper or even damaging breeding techniques, such as inbreeding, or even breeding cats that are born with genetic anomalies. Sometimes our husbandry techniques could use improvement, and the veterinarian is the best person to point out the changes we need to make. We even may be letting the temptation of a cat show come before our dedication to a pregnant cat who is due to kitten. As you can see, a veterinarian who not only permits breeders into his practice but welcomes them is the most valuable ally we can have as we breed pedigreed cats.

The most important aspect in your selection of a veterinarian is not the physical components of his office, but the veterinarian himself.

- Will you be able to build a relationship with this veterinarian?

- Will you be able to talk to him and will you trust him when he prescribes a drug for your cat or recommends a cesarean section?

- Will he be able to trust you enough to give you prescription medications to keep in your cattery and use only when needed?

- Will he learn about your breed?

- Will you follow his advice on husbandry techniques?

All these aspects of your relationship are critical to the success of your cattery. You never want to feel you did something that harmed one of your cats because you felt you could not ask your veterinarian about some information another breeder gave you.

The ideal veterinarian for a cattery is one who has some experience or training in herd management techniques or kennel or cattery courses or experience. Because of this training, he will understand how to care for many cats who are confined in the same cattery. He must also know about the spread of infectious and contagious diseases, fungus and parasites, since some of your cats will be traveling to cat shows or will temporarily spend time in other catteries for stud service. He should be an expert in preventive medicine, because you would rather use the proper techniques to prevent a problem than wait until that problem is present and then try to treat it.

You should make an appointment to meet with a veterinarian you are considering, so you can interview him. When you interview him, you should ask about subjects that are critical to you as a breeder, such as:

- What is his training?

- Has he had previous experience working with pedigreed cat breeders?

- Can you see his facilities for boarding cats who must be at the veterinarian overnight?

- Does he release males who have been neutered the same day they have their surgery? Does he do the same for females who have been spayed?

- Does he permit the breeder to be in the operating room to assist with the kittens during a cesarean section?

- Can he sign a health certificate for a cat who is being shipped by air or will be living in a different state or country?

- Who covers his practice at night and on the weekends?

- Will he alter pet kittens at three to four months of age?

The answers to all of these questions will help you decide whether or not you will be able to work with the veterinarian you are interviewing.

Since you will be breeding your cats, you will want to make sure your veterinarian is trained in ultrasound techniques. This simple procedure will become extremely valuable for you, and you want a veterinarian who has the proper equipment and who knows how to interpret what he sees on the ultrasound. In addition, you will want to make certain he can perform an ultrasound without having to shave too much fur from your queen. While most cats will have to have some hair shaved from the abdominal region, there is no need to shave her entire belly.

Ask the veterinarian you are interviewing for references, especially references from other cat or dog breeders in his practice. Then call those people and ask them how they feel about that particular veterinarian. Have they had any problems with him? Was he available when they needed him? Does he listen to them? Does he learn about their breed?

Once you have selected a veterinarian and have established a relationship, never abuse that relationship. Veterinarians are constrained by law from prescribing medications without examining the sick animal. Your veterinarian may be able to make an exception to this if you have a good relationship, if he knows the cat and if he knows that you are very careful in describing the physical signs of illnesses or problems with your cats. In states where rabies inoculations are mandatory, your veterinarian must inoculate all your cats for rabies unless he feels there is a legitimate health reason not to.

If you and your veterinarian have decided upon a certain procedure for testing your cats for infectious diseases, never violate this procedure, not even "just this once." When your veterinarian certifies that your cattery is free of contagion, he does so as a medical professional who is licensed by the state. When he signs your cattery inspection form for the Cat Fanciers' Association Cattery of Excellence Program, he states that he has inspected all there is to see. *Putting your veterinarian in a*

Pet Health Insurance

Pet health care insurance is still not widely used. However, we think it is useful for many cat owners, if for no other reason than it protects us from ever having to worry that we might hold off on critical medical treatment for financial reasons.

Because of that, do not analyze insurance in terms of its payoff. The best payoff would be never having to have to file a claim, which means your beloved animals would never be sick.

As with your medical insurance, pet insurance is not perfect, but it is much better than nothing. It does not cover routine shots, because the owner should be doing that anyway. It does not cover pregnancy, because either the cat should have been neutered or the pregnancy is a planned breeding, which is a business decision and not a health emergency.

You should consider these issues when you are selling a kitten, because most policies allow you to transfer coverage to a new owner. Not only does this provide protection for the new owner, but it serves as additional protection for you. If a new owner claims the kitten was sick when you sold it, having insurance coverage may protect you from someone claiming you owe them a lot of money for veterinary treatment.

compromising position is never done by a responsible, professional breeder of pedigreed cats.

You must also explain your own cattery management policies and procedures to your veterinarian. If he has a problem with the type of husbandry you practice, explain why you are doing what you are doing. Then listen to his concerns. Try to work things out with your veterinarian. It does not help your cattery to be constantly changing veterinarians. The fact that your veterinarian knows your cats and their health history is critical to their care.

Realize that while your veterinarian has a friendly relationship with you, his patient is your cat. If your veterinarian asks you to leave the room during a cesarean section, or any other procedure, it is because his primary concern is his patient.

DRUGS AND VACCINES

Once you are running a working cattery, you will begin to see just how important it is to control the costs of drugs. Here are a few tips to help you.

Catalogs are a good way to buy drugs you use often. These drugs can range from routine inoculations to medications for eyes. Before you order, make sure to calculate shipping costs (or order minimums) into your evaluations of which supply house offers the best value. Some of these companies are listed in the Appendix.

You cannot always buy everything you need from a catalog. And what you can buy often varies by state, as well as by the type of product you are buying. Some states require that drugs (and syringes) be purchased only with a prescription from your veterinarian. In some states, this applies to drugs that come pre-loaded into syringes. In a few states, rabies vaccines can be given only by veterinarians, and the supply houses will not ship to individuals in that state.

If you have a choice, do not get veterinary products from a human pharmacy (at least until you check the prices and compare them to a veterinary supply house).

Call your order in rather than mail it. When you call, ask if the items are in stock. If they are not, do not back order unless you are not paying a second round of shipping charges for the balance of the shipment, and unless you can establish when the products will be shipped. Also, when you call in you should ask if there are any special charges for shipping the medications. For example, most companies suggest using two-day or faster shipping for refrigerated vaccines (they are shipped with a cooler); a few do this automatically and charge you. Find out first.

Avoid buying drugs from a vendor at a cat show unless you check the expiration date on the product, can be sure the product has been properly stored and already know the catalog price of the product. You will tend to pay extra for the convenience of buying at a show.

If your cat (or cattery) needs a certain product regularly, to be administered when your veterinarian tells you, order a supply and keep it on hand. If the product requires a prescription, check if the catalog house will accept one from your veterinarian and ship the product to you. Most of them will. Then let your veterinarian know you have it on hand. Make sure to keep a copy of the prescription you send to the supply house, since some of them require you to send the original prescription, not a copy.

When your order comes, before you put it away check the expiration dates on products. If you have a product that expires in less than one year, call the company immediately and ask for a replacement (unless you are going to use it all now). Do not settle for short dating.

If you routinely have to get medications from your veterinarian, bring a catalog with you. Compare the price you would pay to the catalog firm with what the vet's office charges you. That means anything from antibiotics to insulin. You can ask to be given a price comparable to the catalog price. If he is not able to comply, get just enough medication from the vet's office to cover you until the catalog order arrives, and get a prescription for the balance.

What Should You Vaccinate Against?

Drug companies have developed many vaccines for use against diseases that affect cats. These vaccines have been used successfully for years and have proven efficacy against these diseases. You should always vaccinate against the most common diseases affecting cats. These diseases include:

- Feline Panleukopenia is the feline version of distemper. It is fatal for 50 percent to 70 percent of cats who contract it. The disease is short-term but severe. Most affected cats die within three to four days after they first show signs of the disease. This disease is highly contagious.

- Feline Viral Rhinotracheitis is a chronic upper respiratory problem that can be fatal in cats and young kittens. However, even if it is not fatal to a particular cat, that cat can continue to shed the disease, especially when under stress. Chronic carriers of this disease can cause real problems in a cattery, because they can continue to infect the other cats.

- Feline Calici Viral Disease, a highly contagious disease, affects the lungs. It causes pneumonia and can be fatal. It is the cause of approximately 40 percent of all respiratory tract diseases in cats.

- Chlamydia Psittaci is a highly contagious bacterial infection that also affects the respiratory system. It is also the cause of many of the eye infections in cats and kittens.

You can buy vaccines that contain the inoculants for all four of these diseases. Kitten vaccines are given as a series of two shots with an annual booster shot. But these "four-way" vaccines enable you to give just one shot to inoculate against all of these diseases. As with everything else in a multiple-cat environment, the traditional vaccination schedule should be discussed with your veterinarian and adapted to your own particular cattery.

While it is easier to keep all the cats in your cattery on the same vaccination schedule, this can be impossible in a cattery. Make certain you keep meticulous records so that you can catch up on your booster shots for any cat you failed to vaccinate at a set time because it was pregnant, ill, or for other reasons.

> **NOTE!**
>
> NOT EVERY VACCINE IS AVAILABLE FOR PURCHASE IN ALL STATES. SYRINGES AND NEEDLES MAY ALSO NOT BE AVAILABLE, DEPENDING UPON THE STATE IN WHICH YOU LIVE.

Killed Versus Modified Live Vaccines

When you look in the veterinary supply catalogs, you will see two different types of vaccines. One type is called *killed* and the other is called *modified live*. The killed vaccine is just that: The inoculant has been completely killed, and this is what you will be injecting into your cat. While the killed vaccines are safer than the modified live vaccines, they also take longer to produce the desired immunity.

The modified live vaccine is altered to produce a faster immune response. While these vaccines provide greater and faster immunity, they may also be shed from the vaccinated cat into the cattery. They should never be used on a pregnant cat.

The choice of which type of vaccine to use should be discussed with your veterinarian, if the breeder you bought your kitten from has not given you explicit instructions on which type of vaccine to use. Some breeds of cats tend to react well to the modified live vaccine, while others can only safely use the killed vaccine.

> ### HINT!
>
> HAVE YOUR CATS TESTED FOR INFECTIOUS DISEASES AT LEAST THREE MONTHS AFTER GIVING ANY VACCINE. VACCINES CAN CAUSE TEMPORARY FALSE NEGATIVE TEST RESULTS.

Traditional Kitten Vaccination Schedule

	FIRST SHOT	SECOND SHOT	THIRD SHOT
Panleukopenia	10 weeks	16 weeks	
Rhinotracheitis	10 weeks	16 weeks	
Calici Viral Disease	10 weeks	6 weeks	
Chlamydiosis	10 weeks	6 weeks	
Feline Leukemia (optional)	10 weeks	12 weeks	24 weeks
Rabies	16 weeks		

If you are giving your own shots, you will need syringes. The easiest way to buy the syringes for your vaccines is through the veterinary supply catalogs. The 3-cc syringes are most easily used to give vaccines. One-cc syringes are also available with a smaller bore needle, but these can sometimes become clumsy to use because the syringe will be almost completely filled with the vaccine.

Vaccine Controversies

Today there are controversies surrounding several of the newer vaccines. Over time, these controversies may diminish in intensity and may even be resolved. However, as new vaccines are developed and introduced, it is likely there will be controversy surrounding them as well. Some of these controversial vaccines are discussed below.

Ringworm vaccine was developed to help prevent ringworm in cats. It has been known to cause lesions at the site of the vaccination, which can create temporary bald spots. This may look like a typical sign of ringworm itself.

Ringworm vaccine should never be used on pregnant queens under any circumstances. In clinical trials by the manufacturer (Fort Dodge Laboratories), no abortions or miscarriages were noted. However, several breeders who have used the vaccine in pregnant queens have lost kittens.

Use this vaccine carefully, only if you have had a problem with ringworm in your cattery and even then, only in consultation with your veterinarian.

While the feline infectious peritonitis (FIP) vaccine is considered to be safe, there are some problems with it.

> **HINT!**
>
> WHEN YOU RECORD THE VACCINES YOU HAVE GIVEN, RECORD BOTH THE LOT NUMBER AND EXPIRATION DATE ON THE LABEL OF THE VIAL YOU USED. SHOULD ANY QUESTIONS ARISE LATER ABOUT THAT MANUFACTURER'S VACCINE, YOU WILL KNOW IF THEY AFFECT YOUR CATTERY.

First of all, the vaccine is formulated for Type II feline coronaviruses, as opposed to Type I, according to Dr. Niels C. Pedersen, DVM, Ph.D., a researcher in the field of contagious and infectious diseases of cats. Dr. Pedersen has found that most field strains of the coronavirus are Type I.

In addition, the vaccine is only effective on kittens 16 weeks old or older who have tested negative for exposure to coronaviruses. Then the vaccine may protect the kitten, especially if he is going into a multi-cat environment. If you have FIP in your cattery, this vaccine will not eliminate it.

Feline leukemia (FeLV) vaccine protects against feline leukemia, which affects the immune system and leaves a cat open to infections from other diseases such as FIP. In fact, the appearance of feline leukemia and FIP in the same cat is not uncommon.

Many breeders do not use this vaccine for pedigreed cats as they believe its use might make the cat susceptible to other diseases, specifically the coronaviruses that exist in all catteries.

HOW TO INOCULATE KITTENS

Intra-nasal Inoculations

Although modified live intra-nasal vaccines are generally used on young kittens, they should not be used on kittens under four weeks of age. These vaccines are administered by placing a drop of the vaccine in the corner of each of the kitten's eyes. The remaining vaccine is then administered in the nose. When you use these vaccines to inoculate kittens, you might want to wrap the kitten in a washcloth or small towel to hold him firmly.

This kind of vaccine can be very difficult to administer to an adult cat, as an adult can move its head away in the time it takes for the drop to fall into his eye or nose.

Parenteral Inoculations

Giving an injection to a cat or kitten is really very easy and very safe, as long as you follow the proper procedure. Always give your vaccinations subcutaneously, which means under the skin (called "subQ"). Giving an injection into the muscle of the cat is more complicated, and you may hit a nerve, which can cause extreme pain or temporary paralysis.

To give a subQ injection, follow these simple steps:

To give an injection, pull up the scruff of the kitten's neck . . .

1. Open the top of the vaccine vial and clean the rubber area with an alcohol swab. If the vaccine must be mixed, you will have one vial of powder and one vial of the liquid component used to mix the vaccine. In this case, open the tops of both vials and clean both with an alcohol swab.

2. Remove the needle cover from the syringe and draw into the syringe an amount of air equal to the

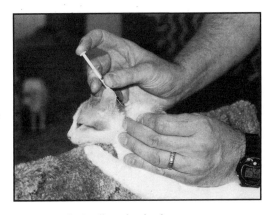

. . . inject the needle under the skin . . .

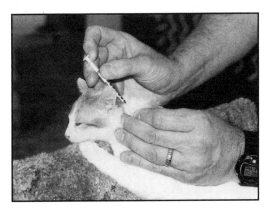

. . . and depress the plunger of the syringe.

amount of the vaccine you need. For example, if the vaccine dosage is 1 cc, draw 1 cc of air into the syringe. Insert the needle into the vial and depress the plunger. With the needle still in the vial, draw the plunger back until you have the proper dosage of the vaccine in the syringe.

WARNING!

DO NOT GIVE ANY VACCINA-
TIONS TO A KITTEN WHO IS ILL.

If you have to mix a vaccine, follow this procedure first with the vial of liquid. Then insert the needle into the vial of powder, depress the plunger to insert the liquid into the powder, withdraw the needle and gently shake the bottle of vaccine to mix it. Once it is mixed, follow the same procedure to draw the vaccine into the syringe.

3. Holding the kitten firmly, grasp the scruff of the neck and lift the skin away from the body.

4. Insert the needle under the skin of the kitten, *but not into muscle.*

5. Depress the plunger to expel the vaccine.

6. Kiss the kitten and rub his neck where you gave the shot.

Testing for Disease

Since you have tested each and every one of your cats for feline leukemia, feline coronavirus, feline AIDS and toxoplasmosis when you brought them into your cattery, and retested if any cat went outside of the cattery or showed symptoms of any disease, you can feel secure that your cattery is free of these diseases.

But when you sell kittens, you will want to assure the new owner of this. The easiest way is to test one kitten from each litter for these conditions. When the test comes back negative, copy this paper and include it with each of the kittens you sell. Include this procedure in your contract and ask that the new owner explain your procedure to the cat's new veterinarian.

In the event that a coronavirus titer is in the positive range, another blood test should be done to determine whether or not the kitten is developing antibodies to the coronavirus. If this test shows increased antibody activity, another blood test should be done. This test is called the PCR (polymerase chain reaction) and is a genetic test to differentiate FIP from other coronaviruses. This test is controversial, and many veterinarians believe it is not actually able to make this discrete a differentiation.

IMPORTANT!

"UNDER NO CIRCUMSTANCES SHOULD A CAT BE EUTHANIZED BASED SOLELY ON THE RESULTS OF A CORONAVIRUS TITER TEST . . . . A CAT CAN BE INFECTED BY FIPV AND *NOT* DEVELOP FIP," ACCORDING TO THE *WINN FOUNDATION REPORT: HIGHLIGHTS FROM THE INTERNATIONAL FIP/FECV WORKSHOP.*

FLEA CONTROL

The best way to control fleas is never to get them in your cattery in the first place. However, this is just an ideal. You may well bring fleas into your cattery from a cat show, from a newly acquired cat or just by having fleas attach themselves to you as you walk in the grass during flea season.

Fleas are not easy to eliminate, but it can be done. You can shampoo your cats with flea shampoos, dust them with a powder made to kill fleas or have your cats wear flea collars. However, all of these products contain poison to kill the fleas, and your cat can react to these poisons. You can use all-natural, herbal products either in the form of shampoos or dips or liquids made to be added to the water dish. Some of these natural substances work very well, but it seems many of the ones that work do so only on specific breeds of cats.

There are now oral medications your veterinarian can give you to help control fleas. These are safer than the sometimes toxic dips and shampoos that are still available. They are also easier to use. These oral agents do not prevent fleas from infesting or biting your cat. Instead, they break the life cycle of the flea by preventing the flea eggs from developing into adults. If you have a flea problem at the time you start these oral agents, it will take a bit of time to rid the cattery of fleas by using these medications alone, but it will happen.

Always consult your veterinarian before you decide to use one of these agents on a pregnant cat. And these oral agents are not recommended for kittens under the age of six weeks.

Another option, which works in a similar way, is a new generation of topical agents offered through veterinarians. These topical agents immediately kill *adult* fleas. As with the oral agents, they do not destroy fleas at all stages. But by killing all adults on a cat, they help you to break the life cycle—when used along with a program attacking the entire environment. What makes them attractive is that they are easy to apply and do not pose the dangers of the older, more toxic types of flea dips and powders.

Since these are just being introduced into the U.S. from Europe, experience with them is still limited. But it appears that most of them are safe for use on both kittens and cats. Before you use them, check with your veterinarian as to options and possible side effects.

DEALING WITH COMMON KITTEN PROBLEMS

Kittens, even the healthiest of them, do get sick. Many of their problems are due to the fact that they are kittens, and are common and very minor. They get food in their eyes when they are being weaned because they seem to have to put their entire face in their food dish. They get little bites when they are wrestling with their litter mates. They tumble off tall places. Kittens are actually quite resilient. When you see one fall off the bed and land on his side, then get up and run away, you are thankful for those soft little bones.

The major problem when dealing with kitten problems is that they progress so very fast. You can look at a kitten in the morning and he appears to have a slight upper respiratory infection but no fever. By that evening, he has a high fever. By the next day, he may well have pneumonia. *Kittens must be treated aggressively and immediately.* While you should always take your kitten to your veterinarian at the first sign of illness, you should also have some medications available at home. And you must know some techniques so that you can intervene right away.

Red Eyes

Red eyes (conjunctivitis) can have many causes. Some are easy to avoid, such as the kitten getting food in his eyes. Just make sure you clean out the kitten's eyes after he eats. You can help to avoid stabs in the eyes of kittens who are playing with each other by being careful to keep their nails clipped.

Kittens also get excrement in their eyes, as well as toys, dust, dirt and cat litter. All you can do about this is to watch the kitten carefully and flush his eyes when the situation demands it. The eyes can be flushed with a veterinary eye wash, which you can buy from one of the suppliers listed in the Appendix. You can also use sterile human eye wash or pH-balanced eye drops, commonly called liquid tears.

> **IMPORTANT!**
>
> NEVER USE ANY STEROID EYE MEDICATION WHEN THERE IS ANY DANGER OF AN INFECTION. STEROIDS CAN VERY RAPIDLY MAKE AN INFECTION WORSE.

When applying eye ointment, be careful that the tip of the applicator does not touch the eye itself.

Oral medication is easy to give when you have the kitten well controlled.

Red eyes are also caused by allergies. Cats and kittens get allergies just as people do. In fact, if you are prone to allergies and you have a cat who is prone to allergies, you might both find yourself reacting to an allergen at the very same time. You can handle this by using an over-the-counter allergy eye drop. Be careful with these, as they can sometimes sting.

You must be extremely careful when you are dealing with red eyes. You should not try to remedy this situation on your own, unless you are sure the cause is something simple such as food in the eye and it clears up immediately. If the eye irritation continues for 48 hours, it is most likely an infection and the kitten should go to the veterinarian.

Eye infections can be caused by various organisms. While there are many eye ointments that are effective in clearing up conjunctivitis, you may need a culture to determine which ointment is best for the specific infection. If you let a red eye go untreated, the eyeball itself can be scarred.

Diarrhea

Diarrhea in kittens can be caused by many things. Sometimes a kitten will develop diarrhea just from going through the weaning process and trying to adjust to food. Sometimes you will find the same reaction when the kitten is learning to eat dry food. Kittens can also be notoriously overindulgent. Everything tastes good to them. This overindulgence can sometimes lead to diarrhea.

> **IMPORTANT!**
>
> IF A KITTEN HAS DIARRHEA, CHECK HIM OFTEN TO MAKE CERTAIN HE IS NOT BECOMING DEHYDRATED. IF HE IS DEHYDRATED, BEGIN REPLACEMENT FLUID THERAPY IMMEDIATELY.

Diarrhea can also be caused by certain organisms such as giardiasis or coccidia. In some cases, these organisms can be difficult to isolate. If your kitten has extremely loose or foul-smelling stools, take him to the veterinarian. You should also do this if you see evidence of blood or mucous in the stool.

If the stool is merely loose but the kitten does not yet have diarrhea, try using acidophilus. This is a culture commonly found in yogurt. You can buy acidophilus at health food stores or, if the kitten will eat it, you can feed the kitten yogurt.

For common kitten diarrhea, you can give some of the remedies available in the veterinary supply catalogs or in pet supply stores. These are mild and should stop the problem. One of these remedies is Pectillin.

Rehydrating Kittens

You can tell when a kitten needs to be rehydrated by pulling up the scruff of the neck and pinching it gently. If the scruff remains up and does not immediately spring back to its normal position, the kitten is dehydrated. When this happens, the situation is critical. Kittens cannot exist for long without enough fluid in their bodies. Not only are they "dry," but the critical electrolytes that help to make the body function normally are depleted. The kitten must be rehydrated.

The quickest and most effective way for you to rehydrate the kitten is to administer an intravenous solution called Ringer's lactate under the

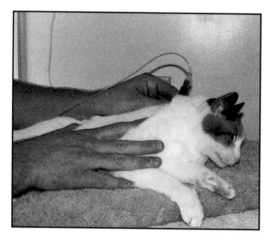

An intravenous system is easy to use when you must rehydrate a cat or kitten.

skin of the kitten. You can get Ringer's lactate solution, along with an intravenous set-up, from your veterinarian.

Take the bag of Ringer's lactate solution and hang it up so that it is at least two feet above your cat. Attach a needle to the end of the tubing. Inject the needle under the skin of the kitten in the scruff area. Open the tube so the solution runs at a slow but steady rate. If at all possible, keep the bag of solution at your eye level. This way you will be able to see very clearly exactly how much solution you are administering.

You will have to judge how much solution to administer. This will depend upon the size of the kitten and how dehydrated he actually is. If a kitten is very dehydrated, you will want to administer what will seem like a very large amount of fluid—perhaps 50 ccs or 75 ccs.

The fluid may cause a temporary lump in the back of the neck. Massage this area after you have finished administering the fluids.

You may have to rehydrate the kitten several times each day to avoid pushing too much fluid into him at any one time. Remember that the more often you have to do this, the more sore his neck will become.

If you are at all uncomfortable dealing with this procedure, take the kitten to your veterinarian, who can administer fluid intravenously. While you are at your veterinarian's office, have him teach you how to rehydrate kittens. This technique is too important to ignore. You must learn how to do this and be ready to act when your kitten needs you. Rehydrating can make all the difference in the recovery of your kitten.

Constipation

Constipation is not as much of a problem with kittens. While your kitten is being weaned, you should expect that he will not defecate for the first couple of days. If you find your kitten still has not defecated after about three days of eating solid food, you may be using too much baby cereal or the kitten may not be really eating as much as you think he is.

If the constipation continues, you can give the kitten Laxatone. This sticky paste can be put on the kitten's tongue or on the roof of his mouth. Do not use too much or he may just spit it out.

Colds

When we refer to a kitten having a cold, we are generally talking about an upper respiratory infection. As a kitten begins to adjust to his new environment, he is constantly encountering the germs that are part of every cattery. As he breathes in these germs, which are still foreign to him, he can develop an upper respiratory infection.

The symptoms of an upper respiratory infection are those of a common cold. There will be some sneezing, lassitude, loss of appetite and a slightly elevated temperature.

Your role in caring for a kitten with an upper respiratory infection is to administer the medication your veterinarian prescribes and to support the

Blizzard spends his nights in the bottom of the Thermocare unit in the birthing cage.

kitten. You should never try to treat an upper respiratory infection yourself, as this can very quickly turn into pneumonia. The medications you may have on hand may not be effective against the particular germ that is causing the upper respiratory infection, and by delaying a veterinary visit you may be putting the kitten at risk.

Your supportive therapy in dealing with an upper respiratory infection consists of trying to get the kitten to eat. This is not as easy as it sounds.

Sick Kitten Diet

- Baby food meat (chicken)
- One egg yolk
- Nutracal, a vitamin supplement in paste form
- Pediatric Stat, liquid vitamins formulated for kittens
- Milk replacer or Cat Sip, a special milk made for cats

Mix this mixture in a small dish. Microwave until the egg yolk is completely cooked. Feed the kitten or use the syringe to place the mixture directly into its mouth.

Feed very small amounts, frequently. Every two hours is usually ideal, including through the night. Store any unused food in the refrigerator and rewarm (do not recook) before using it again. Do not keep this mixture for more than 24 hours.

When a kitten is anorexic, it can be very frustrating trying to get any nourishment in him at all. Before you start to feed him, clean his nose. If his nose is clogged he will not be able to smell the food and will not be enticed into eating. You can sprinkle garlic powder on the food to help give him something to smell. If he does not eat his regular food, switch to the Sick Kitten Diet.

You may also feed a kitten chicken soup or add this to his food. If he still will not eat, try appetite stimulators available through veterinary supply catalogs. While a kitten is anorexic, check him for dehydration and rehydrate him if necessary. If he is drinking his water, switch to Pedialyte in his dish or an electrolyte supplement made especially for cats and kittens. (Pedialyte is an electrolyte solution made for human babies and is available in drug and grocery stores.)

If your kitten is very congested, you may want to make certain you use the vaporizer or nebulizer several times each day (see Chapter Seven). You will also want to keep track of his temperature. To do this, take his temperature at least four times each day at set intervals and keep a record of the temperature and the time you took it. Watch this kitten carefully. Listen to his chest with your stethoscope every time you take his temperature.

Keep this kitten confined and make sure his sleeping area is warm and free of drafts. The confinement is both to make certain he and his environment are controlled, and to isolate him from the other kittens and cats so that his upper respiratory infection does not spread throughout the cattery; any infection in a cattery can spread rapidly, putting other kittens in danger and making the adult cats ill.

Immune System Stimulators

There are times when you may feel that a kitten would thrive better on an immune system stimulator such as ImmunoRegulin. This drug is made from a certain type of bacteria that has been found to enhance a kitten's immune system. It is used when a kitten is undergoing stressful circumstances and may shows signs of lassitude or chronic colds without actually having an infectious process present.

ImmunoRegulin is given in small doses, usually 0.25 cc injected under the skin twice a week for two weeks. The dosage can be less than this in a small kitten.

Many breeders give an injection of ImmunoRegulin before a kitten faces the stress of going to his new home. ImmunoRegulin may elevate the coronavirus titer, however, so the kitten should be tested before this drug is used. You should also make note of any ImmunoRegulin use in your contract and vaccination record, along with the notation that it has been known to elevate blood titers.

HOMEOPATHIC AND HERBAL REMEDIES

Homeopathic veterinary techniques make use of substances that are found naturally in plants, animals or minerals. The principle behind homeopathy is similar to that of vaccines: Like cures like. In other words, you give the patient a small dose of a substance that, in larger doses, would produce symptoms similar to those the animal is already experiencing. For example, you would give a vomiting cat small doses of ipecac. Ipecac is usually used in larger doses to induce vomiting.

While homeopathic remedies are regulated by the Food and Drug Administration and are considered over-the-counter products that are basically harmless, this may change in the future.

Some Natural Remedies for Common Conditions

Condition	Remedy
Mismothering	Pulsatilla
Start milk flow	Urtica urens
No milk	Lac delforatum
Dry up milk	Urtica urens
Mastitis	Aconite along with warm compresses with Calendula lotion
Encourage males to breed	Black cohosh
Stimulate immune system	Echinacea
Depress sexual interest	Hops
Relieve birthing pain	Nettles
Strengthen uterus	Red raspberry
Gastric upset	Slippery elm
Diarrhea	Acidophilus
Regulate hormones in queens	Sepia
Maintain early pregnancy	Viburnum
Maintain late pregnancy	Caulophyllum
Prevent delivery hemorrhages	Arnica

The rise in popularity of homeopathic medicine really began in the 1880s. During that era, homeopathic techniques were used to treat yellow fever, scarlet fever and other human diseases that were commonplace at the time. Homeopathy was very effective in treating these rampant infectious diseases. In addition, the death rate in homeopathic hospitals was significantly lower than in traditional hospitals.

Homeopathy is still considered an alternative to traditional medicine in this country. However, in India, Europe and elsewhere in the world, homeopathic medicine is commonly used and is very much a part of the existing medical community. Homeopathic veterinarians can be found in this country, if that is the kind of veterinary medicine you prefer.

If you are not using a veterinarian who is skilled in using homeopathic and herbal preparations and are using these remedies yourself, you should be aware that very little scientific data is available on their use, and much of the documentation on their efficacy is anecdotal.

Herbal medicine attempts to put the body in tune with nature. Herbs have been used throughout history to relieve symptoms and, hopefully, to effect cures. The herbs used in herbal remedies are considered by the Food and Drug Administration to be foods. Both homeopathic remedies and herbal preparations may be found in health food stores, stores specializing in natural vitamins and supplements, and in specialized catalogs.

You must also be extremely careful when you are adjusting dosages of remedies meant for humans into a dosage that can be safely given to a cat. If you are interested in using homeopathic and herbal preparations for your cats, get a book that specifically deals with this, take the time to find a homeopathic veterinarian who will work with you, or both.

In any case, homeopathic and herbal preparations are not meant to be a substitute for traditional veterinary care. They may be used to relieve minor symptoms or in conjunction with a course of treatment that your veterinarian may be prescribing. In all cases, check with your veterinarian if you are attempting to treat a cat who exhibits any symptoms of illness.

There are also legal constraints when it comes to vaccinations. For example, in states with laws that mandate the use of rabies vaccine in cats, you will be breaking the law if you refuse to comply even though you may prefer to use alternative medicine to treat your cats.

You know you are a cat breeder when . . .

- Your cats' ribbons and trophies fill the mantel, while your families' trophies are stored somewhere with last year's pickles.

- You remember someone's cat's name, but not their name.

- Buying a cat means five minutes studying the cat and five days studying its pedigree.

- You have every registration number of every show cat you own memorized, even though you sometimes cannot remember your own telephone number.

- You can recite the birthdays and birth weights of your last five litters, but can't remember any of your family's birthdays.

- All the supermarket clerks think you have a carnivorous (human) baby ("Why doesn't she ever buy *vegetable* baby food?").

- Your "baby" pictures don't look like other people's "baby" pictures.

- You bury your empty cat food cans in the bottom of the recycle bins so the neighbors can't see how many of them you throw out in a week.

Adapted from *101 Ways to Know You're a Cat Fancier.*

CHAPTER NINE

Raising the Kittens

It is amazing to see just how wonderful cats are when they are mothers. It is even more amazing to see that all the other cats in your cattery have such a wonderful place in their lives for young kittens. Not only will the other whole females adopt and mother the kittens, but so will the spayed females. And sometimes the males make the best mothers of all! The entire tribe will help to raise the kittens, teaching them what they need to know, correcting them when they go astray, playing with them, bathing them and protecting them.

This is a time for you to watch the kittens carefully so you can intervene immediately if something is going wrong. You will also want to make certain your husbandry techniques are excellent and your cattery is spotless—which is not always easy with kittens, as they tend to get into everything.

This is also a time for you to enjoy the kittens, play with the kittens and take many pictures, both for selling this litter and to always remind yourself how wonderful this litter is.

THE CORNELL EARLY WEANING PROGRAM

One of the difficulties with cats in a cattery is the presence of chronic upper respiratory infections. These chronic infections are passed along when one cat has an active infection and sheds the virus in the cattery by direct contact, by contact with the saliva, or through sneezes.

Woodstock, an altered male, takes care of Blizzard as if he were the kitten's mother.

One of the methods breeders use to prevent the spread of these upper respiratory infections is to isolate queens with their kittens. This assumes, of course, that it is not the queen who is infected.

It has also been suggested that an entire litter of kittens be raised in isolation until they are 120 days old. For many catteries, this is unrealistic. True medical isolation would require the cattery owners to disinfect all utensils and litter boxes, as well as themselves, and to wear protective clothing every time they went in and out of the isolation area. This clothing would then have to be placed in a sealed container and washed with disinfectant.

Most of us do the best we can to maintain a clean and healthy cattery environment while still raising kittens who are socialized enough to make the transition to another home.

One easy alternative to incorporate into the cattery to help protect the health of the kittens is the Cornell Early Weaning Program. Be certain you discuss this program with your veterinarian, as he will be able to help you modify the program to meet your specific needs.

The procedures are as follows:

1. Place pregnant queens in their isolation area a few days before their due date.

2. When the kittens are 14 days old, administer one dose of rhinotracheitis and calicivirus vaccine (MLV) to all kittens. (Split one dose among the entire litter.)

3. Around 21 days begin to feed the kittens and start the weaning process.

4. At 28 days administer a full dose of rhinotracheitis, calici and panleukopenia vaccine by subcutaneous injection to each kitten.

5. By day 35 completely wean the kittens and remove the queen, leaving the kittens in isolation from all adult cats.

6. Follow your veterinarian's recommendations regarding completing the routine vaccination schedule.

7. It is safe to put kittens with adults at four months of age, as they should have vaccine protection against upper respiratory diseases. If chlamydia is a concern, then include it in the vaccine as well.

WEANING THE KITTENS

Actually, weaning kittens is delightful and you must have your camera ready. Kittens adore having food all over their little faces. Dishes of food are obviously wading pools when you are a little kitten. Food gets in the strangest places on a kitten, and no matter how closely you watch, you will never be able to figure out just exactly how that kitten managed to get baby food on the back of his neck!

When weaning kittens, you will want:

*   A small dish
*   Strained, mild, meat baby food such as chicken
*   Baby rice cereal

- Feline milk replacement, such as Just Born or KMR, or milk made for cats such as Cat Sip

- A spoon and craft sticks (small wooden sticks, like the sticks ice cream bars come on, available at craft stores)

- A washcloth to clean the kittens and plenty of paper towels to clean the area where they will be eating

Mix a small amount of the baby food in the dish and add some of the milk with some of the cereal to make the mixture relatively thick. Heat this until it is warm but not hot.

Put the kittens next to the dish and place a small amount of the food in their mouths using the craft stick. You may have to gently open their mouths to do this. Continue until each kitten gets a small amount of food.

Remember that the kittens are new to this and will try to suck the food down instead of chewing it. They will probably get food all over their faces, and most kittens will also try to walk in the food dish.

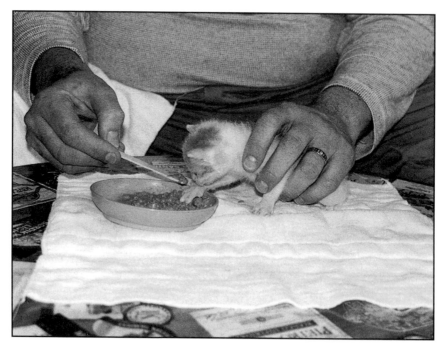

Since kittens will walk in the weaning mixture you give them, they must be thoroughly cleaned after they are fed.

Carefully clean each kitten. You want to be extremely careful to clean the kitten's nose, as he may well have food in his nostrils. During normal breathing, this food may continue to find its way up his nose and can cause him some discomfort. Also, carefully watch his eyes. If you have to do so, clean his eyes with an eye wash to avoid an infection or an irritated eye. Usually any adult cats you may allow in with the kittens at this point will do the best job of washing the kitten.

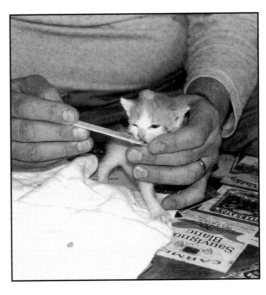

Using a craft stick, place some of the warmed weaning mixture in the kitten's mouth.

Kittens being weaned have baby food all over themselves, and this makes the kitten particularly tasty to wash.

After the kitten has been washed by you, place him in a small litter box so he gets used to the idea of using the box.

Continue this weaning process two or three times each day until the kittens begin to eat. After a couple of days, they may not need to have food put in their mouths anymore; they may start to eat on their own. Some kittens will eat on their own for a day or so and then act as if they have no idea what eating is all about, and you will have to start the process all over again with the craft stick. This is not unusual.

Also, if you put the dish on a table or the floor at the beginning, the kittens may

> ## WARNING!
>
> NEVER USE BABY FOOD THAT CONTAINS ONION. ONION HAS BEEN FOUND TO CAUSE HEINZ BODY ANEMIA IN CATS. THERE IS NO CURRENT DATA ON HOW MUCH ONION A CAT OR KITTEN MUST EAT BEFORE THIS BECOMES A PROBLEM, SO IT'S BEST TO AVOID IT ENTIRELY.

have a bit of a problem keeping their necks down to eat. You may want to elevate the dish to make it easier for the kittens to eat.

When the kitten is just starting to eat, it may help if you lift the dish up to him.

As the kitten grows, gradually lower the dish.

Each day, eliminate some of the milk from the food so that it becomes thicker. After about five days, you may want to add some canned kitten food to the weaning mixture. Eventually, add more kitten food and cut down on the baby food meat. You will want to watch very carefully during weaning time to assure yourself that the kittens are not getting diarrhea. A change in diet can sometimes cause this.

SOCIALIZING THE KITTENS

You want your kittens to be completely socialized and to adapt well to people. This is true whether the kitten is show quality and will be in the judging ring or is pet quality and will be placed in a loving home where she will be a cherished pet. A kitten must grow into a cat who likes people, who is not hostile or aggressive, who will play with people and not be too shy, who is loving and sweet, and who will become a loved companion to whomever is fortunate enough to live with him.

> **HINT!**
>
> TO GET KITTENS USED TO EATING DRY FOOD, MOISTEN THE FOOD WITH VERY WARM WATER, CAT'S MILK OR CHICKEN BROTH UNTIL IT IS THE CONSISTENCY OF MUSH. EVERY DAY, DECREASE THE AMOUNT OF FLUID YOU ADD TO MAKE THE CONSISTENCY DRYER, AND START ADDING THE DRY FOOD TO THE TOP OF THIS MIXTURE. EVENTUALLY THE KITTENS WILL EAT THE DRY FOOD.

Since you will not be breeding a breed with feral blood, any cat should be able to meet these criteria. But you, as the breeder, will have to make certain of this.

Socializing your kittens will be one of the most rewarding jobs you have as a breeder. If you did not enjoy playing with cats and kittens, you would not be a breeder in the first place! This is a very enjoyable time, when your kittens get to explore the world and discover everything that is in it. They will be learning while they are exploring and you

Blizzard is now old enough to eat out of the regular cat food dish.

will be helping them to stay out of trouble, to enjoy people and to become well-mannered cats who will be a joy to own.

Socializing is more than just playing with the kittens, although this is a very important part of socialization. You must actively spend time with each individual kitten, holding him, kissing him and touching him all over his body. Remember that you are preparing him for his entire future. This future involves his going to the veterinarian, where he will be handled for examinations.

If you can, you will want to have other people in your family, or friends when he gets old enough for this, handle him and play with him. If the kitten will be exhibited, he must get used to being handled by several strangers in a day. He must also get used to judges examining him to check the particular characteristics of his breed. For example, in evaluating Himalayans, Persians and Exotic Shorthairs, the judges place their finger in the "break" of his nose. Japanese Bobtails will have to learn to have their tails examined. When you acclimate your kitten to these methods of handling, you will want to praise the kitten afterward. Positive reinforcement is the best way to train kittens.

Blizzard is watched over by Gideon as he sits on the top of a small scratching post.

EXERCISE

Exercise is critical for kittens. It helps to strengthen their muscles and increase their endurance as they play. One of the best pieces of equipment for kittens is a cat tree with a slope. This way they can run up the tree when they are too small to jump up to the top.

You will also want to have plenty of cat trees around so the kittens can learn to scratch their claws on the trees instead of on inappropriate areas of the house such as the sofa. Remember that kittens are young and relatively unknowing at this point in their lives. If your cat trees are wood and they are taught to scratch their claws on them, they may think that all wood is fine for scratching their claws. So, if the wooden banister on the staircase is also made of wood, it is therefore also a fine place to scratch their claws.

The best way to discipline a cat is to squirt it with a water squirt gun while saying the word "No!" in a firm voice. Never, *ever* touch a cat in anger. You can also use spray repellents on the areas where the kittens should not be.

There are many types of toys for your kitten to play with. Many of them contain catnip, which is not a reason to buy them for a young kitten. This is because most young kittens have not yet developed a taste for catnip.

However, the adult cats have, and they will happily play with the toy and the kittens.

You should always be careful before you give your kitten a toy. Look at it carefully to make certain that there are no small pieces that a kitten can pull off and swallow.

There are also many interactive toys that enable you to take part in your kitten's games. Many of these toys feature a bunch of feathers or a catnip mouse at the end of a stick or string. This way you can sit down and "go fishing" for the kittens. They have a wonderful time following the toy in the air and then catching it as it hits the ground. Kittens also tend to jump up in the air to try to catch the

This slanted cat tree enables Blizzard to climb onto the bed.

Cat trees help cats and kittens to exercise as well as scratch their claws.

toy, and this provides wonderful exercise for them.

There are also little things that make wonderful cat toys, such as a bottle of non-toxic bubble solution and a bubble blowing gun. Kittens tend to be totally mystified by these bubbles and will try to catch them and chase them as they land on the floor.

Kittens tend to be their own best toys, and there is probably nothing you can buy that will equal the fun the kittens will have playing with each other. When kittens play, they are actually being little tigers, living in the jungle, fending for themselves and being fierce predators. If you are not careful, you will be walking while the kittens are out playing and will suddenly find your ankle being attacked by one of these wild jungle animals. They never seem to understand why you find it so amusing that you are being attacked by what is, in their minds, a fierce predator (but in your mind, is just a small kitten).

While all of this may look silly, some of it really is not so much play as it is learning. Kitten play teaches these little cats how to hunt and how to take care of themselves. When two kittens wrestle with each other along with the mandatory growling, each kitten is learning how to protect itself. This is why the play should be allowed to continue. Kittens will not purposely hurt each other. You should watch to make certain they do not hurt each other inadvertently, but for the most part, this play is an important part of their kittenhood.

Now that the kittens are around more of the time, you will have to be very careful where they play. You will now have to kitten proof the house even more carefully and cover more areas than you did when the kittens were younger and could not go everywhere. Remember:

Blizzard wrestles with Woodstock in typical kitten play.

- Kittens put anything they find in their mouths, so you must make certain they cannot get something small or sharp and choke.

- Be careful of thread or yarn, which can form knots in their stomachs.

- Watch out that all toilet seats have the lids down so the kittens cannot fall in and drown.

- Never run the clothes dryer without checking first to make sure there are no kittens inside.

- Watch the dishwasher, as kittens are attracted to areas where they smell food.

- Cover the sink disposal unit.

- Keep all trash cans emptied or *securely* covered.

- Make certain all poisons are kept behind tightly closed doors.

- Empty all ash trays.

- Be very careful when you open doors, especially the doors to the outside, as kittens can be very fast.

- Walk carefully yourself, as kittens are always underfoot.

- Always look on the stairs when you are going down them—stairs seem to be favorite kitten sleeping places.

In general, while your kittens are out of their cage you must always be aware that they are out and about, and you should always keep a sharp eye on them.

Grooming

While kittens are learning to play and enjoying the world, this is the time to get them used to being groomed. Brushing the kitten's fur will turn into a game as the kitten tries to attack the brush while you are grooming him.

Grooming is important to keep his fur clean. Kittens are just learning to bathe themselves, so they are not going to be as clean as your adult cats. They also tend to play everywhere and get into some places that are truly amazing. Without regular grooming, kittens will look dirty.

While the kitten is young, you will also want to get him used to having his nails cut. This is a little more difficult to do on kittens, as they tend to wiggle and not cooperate. One simple trick is to hum a little song while you are cutting the kitten's nails. The kitten tends to be interested in what you are singing, and this distracts him from the fact that his nails are being cut.

It is also easier to cut a kitten's nails with a small animal nail cutter or a small human nail clipper. The nails on a kitten are small and not as tough as those on a cat, so the smaller clipper tends to give you more control. Be certain you have plenty of light as you clip the nails, because the quick of the nail is more difficult to see in a kitten.

It is critical to keep the nails clipped on a kitten for many reasons. First, with the way they play, you can end up with nails scratching eyes as the kittens play and wrestle. They know they are supposed to use their claws to protect themselves, but they do not have the control an adult cat has and can inadvertently stick their claws into the eyes of a playmate. Keeping the nails short can help to prevent the more serious accidents that can happen.

Kittens also tend to play and try to climb everywhere. Having long nails can enable the kitten to be rather destructive. And climbing everywhere includes climbing on you. You can end up very scratched up as your kittens try to climb up your legs.

While kittens generally do not need bathing, it is good to get the kittens you will be keeping for show accustomed to the water at this point.

They tend to adapt to having their show bath more easily if they are bathed when they are young.

LITTER TRAINING

Your queen will be the one to teach the kittens how to use the litter box. One way to make sure they do not lose this training is to place a litter box near the kittens when they are out playing. If their box is ordinarily kept upstairs and the kittens are downstairs playing, make sure there is a box downstairs with them.

You will also want to make sure they know where the box is. To do this, put the kittens right into a litter box as soon as they have finished eating. Even though they may leave it immediately, putting them in the box will reinforce their knowledge of where it is.

Be very careful what type of litter you use for kittens. Kittens have a tendency to play in the litter box. They also have to taste the litter. In general, clumping litter is not good for kittens, as they may get it in their lungs or clump in their stomachs if they eat it. There are many other types of litter that are perfectly safe for the kittens to eat. Some of these are made from recycled newspaper or plant fibers. You can also use rabbit pellets.

Check the litter box often to make certain the kittens do not have diarrhea. If a kitten makes a mistake and uses an inappropriate place to eliminate, take him to a proper litter box. Then clean and deodorize the spot where he went to the bathroom and use a repellent on the area.

Never put a litter box where the kittens eat. Even kittens tend not to eliminate where they eat.

YOU KNOW YOU ARE A CAT BREEDER WHEN . . .

- You ask people where the litter box is whenever nature calls.

- You adopt a bored expression and answer automatically, "several," to the frequently asked question at the supermarket: "How many cats *do* you have?"

- Your cat albums have more quantity and quality pictures and are far better annotated than any album you started for your human children and never kept up.

- You find yourself saying to your friends, "I can't go out Friday night; I have to wash my cat," and you *mean* it.

- You don't bother with lint rollers because "tweed" clothes seem normal to you.

- You have claw marks up your arm and can't understand why some people look so horrified when they see them—doesn't everyone occasionally have a day that doesn't go quite as planned?

- Your car needs new tires and you say the car's paws need more traction.

Adapted from *101 Ways to Know You're a Cat Fancier.*

CHAPTER TEN

Registering and Selling Kittens

A remark attributed to the late Don Shaw, a cat geneticist and judge, says it all:

"Just because you can breed a cat does not mean that you have an absolute right to register the kittens. And just because you have been given the right to register the kitten does not mean that you have an absolute right to show it."

MASTERING THE PAPERWORK

Mastering the art of registry paperwork is critical. The reason it must be done correctly is that the entire process of registering, buying, selling and breeding pedigreed cats hinges on the underlying foundation of the registration process. Remember, a pedigreed cat is one with a pedigree—that is, one that has been registered for generations.

The decision of where to register a kitten or a litter is very similar to the decision of where you want to register your cattery (see Chapter Two). In general, the safest thing to do is register a new litter in one of the national registries. That way you make sure the kittens can be registered in any one of the other two (as we will show later in this chapter), assuming the other registries accept your breed for registration.

If you have a buyer who wishes to have the kitten registered in the association you've chosen, you have done the needed work. If the buyer wants to show that kitten in one of the other two national associations, that can be accomplished even if the parents are not already registered there. But that cross-registration is usually not so easy (or even available)

The Cat Fanciers' Association, Inc.

1805 Atlantic Avenue, PO Box 1005 • Manasquan NJ 08736-0805 • 908-528-9797

SUPPLEMENTAL TRANSFER

Side 1 OR side 2 of this form must be completed and submitted with the blue CFA Cat Registration Application (blue slip) OR the CFA Registration Certificate when a cat has been transferred before applying for registration in the name of the current owner. A separate form must be completed and signed to record EACH transfer after the first one recorded on the application or the back of the registration certificate. Please TYPE or PRINT, do not use pencil.

Part 1 – Blue Slip Supplemental Transfer

If you possess a cat registration application (blue slip), and the ownership information contained on the application has changed, please complete this part of the form. Attach this form to the blue slip and send to CFA. Owner(s) transferring the cat identified below must complete and individually sign this section. The name of the new owner(s) should be printed below as they are to be registered.

CFA Litter #: _____ Cat's Name: _____

Date of Transfer: _____

Name(s) of New Owner(s): (30 spaces)

Address: _____

City: _____ State: _____ Zip: _____

I/we transferred the cat identified above directly to the New Owner(s) listed above on the date indicated.

Former Owner(s) Sign Here: _____

New owner(s) complete the following:

I (we) apply to The Cat Fanciers' Association, Inc. to have a Registration Certificate for this cat issued in my (our) name and certify that I (we) acquired this cat on the date stated above directly from the Former Owner(s). I (we) agree to abide by all rules and regulations of CFA and understand that if the Not for Breeding section in Section E of the Cat Registration Application has been checked by the breeder, I (we) will receive a Not For Breeding registration.

New Owner(s) Sign Here: _____

FEE: $7.00 for EACH transfer.

Please see reverse side if you possess a cat that has already been individually registered.

Part 2 – Registered Cat Supplemental Transfer

If you possess a **certificate** for an **individually registered cat** (green certificate), and the ownership information contained on the transfer portion of the application has changed, please complete this part of the form. Attach this form to the registration certificate and send to CFA. Owner(s) transferring the cat identified below must complete and individually sign this section. The name of the new owner(s) should be printed below as they are to be registered.

CFA Registration #: _____ Cat's Name: _____

Date of Transfer: _____

Name(s) of New Owner(s): (30 spaces) [ ][ ][ ][ ][ ][ ][ ][ ][ ][ ][ ][ ][ ][ ][ ][ ][ ][ ][ ]

Address: _____

City: _____ State: _____ Zip: _____

I/we transferred the cat identified above directly to the New Owner(s) listed above on the date indicated.

Former Owner(s) Sign Here: _____

New owner(s) complete the following:

I (we) apply to The Cat Fanciers' Association, Inc. to have a Registration Certificate for this cat issued in my (our) name and certify that I (we) acquired this cat on the date stated above directly from the Former Owner(s). I (we) agree to abide by all rules and regulations of CFA and understand that if the cat already has limited registration I (we) will receive a Not For Breeding registration.

New Owner(s) Sign Here: _____

FEE: $7.00 for EACH transfer.
Please see reverse side if you possess a blue slip.

21078-95©

if the kitten is first registered in one of the regional or state registries, because these associations are not considered to be part of the national and international cat fancy.

In the following paragraphs, we will walk you through the paperwork process. If you have any questions or problems, do not be afraid to call the registry's office and ask for help. All of the registries work hard to help breeders get the paperwork right.

Registering a Litter

Once you choose which national association to register your litter with, you face three possibilities:

- Neither parent is registered with the registry.
- Only one parent is registered with the registry.
- Both parents are registered with the registry.

If neither parent is registered with the registry, you cannot register the litter directly. Either you must register the parents retroactively, or you must register the litter and the individual kitten elsewhere and then transfer that registration.

In some cases, it may be cheaper for you to register the dam and sire of a litter with a registry so that you can register the kittens there, than to separately register a kitten. This is known as a retro registration. It most often occurs when the grandparents are registered with the desired registry, but the parents are not. If you own both parents, or can get their owners' written consents, you can register the parents of your new litter at the same time you register the litter. While this is complex, it can be done all at once. Be warned, however, that although the national registries allow such retro registrations now, they can change this at any time.

If only the dam is registered with the registry, you can usually register the litter directly, as long as you have a full pedigree on the sire. If it is only the sire who is registered with that registry, you will have to proceed as if both parents were not registered with the registry.

If both parents are registered with the registry, you will be able to register the litter directly, on an approved form.

Remember, when you register the litter, you do not have to select names for each of the kittens. You are permitted to do so (in fact, the registries adjust their fees to encourage this), but it is not necessary.

There are several keys to making sure the litter registration goes through the first time:

- Fill out every part you are asked to complete. Never assume "the office knows that."

- Go back to the original paperwork to make sure you are using the correct numbers and other information for each cat shown on the registration form.

- Make sure the owner of the queen and owner of the sire each sign everywhere they are supposed to.

- When asked for registration numbers, use those of the registry you are dealing with, if they are available.

- If you are asked to give a pedigree, make sure you show the name, breed, color pattern and registration number for every cat on the paperwork.

- Always double-check how many generations are needed on the pedigree, whether or not the association requires that the pedigree be certified, and if it must be certified, by whom—the owner or another registry.

- Use only the terms approved by the registry you are dealing with. Do not call a cat ebony if the official color is black; find out if the cat is a Colorpoint Shorthair or a Siamese, and whether or not the registry recognizes the "van" pattern. Failure to do this is one of the most common reasons paperwork is returned.

- Enclose a check for the full amount. If you are not sure of the proper amount, call the registry office and ask.

Registering an Individual Kitten

Once a litter has been registered, you will receive an individual registration slip for each kitten showing that the kitten's litter has been registered

LITTER REGISTRATIONS

GENERAL INSTRUCTIONS: Litter registration is encouraged even if no kittens are being individually registered. Individual kitten registrations can be processed more quickly if a litter has already been registered. The Official ACFA Litter Registration Application Form [or a copy] **must** be used. Additional application forms may be obtained from our Office at no charge.

PRINT OR **TYPE**, EXCEPT where signatures are required. Signatures, when required, **attest to the accuracy of the information contained** on this application.

COMPLETING THE APPLICATION - The application form must be completed and **signed** by the breeder of the litter. The breeder is: [1] the registered owner of the dam on the date of mating OR [2] the lessee of the dam on the date of mating. **If cat is leased, you must append:** [1] A COPY OF THE LEASE AGREEMENT, [2] A SIGNED LEASE STATEMENT, OR [3] FILL OUT, COMPLETE WITH REQUIRED SIGNATURE, THE LEASE STATEMENT APPEARING BELOW! All appropriate spaces must be filled in and the application MUST contain:

- The number of males/females in the litter
- The birthdate of the litter
- The sex and color of **each** kitten in the litter

- The breed of the litter
- Signature of Breeder
- Signature of the Owner of the Litter

- Signature of the Owner of the Sire
- Address of the Owner of the litter
- Breeders Cattery Name & #, if registered with ACFA

Information on SIRE and DAM - Their full registered name, ACFA registration number [if registered with ACFA], breed, color, pattern, eye color, birthdate.
- If SIRE or if DAM, or both are not registered with ACFA- A photographic copy of the registration certificate from the association with which the cat[s] is/are registered MUST accompany the litter registration application. You must also: [1] Fill in the 3 generation pedigree of the sire and/or dam not registered with ACFA, COMPLETE WITH FULL REGISTRATION NUMBERS and the initials of the association in which all cats in the pedigree are registered. OR: [2] Send a photographic copy of the 3 generation pedigree of the sire and/or dam not registered with ACFA, making sure all cats in pedigree have full registration numbers listed.

LITTER REGISTRATION FEES EFFECTIVE JANUARY 1, 1991:
- SIRE and DAM **registered** with ACFA ~ ~ ~ ~ ~ ~ $ 7.00
- SIRE and/or DAM **NOT registered** with ACFA ~ ~ ~ ~ $14.00
- Individual Registration of Kitten ~ ~ ~ ~ ~ ~ ~ $ 7.00

REGISTRATION OF KITTEN AT TIME OF LITTER REGISTRATION

Kit No.	Name Choice May not exceed 35 letters, characters and spaces	Owner's Name and Address

LEASE STATEMENT

I, as the owner of record of the dam [Please print cat's name] _____

Registration # _____ do state that _____
                                                       Name of Lessee [Please Print]
was a lessee of the above named cat when the litter was bred and for which they are applying for registration.

_____   _____   _____
    Date   Signature of Owner/Lessor   Print Name of Owner/Lessor
Mail to:

     AMERICAN CAT FANCIERS ASSOCIATION, INC.   P O BOX 203   POINT LOOKOUT MO 65726
     Phone 417/334-5430   Fax 417/334-5540

Application will be returned for lack of sufficient funds or lack of necessary information. Delays may occur because of illegible writing, so please PRINT or TYPE information. Completed registration forms [including registrations forms for the unregistered individuals in the litter] will be mailed to the litter owner. Please allow us at least 3 weeks from the day you mail the application.

A C F A - The FRIENDLY ASSOCIATION

No. of Males	No. of Females	Breed		Date Registered	Litter Registration Number
			Office) Use) Only)		

Birthdate

month	day	year

Kitten Serial No.	Sex	Color of Kitten
1		
2		
3		
4		
5		
6		
7		
8		
9		

Signature of Breeder

Signature of owner of litter

Address

Signature of owner of Sire

Breeder's Cattery Name and No.

Sire _____
ACFA No. _____
Breed _____
Color/Pattern _____
Eye Color _____
Birth date _____
Other Reg. No. _____

3. Sire _____
Reg. No _____
Breed & Color _____

4. Dam _____
Reg. No. _____
Breed & Color _____

7. Sire _____
Reg. No. _____
Breed & Color _____

8. Dam _____
Reg. No. _____
Breed & Color _____

9. Sire _____
Reg. No. _____
Breed & Color _____

10. Dam _____
Reg. No. _____
Breed & Color _____

This application will become a permanent record in the files of the American Cat Fanciers, Assn.

Dam _____
ACFA No. _____
Breed _____
Color/Pattern _____
Eye Color _____
Birth date _____
Other Reg. No. _____

5. Sire _____
Reg. No. _____
Breed & Color _____

6. Dam _____
Reg. No. _____
Breed & Color _____

11. Sire _____
Reg. No. _____
Breed & Color _____

12. Dam _____
Reg. No. _____
Breed & Color _____

13. Sire _____
Reg. No. _____
Breed & Color _____

14. Dam _____
Reg. No. _____
Breed & Color _____

American Cat Fanciers Association, Inc.
P.O. Box 203, Point Lookout, Missouri 65726
Application for Litter Registration

APP-1 Revised 6-82

THE CAT FANCIERS' ASSOCIATION, INC. LITTER APPLICATION
Please read instructions on reverse side before completing application.

Please Type or Print   **SECTION A — Birth Information**

Date of Birth   # of Living

_____   _____   _____ _____
Breed   Month/Day/Year   Females Males

SECTION B — Sire Information

Registered Name of Sire

CFA Registration Number   Signature of Sire's Owner/Lessee

Owner/Lessee of Sire at Time of Mating

Address

City   State/Province   Zip/Postal Code

SECTION C — Breeder & Dam Information

Registered Name of Dam

CFA Registration Number   Signature of Breeder of litter

Name of Breeder of Litter

Breeder's Address

City   State/Province   Zip/Postal Code

Breeder's CFA Registered Cattery Name (if any)   Breeder #/ Cattery #

Please check [ ] This is my first litter registration with CFA.
if applicable.
[ ] I have recently moved. My previous zip code was _____.

OPTIONAL   SECTION D — Lease
On the date of mating, this dam was leased to the person listed in Section C.

Signature of the Registered Owner of the Dam on the Date of Mating.   Date

OPTIONAL   SECTION E — Litter Owner
(Complete only if owner different from breeder.)

Name of Owner

Owner's Address

City   State/Province   Zip/Postal Code

Owner's Cattery Number   Signature of Owner of Litter

Office Use Only   Office Use Only   Office Use Only

SECTION F — Kitten Registrations   (Complete this section ONLY to register individual kittens)
(Enter 2 choices of name, and name and address of owner)

Name of Cat (1st Choice)

Name of Cat (2nd Choice)

Sex: Color: Eye Color: Office Use Only

Owner Name
Address:

City: State/Province: Zip/Postal Code:

Name of Cat (1st Choice)

Name of Cat (2nd Choice)

Sex: Color: Eye Color: Office Use Only

Owner Name
Address:

City: State/Province: Zip/Postal Code:

Name of Cat (1st Choice)

Name of Cat (2nd Choice)

Sex: Color: Eye Color: Office Use Only

Owner Name
Address:

City: State/Province: Zip/Postal Code:

Name of Cat (1st Choice)

Name of Cat (2nd Choice)

Sex: Color: Eye Color: Office Use Only

Owner Name
Address:

City: State/Province: Zip/Postal Code:

LITTER REGISTRATION APPLICATION

TICA

MAIL APPLICATION WITH FEE TO

THE INTERNATIONAL CAT ASSOCIATION

P.O. BOX 2684
HARLINGEN, TEXAS 78551
(210) 428-8046

(Please read instructions on reverse side before completing application).

TYPE OR PRINT   SECTION A

NO. OF LIVING

BREED   DATE OF BIRTH   FEMALES   MALES

SECTION B — SIRE

BREED   REGISTERED NAME OF SIRE

REGISTRATION NUMBER   COLOR

OWNER OF SIRE AT TIME OF MATING

STREET ADDRESS

CITY   STATE   ZIP

SIGNATURE   CATTERY NAME (IF ANY)

SECTION C — DAM

BREED   REGISTERED NAME OF DAM

TICA REGISTRATION NUMBER   COLOR

OWNER OF DAM AT TIME OF MATING (OR LEASEE)

STREET ADDRESS

CITY   STATE   ZIP

SIGNATURE   CATTERY NAME (IF ANY)

I hereby certify that the above statement is true and correct.

SECTION D | **SECTION E** (Complete this section ONLY to register individual kittens) (Enter 2 choices of name and name and address of owner)

1

SEX   NAME (1ST CHOICE)

NAME (2ND CHOICE)

COLOR   OWNER

EYE COLOR   STREET ADDRESS

LH☐ SH☐
CE☐ SE☐   CITY   STATE   ZIP

SECTION D CONTINUED | **SECTION E CONTINUED** (Complete this section ONLY to register individual kittens) (Enter 2 choices of name and name and address of owner)

2

SEX   NAME (1ST CHOICE)

NAME (2ND CHOICE)

COLOR   OWNER

EYE COLOR   STREET ADDRESS

LH☐ SH☐
CE☐ SE☐   CITY   STATE   ZIP

3

SEX   NAME (1ST CHOICE)

NAME (2ND CHOICE)

COLOR   OWNER

EYE COLOR   STREET ADDRESS

LH☐ SH☐
CE☐ SE☐   CITY   STATE   ZIP

4

SEX   NAME (1ST CHOICE)

NAME (2ND CHOICE)

COLOR   OWNER

EYE COLOR   STREET ADDRESS

LH☐ SH☐
CE☐ SE☐   CITY   STATE   ZIP

5

SEX   NAME (1ST CHOICE)

NAME (2ND CHOICE)

COLOR   OWNER

EYE COLOR   STREET ADDRESS

LH☐ SH☐
CE☐ SE☐   CITY   STATE   ZIP

6

SEX   NAME (1ST CHOICE)

NAME (2ND CHOICE)

COLOR   OWNER

EYE COLOR   STREET ADDRESS

LH☐ SH☐
CE☐ SE☐   CITY   STATE   ZIP

7

SEX   NAME (1ST CHOICE)

NAME (2ND CHOICE)

COLOR   OWNER

EYE COLOR   STREET ADDRESS

LH☐ SH☐
CE☐ SE☐   CITY   STATE   ZIP

CAUTION!

YOU CANNOT ALWAYS USE ONE
ASSOCIATION'S LITTER REGIS-
TRATION TO REGISTER A KITTEN
IN ANOTHER REGISTRY. DE-
PENDING ON THE REGISTRY,
YOU MAY HAVE TO REGISTER
THE KITTEN WITH THE REG-
ISTRY WHERE THE LITTER IS
LISTED, AND THEN TRANSFER
THAT KITTEN TO THE NEW REG-
ISTRY. IF YOU ARE TRYING TO
DO THIS, YOU MUST CONTACT
BOTH REGISTRIES FIRST.

with the registry, together with other important information. Each kitten must then be individually registered. It is this slip that is usually given to new owners.

If you want to register the kitten with the same association that registered its litter, simply fill in the slip, enclose the required fee and send it off. If you want to register the kitten with a different registry, it will have to be litter registered in its primary registry first.

There are several keys to making sure that an individual registration goes through the first time (some of these may look familiar):

- Fill out everything you are asked to complete. Never assume "the office knows that."

- Go back to the original paperwork to make sure you are using the correct numbers and other information for each cat shown on the paperwork.

- Make sure the owner of the queen and the owner of the sire each sign everywhere they are supposed to. Double-check the litter registration slip to make sure the breeder has signed, if necessary.

- Include all paperwork the form requires. Do not make any changes on that paperwork. If it is wrong, call the registry office and find out how to correct it.

- Use only the terms approved by the registry you are dealing with. Do not call a cat ebony if the official color is black; find out if the cat is a Colorpoint Shorthair or a Siamese, and whether or not the registry recognizes the "van" pattern. Failure to do this is one of the most common reasons paperwork is returned.

ACFA

BREEDER'S ACFA CATTERY NAME AND NUMBER | LITTER REG. NUMBER

FIRST NAME CHOICE

SECOND NAME CHOICE

OWNER'S NAME(S)

ADDRESS

ADDRESS

CITY _____ STATE _____ ZIP

OWNER(S) CATTERY NAME _____ NUMBER _____

TO BE COMPLETED BY BREEDER - Complete Items #1, #2, #3, others as necessary

1. COLOR: _____

☐ MAY be used for breeding

2. SEX: _____ EYE COLOR: _____

☐ MAY NOT be used for breeding

3. BREEDER'S SIGNATURE(S): _____

☐ ONLY record as Household Pet

BREED

BREEDER

OWNER

SIRE

DAM

BIRTHDATE

OWNER'S SIGNATURE _____

The Cat Fanciers' Association, Inc. – CAT REGISTRATION APPLICATION ©

**** SEE REVERSE SIDE FOR COMPLETE REGISTRATION INSTRUCTIONS ****

Your cat is NOT REGISTERED until this application is filed with CFA.

Registration Fee $7.00

SECTION A – Cat's Name – Limited to 35 spaces including breeder's CFA registered cattery name prefix, if any. Add your cat's name after the cattery prefix, if any.

PRINT ONE
LETTER PER
BOX – SKIP A
BOX BETWEEN
WORDS –
PUNCTUATION IN
ITS OWN BOX.

1st CHOICE

Breeder's registered cattery name, if any.

2nd CHOICE

Do not write in box.

SECTION B
BREED:

DATE OF BIRTH:

SIRE:

DAM:

BR./CATTERY #:

LITTER #:

BREEDER:

ISSUE DATE:

SECTION C – PURCHASER's/OWNER's NAME(s) [First, Last – No Mr./Mrs.] – Limit 30 Spaces. No ERASURES OR ALTERATIONS TO THIS SECTION PERMITTED. Use this form for recording ORIGINAL transfer from breeder to first purchaser/owner only – for subsequent transfer contact CFA for supplemental transfer statement form.

STREET

CITY   STATE/PROVINCE   ZIP/POSTAL CODE

SECTION D   THIS AREA MUST BE COMPLETED BY BREEDER

COLOR OF CAT:
(See reverse #6)

COAT LENGTH: Long   Short
(Circle one)

SEX: Male   Female   Neutered*   Spayed*
(Circle One)   Male   Female

EYE COLOR:
(White cats only)

DATE   Month   Der   Year
OF SALE:

*A surgically sterilized cat.

SECTION E – EITHER #1 OR #2 MUST BE COMPLETED by the breeder/owner. See instructions #8 and/or #13 on reverse. Any erasure or alteration to this section may void this certificate.

1. ☐ This cat MAY be used for breeding.

SIGNATURE OF BREEDER (See Item 8 on reverse)

2. ☐ This cat MAY NOT be used for breeding.

SIGNATURE OF NEW PURCHASER(S)/OWNER(S) (See Item 13 on reverse)

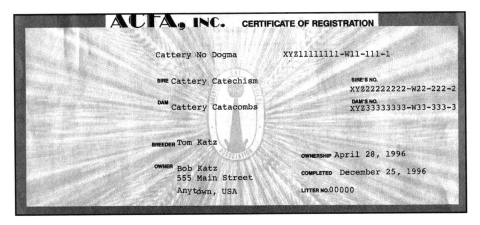

These are sample Certificates of Registration. Both have forms on the back that must be filled in and sent to the registry if the cat's ownership is transferred.

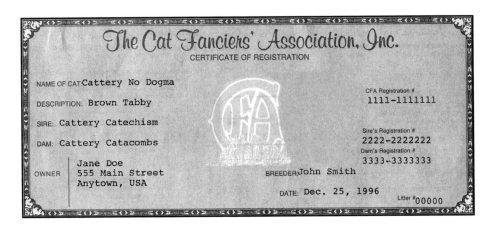

- Enclose a check for the full amount. If you are not sure of the proper amount, call the registry office and ask.

Registering Cats and Kittens from Other Associations

No cat automatically has the right to be registered in an association merely because it is registered elsewhere. The acceptance of such a registration, commonly called reciprocity in the fancy, is a matter of courtesy, not a right. That means Registry A can accept cats registered in Registry B while declining all cats from Registry C. In turn, Registry B might accept only some cats from Registry A. And each registry has the right to change its rules at any time, as it sees fit.

The chart shows the current reciprocity relationships among the national registries.

Given this, there *are* ways cats registered with one registry can have their registration formally transferred to another. But the requirements can be strict:

> **CAUTION!**
>
> BECAUSE IT IS EXTREMELY DIF-FICULT, AND IN SOME CASES IMPOSSIBLE, TO TRANSFER A CAT'S REGISTRATION FROM RE-GIONAL AND LOCAL REGISTRIES TO THE NATIONAL REGISTRIES, YOU ARE BETTER OFF BUYING A KITTEN WHOSE LITTER IS ALREADY REGISTERED WITH ONE OF THE NATIONAL REG-ISTRIES.

- The cat in question must be properly registered in the "primary" registry.

- It must be of a breed, color and pattern accepted for registration in the other, or "secondary," registry.

- At this time, none of the three national registries allow supplemental registration based solely on proof of registration in one of the other two associations. In other words, you cannot register an ACFA-registered cat in TICA simply by sending in a copy of the ACFA registration. More is required.

REGISTRATION RECIPROCITY			
	ACFA	CFA	TICA
Will register cats and kittens initially registered in the other two associations (assuming the breed, color and pattern are registerable).	Yes	Yes	Yes
Is a pedigree certified as true by the breeder sufficient?	Yes; must show registered names and registration pedigree numbers for all cats on the pedigree	No	Yes; three-generation required
Is a pedigree certified by the original registry required?	No	Yes	No
Other special requirements.	Must have a copy of the original registration certificate	Can register using a certified pedigree only when the cat is not eligible to be registered using standard procedures	No

APPLICATION FOR REGISTRATION OF CAT
NOT LITTER REGISTERED WITH ACFA

Registration Procedures for Cats Registered with Another Association:

PLEASE complete the application in full. ACFA rules state that we must have a minimum of **three generations of ancestry** [entered in blocks 1-14-note exception below] complete with registered names and COMPLETE registration numbers. Please use ACFA registration numbers wherever possible.

Exception: A photocopy of the cat's three generation pedigree may be submitted in lieu of completing blocks 3-14 of the application.

A photocopy of your cat's **registration certificate** from the association with which your cat is registered MUST accompany your application. This certificate **must** list you as owner.

Complete the **owner's name** as you wish it to appear on the Registration Certificate. Ensure that you provided your **complete address** as the owner, on the application.

Registration Procedures for Cats Not Litter Registered OR Individually Registered in Any Association:

PLEASE complete the application in full. ACFA rules state that we must have a minimum of **three generations of ancestry** [entered in blocks 1-14-note exception below] complete with registered names and COMPLETE registration numbers. Please use ACFA registration numbers wherever possible.

Exception: A photocopy of the cat's three generation pedigree may be submitted in lieu of completing blocks 3-14 of the application.

If the sire is not registered with ACFA, we must have a photocopy of the sire's **registration certificate** from the association with which he is registered. **The owner of the sire also must SIGN the application.**

If the dam is not registered in ACFA, we must have a photocopy of the dam's **registration certificate** from the association with which she is registered. The owner of the dam, at the time of breeding, **must sign as the breeder.**

If either or both sire and dam are registered with ACFA, the signature of the owner of those cats is required on the application.

REGISTRATION APPLICATION FEES, EFFECTIVE JANUARY 1, 1991: $14.00

Mail to: **AMERICAN CAT FANCIERS ASSOCIATION, INC**
P O Nox 203, Point Lookout MO 65726
Phone: 417/334-5430 FAX: 417/334-5540

Application may be returned due to lack of complete information and/or lack of sufficient funds. Delays may occur because of illegible writing, so please PRINT or TYPE all information. Make sure photocopies are legible. Completed registration certificate will be mailed to the owner of record. Please allow at least 3 weeks from the day you mail the application.

A C F A - The FRIENDLY Association

PROVIDE THREE NAME CHOICES.
[Please PRINT or TYPE.]

Date Registered _____   Registration Number _____

1. _____

2. _____

3. _____
Association
Initials &
Reg. No. _____

Color _____

Sex _____ Eye Color _____
Date of
Birth _____

_____

Owner(s) of Cat to be Registered - IF MORE THAN ONE OWNER AND ALL MUST SIGN TRANSFERS/LITTER REGISTRATIONS, use an "&" between owners' names. If only ONE SIGNATURE IS REQUIRED FOR TRANSFERS/LITTER REGISTRATIONS, use a "/" or "-" between owners' names.

Street Address _____

City/State/Zip Code/Country _____

Owner's Cattery Name & ACFA Cattery No. _____

Breeder's Cattery Name and ACFA Cattery No. _____

Breeder's Signature: REQUIRED, if dam is ACFA registered and/or if cat is not registered with a recognized association.

Owner of Sire's Signature: REQUIRED, if sire is not registered with recognized association.

PARENTS:

1. Sire: _____

_____

Reg No _____

Breed _____

Color _____
Eye _____   Birth
Color _____   Date _____

NOTE: If Sire and/or Dam are not registered in ACFA then the Ancestry in Blocks #3, 4, 7-10 and/or 5, 6, 11-14 must be completed.

2. Dam: _____

_____

Reg No _____

Breed _____

Color _____
Eye _____   Birth
Color _____   Date _____

PROOF OF REGISTRATION: If the cat to be registered is registered with another Association, a photocopy of its registration certificate must be submitted with the application. If the cat is not registered than proof of registration will be submitted for the Dam and/or Sire if not registered with ACFA.

GRANDPARENTS:

3. Sire: _____

_____

Reg No _____
Breed &
Color _____

4. Dam: _____

_____

Reg No _____
Breed &
Color _____

5. Sire: _____

_____

Reg No _____
Breed &
Color _____

6. Dam: _____

_____

Reg No _____
Breed &
Color _____

GREAT-GRANDPARENTS:

7. S: _____

Reg # _____
Brd/Clr _____

8. D: _____

Reg # _____
Brd/Clr _____

9. S: _____

Reg # _____
Brd/Clr _____

10. D: _____

Reg # _____
Brd/Clr _____

11. S: _____

Reg # _____
Brd/Clr _____

12. D: _____

Reg # _____
Brd/Clr _____

13. S: _____

Reg # _____
Brd/Clr _____

14. D: _____

Reg # _____
Brd/Clr _____

American Cat Fanciers Association Inc
P O Box 203, Point Lookout MO 65726 PH: 417/334-5430 FAX: 417/334-5540

- You must strictly comply with the paperwork requirements of the secondary registry. For example, you will have to provide a multi-generation pedigree for the cat. Check on how many generations are required (it can range from three to five or even more); whether the pedigree has to be certified by the primary registry or merely by the breeder (or owner); what information has to accompany each cat on the registration form, such as a note of the breed and color/pattern for every cat on the pedigree.

- If you have to get a pedigree certified by a registry, allow enough time to have it prepared. Registry-certified pedigrees can cost from $20 to $75 at current prices.

- The cat will be registered under the breed name, color and pattern nomenclature of the secondary registry, regardless of the terms and breed designations used in the primary registry.

HINT!

WHEN PROVIDING A PEDIGREE FOR AN ASSOCIATION, MAKE SURE FOR EVERY CAT ON THE PEDIGREE YOU HAVE SHOWN THE CAT'S FULL REGISTERED NAME; THE BREED, COLOR AND PATTERN OF EACH CAT (EVEN IF THAT INFORMATION IS CODED IN THE REGISTRATION NUMBER); AND ITS REGISTRATION NUMBERS IN THAT REGISTRY. IF THIS IS NOT POSSIBLE, THEN INCLUDE REGISTRATION NUMBERS FROM OTHER REGISTRIES, BUT ALSO INDICATE FROM WHICH ASSOCIATION THE NUMBERS COME.

In registering in the secondary registry, you do not surrender your registration in the primary registry. Instead, your cat is now registered in two registries.

Now that you have all this information, remember that the rules of the individual registries are subject to change at any time. These changes may affect how the registry handles its own paperwork and what you must do to get it to accept paperwork from another registry. That means before you enter into any transaction that involves registering a cat at some point, such as buying a kitten or arranging for stud service, *check with all of the relevant registries before you sign any agreement.* By doing so, you will avoid many of the problems that can arise because one of the parties assumed the paperwork "would be okay."

EVALUATING KITTENS

A Pet or Show Quality?

While as exhibitors we are comfortable with the difference between a show cat and a pet, many potential kitten buyers are not. To help them understand what a pet is, the key is to remind them that there is no standard definition of show quality, or of any of the other terms often used by breeders to describe the quality of registered cats.

So you can understand what a range these concepts can cover, here are the definitions our cattery uses in its contracts:

- *Top Show* means the cat is expected to be able to grand—that is, achieve a Grand Championship—in a specified cat association in a reasonable number of shows.

- *Show* means the cat is expected to be able to achieve a Champion-ship in a specified cat association in a reasonable number of shows.

- *Breeder* means the cat is not expected to be able to achieve a Championship in a specified cat association in a reasonable number of shows. However, the cat is of good health and quality, and provides some assets to a breeding program (such as color, lineage, etc.).

- *Pet quality* means that, while the cat is a pedigreed, we believe the cat is not suitable for show competition against other pedigreed cats of the same breed for one or more of several reasons. These reasons include color and markings, relative size or physical features such as ears, tail, etc., and other subjective, cosmetic features, measured against the standards of perfection as adopted by a specified cat association. Pet quality does not mean the kitten is unhealthy but merely that we do not believe it is suitable either for showing as a Championship cat or for breeding.

The best way to educate potential buyers about a pet quality kitten is by referring to all of these definitions. Then, having explained these terms, remind the potential buyer that the quality of the kitten is based on the cattery's evaluation of the kitten. That is, the evaluation represents only an opinion of the kitten's potential as a cat, and is not a guarantee. This is because many factors, such as presentation, nutrition, personality and the rest of the competion can affect a cat's success in the show ring.

Altered Versus Whole Kittens

As a responsible breeder, you must take every step possible to ensure that any cat not specifically sold to be used in a breeding program will be altered. That means:

- Putting a requirement in your contract that all pets be altered and that they may *never* be bred. One way to do this is to collect a deposit that will be refunded when you get proof of the surgical procedure.

- Having your veterinarian alter these kittens before they leave. While this increases your costs slightly, remember that otherwise your buyers would have to do this; there should be no problem asking a new buyer to pay a little extra when you remind them of this.

- Marking on all paperwork that the cat cannot be bred. Each registry has its own way of ensuring this.

- Placing a no-breeding statement on the signed pedigree that you give the new owner. The best place to do it is right near your signature, like this: "I certify that this pedigree is true and complete to the best of my knowledge. This cat is sold on the condition that it is (to be) altered and is not for breeding."

MARKETING

When you set out to breed pedigreed cats, you must immediately consider how and to whom you are going to sell pet kittens, as well as show or breeder cats. Advertising to each potential group of buyers is radically different. In general, buyers of show-quality cats are interested in your record at shows, the lines that are behind your breeding program and the restrictions you may impose on new buyers. Pet buyers, on the other hand, are interested in the breed and its unique characteristics, the temperament and personality of the breed, and in many cases, how near you are to them. Since no breeder can produce only top show cats, most of the marketing you do will be of pet-quality kittens.

Printing Your Own Material

Consider developing your own simple one- or two-page flier on your breed and your cattery. On it, list the special characteristics of your breed, such as "small, lively," as well as information about your cattery such as how long you have been a breeder, whether you have passed an inspection program and so on. While information on your success in the show ring is interesting, it is more important to someone buying a show alter or a whole cat than to the average pet buyer.

Advertising in Magazines and Newspapers

There are any number of outlets for print advertising. The Appendix lists some major national publications that accept advertisements. In addition, consider advertising in your registry's membership publication, your registry's yearbooks and your breed association's newsletter.

When you are considering print advertising, think about the following:

- How often do I have to advertise—monthly or just one time?
- When will my advertisement come out? Will I have kittens then?

- What is the publication's audience—owners of other breeds, owners of my breed, pet buyers or potential buyers of pedigreed show cats?

If you do not want to spend money on regular print advertising, you have other options. You can advertise jointly with other breeders you are working with. You can advertise in monthly magazines only every three or four months. Or you can try to convince your breed society to take out an advertisement featuring a list of all active breeders of your breed, or offering to provide that list on request.

Marketing at Shows

Going to cat shows is one of the most effective and important ways to advertise your cats and your cattery. By exhibiting at a show, we become representatives of the cat fancy in general, and since we're going to be at the shows anyway, it makes sense to market the fancy while we are there. This is easily accomplished. Most people who come to see a cat show are interested in what is going on and ask a lot of questions. As representatives of the fancy, we should try to answer their questions and encourage them in their interest in cats.

> **CAUTION!**
>
> SOME BREEDERS BRING KIT-TENS THAT ARE FOR SALE TO A SHOW, SO THAT POTENTIAL BUYERS CAN SEE THEM. OTHERS SELL DIRECTLY FROM THE CAGE. WHILE BOTH ARE PERMITTED BY REGISTRY RULES, WHEN YOU SELL A KIT-TEN AT A SHOW YOU HAVE NO OPPORTUNITY TO EVALUATE A POTENTIAL BUYER OR CHECK A VETERINARY REFERENCE, AND YOU RUN THE RISK OF TAKING A BAD CHECK.

As exhibitors, we have an obligation to the fancy, the sponsoring cat federation and the show management to dress nicely. In addition to that obligation, we have the same obligation to our cattery. If you look dirty and sloppy, the spectators may think your cattery is also dirty and sloppy.

When you are at any show, be prepared to answer questions about showing and about your breed. Many people will ask you how you go about showing a cat. This is a good opportunity for education. It is possible to promote your breed and your cattery at every show you attend. Here are some way to accomplish this:

- Have fliers explaining all about your breed, whether you make them yourself or get them from a registry or a breed society.

- Keep a notebook with articles about your breed, together with photos showing your cats at play.

- Have a sign with the cat's registered name for each of the cats you are showing. At the show, put the sign on the cage.

- Bring business cards to all the shows where you exhibit, even if you don't have kittens available for sale, and keep them easily available for the spectators to take.

If you have kittens for sale that you're bringing to the show, have a sign on their cage to let the public know. And make sure that the sales cage makes a nice impression. It should be just as pretty, or prettier, than the cage for the cats that are being exhibited.

With that in mind, remember the cage shouldn't be so busy or garish that you can't see the kitten for the curtains. When you use a bed in the sales cage, a low-sided one is better than an igloo-type bed because the kitten can hide in an igloo bed. The kitten should always be visible.

215-916-2079   Carolyn Vella
Fax 215-916-2078   John McGonagle

Jacat
Japanese Bobtails

P.O. Box 737   CFA Approved Cattery of
Blandon, PA 19510   Excellence

Your business card can be plain or fancy.

Keep the cage clean. As the kitten scatters the litter, it must be swept up. For example, feed canned food to the kitten in a dish with a paper towel under it. This can help avoid getting food all over the cage.

Before a kitten is taken to a show, she should be groomed as if she were being shown. Remember, not every buyer has lived with a kitten before. They do not realize that kittens are naturally playful and curious, and this can result in the little ones getting dirty.

The kitten should be played with during the show, especially when the crowd is really thick. Remember, kittens are delightful little creatures, and a cavorting kitten will attract the spectators.

If the kitten is not too playful, and some are not, take her out and groom her. If the kitten is sleeping and will not cooperate in any way, hold her on your lap. A sleeping kitten is the epitome of security and relaxation.

There seem to be two schools of thought about posting prices on the sales cage. Some exhibitors believe stating the price up front can scare away buyers. This is especially true if other exhibitors see your posted prices before they decide how much they will ask for the kittens they have for sale. How can you sell a kitten for $300 or $400 if one can be bought the next aisle for a lower price?

Other exhibitors believe posting the prices means those who stop at the cage to ask about the kittens are not going to be discouraged by your prices. If you want, you can always note that the prices are negotiable. You can also post a sign saying, "Asking $250." Most people know that means that you might consider a counteroffer.

When selling a kitten, do not give her a final name that you never want changed. Part of the fun of owning a cat is choosing the name that is perfect for her. Don't take this pleasure away from the potential owner. When you get right down to it, they will call the kitten what they want anyway.

Tell other exhibitors that you are friendly with that you have kittens for sale. If they

---

> ## REMEMBER!
>
> WE SELL KITTENS BY CON-
> TRACT ONLY. THIS MEANS WE
> HAVE TO HAVE THE CONTRACT
> WITH US WHEN WE EXHIBIT AT
> A SHOW.

are asked about kittens for sale, they may refer the potential buyer to your cage. Do not forget to do the same for them when they are in the same situation.

While we have been discussing ways to help you make your kittens attractive at a cat show, and while you will see other breeders selling kittens from their sales cage, we discourage you from trying to sell your kittens at a show. Shows are a good place to let people see your kittens. You can sell them later, after you have checked a buyer's veterinary references and made sure they are not simply buying a kitten on impulse.

When we put a queen together with a sire, we are responsible for each and every one of the resulting kittens that are produced. In most cases, your hands will be the very first contact this kitten has with a human. That contact and the way we raise our kittens teaches them that humans are kind and caring. How caring are we really if we take our precious kittens and hand them over to anyone who comes to a cat show and has the money to pay for them?

Every buyer must be carefully checked. It would be a tragedy for you to one day find out that one of the kittens you caused to be born had been set loose to end up killed by a car or was abused or wound up being killed at an animal shelter. There are ethics surrounding the breeding of pedigreed cats, and these ethics apply as much to

Selling an Older Cat

Selling an older cat can be more difficult than selling a kitten, but you may be able to compensate for it. Maybe a change of approach is needed. Emphasize the benefits of acquiring an older cat. The cat is thoroughly litter trained and has been neutered. It is used to travel, changes in diet, the commotion of a breeding cattery, and it tends to be less spooky than a kitten. An older cat is more settled and easier for people to take care of, especially if they work all day, are handicapped or are older.

But realize that the show hall may not be the ideal place to sell an older pet-quality cat. Housing for senior citizens is no longer able to forbid residents from keeping pets, although they can restrict the number and kinds of pets that are kept. Perhaps older, neutered cats can be found loving homes by advertising on bulletin boards in senior citizens' apartment buildings or through their social groups.

our pet-quality kittens as they do to our show-quality kittens. If you are not prepared to keep every kitten you produce, should you be unable to find suitable buyers, you must stop breeding immediately.

Online Marketing

The latest way of contacting breeders is through the online computer services such as America Online, Compu-Serve or Prodigy. Here you will find bulletin boards listing pedigreed kittens for sale, or you may place your name on the bulletin board inquiring for pedigreed kittens. Many breeders will routinely check these electronic bulletin boards and will respond directly to you on your computer.

In addition, since breeders know each other and generally know who may have kittens available, most breeders can refer you to other breeders who may have kittens at the time you are looking. Once you have the name and telephone number of the breeder from the computer, you can call them and speak with them directly.

Find out where these bulletin boards are located in your online service (look for a pet forum or something similar), and they can become valuable tools for you to buy and sell kittens.

Referrals

Referrals are a very good source of potential pet buyers. When someone sees one of your kittens at someone else's home and asks, "Where did you get that wonderful kitten?" it is your name that will come up. To make sure, keep in touch with your new pet owners, so that they know where your are. Keeping in touch will also help you make sure your kittens grow up in a loving, responsible home.

Unless you literally have a litter underfoot, and that is where they usually will be, you will have to try and keep a waiting list. If you are going to do that, develop a form you can keep, and make sure your caller is willing to wait and that you keep up with them. If you do not, they will go elsewhere.

Pricing

Every one of us in the fancy who has ever sold a kitten or been benched next to someone who was trying to sell kittens has probably heard the question, "Why does that kitten cost $300 or $500 or $1,000 or $50?"

The current prices for pet-quality pedigreed cats run from $250 to $500, a price range that has not changed for almost 10 years. Why so much? We estimate that it can cost from $175 to $250 to bring that kitten to four months of age, which is the age at which it can be sold. So that means most breeders are not making much profit on the sale of pet-quality kittens.

In addition, breeders are somewhat suspicious of potential buyers who seem to be too cost sensitive. Since it is now estimated to cost from $300 to $700 (see *Cats* magazine, May 1996) to take care of a new cat and its necessities during its first year of life, breeders rightfully wonder about buyers who cannot afford the purchase price. How will they be able to care for that kitten later on?

Now, the next time you see a breeder selling a pedigreed kitten for $350, $450 or more, you should not ask yourself why so much. Maybe you should ask why so little. Conversely, if you see a pedigreed kitten for sale for, say, $75 or $100, ask why so low.

WHAT POTENTIAL BUYERS MAY ASK YOU

When you are dealing with a potential buyer, realize that how much each person knows about your breed, or even cats in general, can vary widely. So treat each question as if it were a very intelligent one. Few things put off a potential buyer more than being made to feel they are stupid.

Think through how you would answer each of these questions below. Remember, you are trying to sell your breed and your kitten, but you must be honest and also keep your response simple.

- What is the personality of this breed? Is it active or placid?
- Are there any genetic problems with this breed that may affect the cat in the future?
- What types of food does it and should it eat?
- Are there any special dietary needs of this breed?
- How much and what kind of grooming or other care does it need?
- How big will the breed generally get when it is fully grown?
- How does this breed get along with other pets or with children?
- How much does it need the companionship of another cat, another animal or a person?

- Is there any difference in the disposition of the males and the females?

- Do you participate in a cattery inspection program?

- What is in your contract?

- Do you guarantee the health of your kittens?

- Does the kitten come with a certificate of health signed by a veterinarian?

- Do you provide copies of the blood tests you have done to show that your cattery is free from contagious or infectious diseases?

- Do you have the names of some people who have bought kittens from you who can be asked about the breed and your cats?

If the potential buyer does not ask all of these questions, tell them the answers anyway to be sure they know what they should about the breed and why they should have one of your kittens.

Always try to avoid complex answers or ones that use a lot of technical jargon. For example, when asked to describe our breed, most of us will fall back on to the language of the breed standard of the association in which we show most. But think, how well does the average person who does not breed or exhibit understand terms like *cobby* or *almost equilateral*? And even if they do, does using these terms actually tell them why you love this breed?

WHAT SHOULD YOU ASK A POTENTIAL BUYER

In your discussions with a potential buyer, there are a lot of issues you should consider. Ultimately, you want to establish at least the following:

- Will this person provide your kitten with a good home?

- Are they able to care for a kitten and will they do so?

- Will they be satisfied with the kitten they are buying, that is, can they care for it properly and is it the right breed for them?

Ask potential buyers the following questions:

- Are you buying this kitten for yourself?

- How many cats do you have and how do you take care of them?

- Are they neutered and kept indoors?

- What do you feed your cats?

- If you had a cat who died recently, how did it die and at what age?

- Do you have children or other pets?

- Are you out of the house during the day?

- What is your lifestyle? Do you like quiet or do you like some activity?

- Are you familiar with this breed?

- Are you able to physically take care of a cat?

- Do you understand that you will have to sign a contract to buy this kitten?

- Do you realize that this kitten will have to be neutered and never used for breeding?

- Are you prepared to keep this cat as a strictly indoor cat?

- May I call your veterinarian and have him recommend you as an owner of a purebred kitten?

- Do you understand that this kitten is not to be resold or given away?

- Do you plan to declaw this kitten?

- Do you understand that either the state law or both the state law and the contract requires you to take the kitten to your veterinarian as soon as you get him?

Feel free to add your own questions. Remember, find out what you need to know *before* the sale. That avoids any problems following the sale.

Shipping a Kitten by Air

In most cases, your buyer will come to your cattery to get their new cat, or you will meet them at a show and transfer the cat there. You can also ship a cat to its new owner by air. However, there are a number of things you must check into before shipping by air. Make sure the airline will take cats in the cargo hold, as that is where they will go. Find out when and where you have to bring the cat to the airline. It may be to the cargo operations area, not to the ticket counter.

Make sure you are using a carrier approved by the airlines. They are very specific on what kinds can be used. Also, double-check the paperwork you must have. For some airlines, you have to put papers in the carrier; for others, you put them on the outside. For some, you do both. All airlines require current health certificates and rabies shots. Ask if you can or must put a bowl for water in the carrier, even if you will not be putting in water.

How much will it cost? Usually cats cannot be shipped collect, and you may want to pass the shipping costs on to the buyer.

Check the flights you are using so that you avoid connecting flights. A connecting flight means the kitten will have to wait in a cargo area for the next flight. Check on the weather. Airlines will not transport live animals if the temperatures are too high or too low. That can be at either airport.

Find out when and where the new owner can pick up the kitten, and make sure the owner is clear about this so the kitten does not spend time unattended at the airport. Find out how you can check on delivery, since the airlines will usually not insure a cat in a carrier.

CAUTION!

DO NOT PUT ANY TOYS OR EXTRAS IN A CARRIER THAT IS BEING SENT BY AIR. IT IS NOT SAFE FOR THE CAT.

In general, spend time with a cargo specialist who understands shipping live animals so that you can ship your cat as quickly and safely as possible. You should also get the most current information on this from the AVMA (see the Appendix).

ADDING EXTRAS

Many breeders try to do a little something extra for the kittens they sell as pets, which makes the experience that much better for the new owner. Perhaps they have the pedigree written in calligraphy, or they give a special toy or cat bed with the kitten. Maybe they follow up by phone with the new owner in a couple of weeks to see how the kitten is getting along. All these things help the breeders feel they have done well by the kittens they have sold.

Kitten Kits

The major premium cat food companies, such as Nutro Products, periodically provide special services to cat breeders. These services benefit not only the breeder, but the new owner as well. Most importantly, these programs benefit the kittens who are being sold. While they vary from time to time, they usually have one or more of the following features.

They help the kitten adjust to its new home by providing food that the kitten is used to eating. That can be a sample, or a coupon for free or discounted food. They encourage new owners to feed their food by offering the breeder discounts or rebates on purchases of kitten food.

Cat care books are also provided to help answer any questions the new owners may have.

Pedigree forms, cat carrier name and address labels, and health and inoculation record forms may also be provided by the companies.

As a group, these are known as kitten kits. They are available to breeders who have previously registered with the cat food companies, and are designed to promote the sale of premium foods.

To find out exactly what types of programs are available, contact the companies themselves, or their representatives at the cat shows. Usually these representatives are very knowledgeable about current breeder programs.

Toys, Beds and Carriers

If you will be sending a toy or special bed with your kitten to its new home, make sure to tell the new owner you are doing this. If they have a cat at home, they may want to make sure their new kitten gets to keep its present. Also, they may want to take these out of the carrier for safety reasons.

You know you are a cat breeder when . . .

- Your spouse tells you they'll leave if you buy one more cat, and you reply wistfully that you'll miss them.

- You can name all your cats, but don't think it's strange when you don't know the exact count.

- Neighbors stop you in front of the house and say, "How many cats do you have? Every day I see a different color cat in the window."

- Something angers you, and you describe it later by saying it raised the fur on the back of your neck.

- You shop at several different stores for canned food or litter to avoid attracting attention, or so you can use as many coupons as possible.

- When someone ticks you off you say, "He gives me a hairball!"

- You express annoyance by hissing.

Adapted from *101 Ways to Know You're a Cat Fancier.*

CHAPTER ELEVEN

Legal Issues Facing the Breeder

Every business or hobby comes complete with its own legal issues. For the responsible breeder, the majority of these concern the way he or she deals with cat registries, other breeders and buyers of both pet- and show-quality kittens. However, there are some other areas where legal issues can also come into play.

CONTRACTS

Whether you like it or not, you will need to develop a contract to cover the sales of some, if not all, of your kittens. There are several reasons for this:

- More and more states have passed "lemon laws," laws protecting the rights of pet buyers if they buy a sick cat or dog (more about them later in this chapter). While the laws are aimed at pet shops and puppy mills, in some states they may also cover individual breeders, even if they breed very few litters per year. And these laws specifically require that the new owner be given written notice of their rights under the law, along with information on the cat, medical records, etc. So you might as well have a contract.

- TICA's ethical breeder program requires that all cats being sold by breeders covered by this program are sold only with a written contract.

- Increasingly, the registries and non-affiliated breed groups are encouraging breeders to urge new owners to spay or neuter pets as soon as possible. One effective way to do this is to agree, via a contract, that the breeder will hold the registration papers and a separate deposit, both of which will be returned when the breeder receives proof that the cat has been altered.

- If you are acquiring a cat for your breeding program or arranging for stud services, you should also have a contract to spell out what each party expects and will receive under what set of circumstances. While that is not a sales contract, it will involve some of the same elements as a sales contract.

Taxes

The relationship between a cattery and taxing authorities varies widely and wildly from state to state. As a responsible breeder, you must find out what the requirements are.

Are you required to collect and remit sales tax on the sales of your kittens? Check with your state's department of revenue for information on sales taxes.

How are you taxed by the state and federal government on your income from sales of your kittens? On this complex and ever-changing issue, you should check with a tax preparer or advisor.

Many people are put off by the idea of a contract. They should not be. Later in this chapter we'll give you specific advice on sales contracts, including some reminders about subjects you should consider covering in your sales contract.

In dealing with contracts and cats, or with contracts in any context, always remember that the contract is there to reflect what both parties have decided on. In addition, the very act of having both parties in a transaction focus on a written document helps avoid the all-too-frequent problems that arise with just a verbal agreement. These problems include misunderstandings between the parties ("I did not know she was going to take my cat to that male"), as well as subjects neither side had considered ("If I had known she might be allergic to cats, I would have arranged to take the cat back after a week or so. But I can't do that now"). Finally, a written contract is proof that you have met whatever requirements are imposed on you, whether by your state, your registry or your breed association.

One of the most common excuses for not having a contract is that the other person is "special": you have been dealing with them for years, they are a friend, they are well-known in the fancy, and so on. In fact, it is more critical to have some written reminder, which is exactly what a contract is, when dealing with friends, if for no other reason than because you are friends. Few things break up a good friendship faster than an avoidable misunderstanding about a cat because nothing was in writing.

> **NOTE!**
>
> CAT REGISTRIES ARE NOT PO-LICING BODIES FOR DISPUTES BETWEEN BREEDERS. HOW-EVER, SOME BREED SOCIETIES ARE. THESE ARE PRIVATE GROUPS, AND NOT ALL BREED-ERS ARE REQUIRED TO BE MEMBERS OF THEM, NOR CAN THEY HANDLE ALL PROBLEMS. BUT IT IS WORTHWHILE TO CONTACT THEM IF YOU HAVE PROBLEMS.

As a breeder, the key in using a contract is to make sure it protects both you and the other party to the transaction. In every situation that requires a contract, there are a few basic principles you should keep in mind:

- Clearly identify the parties to the contract.

- Make sure any important points are written down, not just "understood" between the parties.

- There is no such thing as a standard agreement, or something that "everyone knows" to be the practice.

- If you both agree to change a part of the contract, make the change in writing.

- Let the written text express exactly what you have agreed upon; do not just put in language developed by someone else for another context unless you know exactly what it means and you want your contract to do exactly what the other contract does.

- When considering what to cover in your contract, first make sure both sides clearly understand what is going on and who is bearing what risks.

The most common cause of disputes about cats is the failure of the parties to actually agree upon what is going on. For example, if you expect that you will get a kitten back from a stud service who is able to be registered in CFA, do not assume it; say it in the stud contract. If you follow

REMEMBER!

IN SPITE OF THE BEST EFFORTS OF BOTH SIDES, YOU CANNOT DEVISE A CONTRACT THAT PROTECTS AGAINST EVERY CONTINGENCY, SIMPLY BECAUSE YOU CANNOT ANTICIPATE EVERY SINGLE THING THAT COULD HAPPEN. THAT'S WHY LAWYERS HAVE DEVISED PHRASES LIKE "ACCIDENTS," "UNEXPECTED EVENTS," AND "ACTS OF GOD." IF SOMETHING YOU COULD NOT HAVE FORESEEN DOES HAPPEN, YOU HAVE TO CALMLY SIT DOWN AND WORK THINGS OUT WITH THE OTHER PARTY.

that rule, you will avoid 95 percent of the problems that arise in the fancy.

Do not put in clauses that are not important, that is, that you would not go to court to enforce. And going to court is an expensive and long process. That means do not put in clauses you really could not enforce if it came to a dispute, such as restricting the way second-generation offspring of the cat you sold can be bred. Even when you get a hearing, you will have to show that the clauses in dispute were agreed to by both sides; that one side failed to comply, which is called a breach of contract; that the other side was actually harmed in some way; and what the monetary value of that harm was, which is a very difficult matter to determine in things like stud and breeding contracts.

The four most common situations in which you, as a breeder, will need a contract are the sale of a kitten as a pet, the purchase or sale of a show or breeder kitten, stud service and leasing agreements. To help you in this process, for each type of contract we have listed the most important topics that must be covered in the contract followed by a list of other topics you should consider covering.

Pet Kitten Sales Contracts

The most important topics to cover are:

- The breed, sex and age of the kitten.
- The price and payment terms.
- The new owner's obligation to spay/alter the kitten, including when and how they are going to provide you with proof that it was done.

- When the kitten leaves for its new home.

- Who pays for shipping.

- A health guarantee and current health records.

Other subjects you may want to cover:

- Will the seller or buyer pay a penalty if they cancel the sale?

- Will the kitten be registered? Where?

- Obligations of the new owner to care for the kitten properly.

- Can the kitten be returned? If so, under what circumstances?

> ### HINT!
>
> THE BEST WAY TO PREVENT A CAT YOU HAVE SOLD FROM BEING BRED, ON PURPOSE OR ACCIDENTALLY, IS TO HAVE IT ALTERED BEFORE IT LEAVES YOUR CATTERY.

- Does the new owner have to take the kitten to the veterinarian immediately?

- Can the new owner resell the kitten?

- If the kitten is shown as a household pet, do you want to be kept informed about awards?

- What are the damages for a breach of contract?

- What state's law covers the contract?

In addition to what you have put in writing, remember that you may have to add specific language on the buyer's rights if there are health problems if this sale is covered by a state lemon law.

Show/Breeder Kitten Sales Contracts

The most important topics to cover are:

- The breed, sex and age of the kitten.

- Where it is registered or can be registered.

- When will the new owner get the registration papers and a signed pedigree?

- Name, color, pattern and registration information on the kitten's parents.

- The price and payment terms. If you are getting a kitten back from a breeding, make sure all of the details of the breeding are set out.

- What is the quality of the kitten/cat? If you use terms such as *show* or *breeder*, define what you mean by them.

- When the kitten leaves for its new home.

- Who pays for shipping.

- A health guarantee and current health records.

Other subjects you may want to cover:

- Will the seller or buyer pay a penalty if they cancel the sale?

- Must the kitten be registered? Where?

- Obligations of the new owner to care for the kitten properly.

- In what association(s) will the kitten/cat be shown? Must it be shown until it achieves a particular title? Are you guaranteeing that it can achieve a title?

- Do you want to be kept informed about its show results?

- Can the kitten be returned? If so, under what circumstances?

- Is the kitten guaranteed to be able to breed? What do you mean by that? If it cannot, what will happen?

- Does the new owner have to take the kitten to the veterinarian immediately?

- Are there restrictions on breeding the cat? What are they?

- Can the new owner resell the kitten?

- What are the damages for a breach of contract?

- What state's law covers the contract?

In addition to what you have put in writing, remember that you may have to add specific language on the buyer's rights if there are health problems if this sale is covered by a state lemon law.

Stud Service

The most important topics to cover are:

- Specifically which cats are involved in the stud service, both male and female.

- Which cat goes where? Does the male travel or does the female?

- Certification of the health of each cat. Has each cat been blood-typed before the breeding to avoid producing litters that fade?

- If either the queen or the stud will be housed away from its cattery, the person with custody should have a written consent from the owner allowing emergency treatment of the cat.

- How long will the queen or sire be kept?

- What is the owner of the stud getting for the stud service? A fee? A pick from the litter? Is it first pick? What if there is only one kitten?

- When is the owner of the queen entitled to a rebreeding? Only if the first breeding does not take? If there are fewer than an agreed-upon number of live kittens? (The custom is that there must be at least two live kittens to avoid a rebreeding.)

- Health issues on the return of the cat: Will you require a veterinarian to examine the cat before it comes back? Will there be retesting for exposure to disease? Who pays for it?

- What if the cat has or develops some health problem while it was away? Who pays for the treatments?

Other subjects you may want to cover:

- Should you require that the matings be witnessed? Is that really feasible if the other party is at work during the day?

- Health issues on the return of the cat: What if the cat with a problem is the pregnant female, and the treatment is not appropriate for a pregnant queen (for example, the drug of choice for ringworm cannot be used on a pregnant cat)?

- If you cannot take the cat back right after the breeding, will you be paying boarding fees to the owner who is housing the cat? How much will you pay each day?

Leasing Agreements

Subjects you should cover in every leasing agreement include:

- Cat's name and registration number(s).

- Names of leasor (owner) and leasee (the one who will get possession).

- How long the lease runs for. When is the leased cat to be returned to the owner, and after what tests?

- Which veterinarian examines the cat, what tests must it pass, and who pays for the tests before it leaves the leasor and before it returns to the leasor?

- Who pays for shipping costs and the necessary health certificates—both at the beginning and at the end of the lease?

- Who pays what portions of expenses while the cat is away from home?

- What happens if the leased cat becomes ill; that is, who pays for expenses, who determines what treatment is needed, and what happens if the cat dies?

- Can the leased cat be shown? If so, under what conditions?

- What cat(s) may be bred to the leased cat? What cat(s) may *not* be bred to it?

- In what registries will litters be registered?

- What is the compensation for the lease—pick of the litter (by whom and when) or payments of how many dollars? Who owns any other kittens? Can the owner sell the kittens?

STATE LEMON LAWS

Since 1990, more and more states have enacted lemon laws covering the sale of pets. These are called *lemon laws* because they are modeled, in large measure, on the lemon laws passed many years ago giving car buyers the right to return defective cars, which are generally known as lemons.

These laws are usually statutes, which means they are enacted by the state's leg-islative body, signed by the governor and can be found in the codified laws of the state.

> **NOTE!**
>
> A LEMON LAW MAY APPLY NOT ONLY TO BREEDERS WHO LIVE IN THE STATE, BUT ALSO TO BREEDERS WHO SELL INTO THAT STATE.

In a few states, pet lemon laws have been enacted as regulations by state departments of agriculture or consumer protection. That means they do not appear in the statute books; they are collected in what are called *administrative codes* or *agency rules and regulations*.

Pet lemon laws are found, in one form or another, in almost a dozen states at the time this book was written, and more states can be expected to enact them.

Whatever the state, these laws generally share many features:

- They cover the sale of pet dogs, cats and sometimes other species.

- They require that the buyer be given a statement of the buyer's rights to relief if the pet they buy is sick.

- If the buyer claims the pet was sick when it was purchased or if it had a genetic problem, any claim has to be made after an examination by a veterinarian.

- They permit the pet buyer to collect for veterinarian bills, but only up to the price of the pet, or to return the pet for a refund, or to exchange the pet for another pet of equal value. The option selected is up to the buyer.

The reason these laws are important to breeders is that some of them, such as those in New York and New Jersey, cover not only pet stores but also breeders who sell pet kittens to the public. To find out if your state has one of these laws, you can call the state's consumer protection office. Usually it is that office, or the state department of agriculture, that enforces such laws and tells sellers what kinds of forms they must use.

Many states require you to inform the buyer of what their rights are under the law. To the left is a composite disclosure statement based on how these laws operate. In some states, you may actually be required to have a buyer sign a document outlining all of this information before he or she can buy a kitten from you.

If your state has a lemon law, check if the law covers

Composite Lemon Law Disclosure Statement

If, within 14 days following the sale and delivery of the kitten to the buyer, a licensed veterinarian certifies, in writing, that the kitten is unfit for purchase due to a non-congenital cause or condition, or within six months certifies, in writing, that the kitten is unfit for purchase due to a congenital or hereditary condition or cause, the buyer may do one of the following:

1. Return the kitten and receive a full refund of the total purchase price.

2. Keep the kitten and receive reimbursement for reasonable veterinary fees associated with the cause or condition incurred prior to the receipt of the veterinary certification. The seller's liability under this option will not exceed 75 percent of the purchase price.

3. Return the kitten and receive, in exchange, a kitten of comparable quality selected by the seller.

The selection of the relevant option is up to the buyer.

"Unfit for purchase" means any disease, deformity, injury, physical condition, illness or defect that is congenital or hereditary and that severely affects the health of the kitten, or that was manifest, capable of diagnosis or likely to have been contracted on or before the sale and delivery of the kitten to the buyer.

Any veterinary certificate of unfitness must contain all of the following:

- The name of the owner of the kitten.

- The date(s) of all examinations of the kitten.

you. Just because it only mentions pet stores does not mean it doesn't cover breeders. Read the definition of *pet store* and see if it covers you. If you're not sure, ask. If it does, you *must* do everything the law requires, including giving new buyers the required disclosure statements. The best way to do that it to put them in or with your contracts.

If your state does not have a lemon law, you should still consider including lemon law language in your contract. That way, if your state should

(continued)

- The breed, color, sex and age of the kitten.

- A clear statement of the veterinarian's findings and/or diagnosis, including the clinical bases for them, and copies of all relevant reports and tests.

- A specific statement that the veterinarian certifies the kitten is "unfit for purchase," as defined above.

- An itemized statement of all veterinary fees incurred as of the date of the certification.

- If the kitten is curable, the estimated fee(s) to cure the kitten.

- If the kitten has died, a statement setting forth the probable cause of death and the clinical bases for that conclusion.

pass a law that later applies to you, you at least can show that you have tried to comply with it. In addition, by using these kinds of clauses you have spelled out what will happen if an unhappy pet buyer claims that you sold them a sick kitten.

PET POPULATION AND LICENSING INITIATIVES

An area of increasing concern to responsible breeders is the gradual rise in the number of laws that, under the guise of protecting animals or the public health, try to limit how many animals can be kept in a private home, or try to limit or even ban the breeding of pedigreed cats and dogs.

These laws appear in several guises. Zoning laws are amended to limit the ownership of more than a certain number of "domestic animals" (of any sort). The limited litigation involving these laws so far seems to indicate that they are not legitimate unless the township that passed the law

-Cat Overpopulation- CFA's Position

The Cat Fanciers' Association, Inc.
World's Largest Registry of Pedigreed Cats
PO Box 1005
Manasquan, NJ 08736-1005
908-528-9797

CFA's Position On Cat Overpopulation

The Cat Fanciers' Association, the United States and world's largest registry of pedigreed cats and the largest sanctioning body for pedigreed cat shows, wishes to reaffirm its commitment to the promotion and protection of all cats, pedigreed or otherwise, with the following representing our position on cat overpopulation.

— Needless euthanasia of healthy, adoptable cats is offensive to all cat lovers.

— To reduce the numbers of animals euthanized in the United States, cat lovers should be willing to cooperate with others in the animal field to find solutions which will:

1. Decrease the number of unwanted births of cats, both random bred and pedigreed.

2. Decrease the number of homeless stray cats and increase the return of lost cats to their homes.

3. Increase the number of cats adopted into permanent homes and decrease the number of animals surrendered to the shelters.

— The responsible breeding of pedigreed cats is of value to society in order to preserve the domestic cat breeds and to provide animals with desirable and predictable physical and personality characteristics. Further, our position is that we are opposed to any law or regulation which would prevent the exercise of these activities.

— Those who are involved in the responsible breeding of pedigreed cats should recognize that, while the proportion of pedigreed kittens produced is small compared to kittens born to random bred cats as a result of indiscriminate or unplanned matings, this group should promote ethical breeding practices which will help reduce the number of unwanted cats.

Adopted by CFA Board of Directors on June 20, 1991 in Philadelphia, PA.
9/91

can show that it is unsafe or unhealthy for anyone to house that number of animals under any circumstances.

Local governments are being pressured to amend local laws to accomplish the same thing, or to prevent the ownership of whole animals, whether or not they are used for breeding. These laws are usually advanced as a solution to pet overpopulation in local shelters. The argument goes that the shelters are overflowing with non-pedigreed cats because there are people breeding pedigreed cats; so if breeding is prohibited, the shelters would be empty. While it's not a very convincing argument, and while responsible breeders accept responsibility for every cat they breed for its entire life, many well-meaning people concerned about animals in shelters are swayed by this reasoning.

City governments are also being convinced that licensing cats, as states do with dogs, will somehow cut down on the population of free-roaming cats, that is, cats without owners. It is those free-roaming cats that contribute to the cat population at shelters. But the proposed laws are aimed at cats that are kept inside and which are, by definition, not a part of the problem.

In fact, despite the sometimes good intentions of some people who support these laws, they are actually driven by animal rights activists in a national effort to slow down and eventually halt the breeding of pedigreed cats and dogs. Their next goal—and they have repeatedly stated this in writing—is to ban the ownership of all pets of any kind. To the average breeder, this sounds almost comical. But the organizations that are behind them are anything but humorous—they are motivated, dedicated and well-financed.

> ## What the Animal Rights Activists Have to Say
>
> "Pet ownership is an absolutely abysmal situation brought about by human manipulation."
> —Ingrid Newkirk, co-founder of People for the Ethical Treatment of Animals, from *Washington Magazine*, August 1986.
>
> "One generation and out. We have no problems with the extinction of domestic animals. They are creations of human selective breeding."
> —Wayne Pacelle, vice president, Humane Society of the U.S., from *The Detroit News*, Sept. 27, 1995.

Anyone who breeds pedigreed cats should be prepared for attacks like this one from The Fund for Animals. In their booklet *Point-Counterpoint:*

Pedigreed Cats Face Extinction

The Cat Fanciers' Association, Inc.
PO Box 1005
Manasquan NJ 08736-0805
908-528-9797

Pedigreed Cats Face Extinction

The distinctive and valued cats you see here today could become extinct unless the repressive laws currently being proposed in many communities are stopped.

These laws are often initiated by well-meaning but misguided individuals and groups who are influenced by the intolerant attitudes of animal rights extremists.

Restrictive breeding ordinances, possession limits, burdensome cat licensing and breeder permit laws, as well as restraints on the display/exhibition of animals, have been presented as a means to reduce the number of animals being killed by shelters or to alleviate animal suffering.

Homeless cats seen throughout our communities and in shelters are not the offspring of planned breeding programs. They are the result of careless or unknowing people who allow their free roaming cats to indiscriminately reproduce. They are caused by random mating among feral/free-roaming cats with no owners to comply with laws.

Misdirected, costly and ineffective, these laws are punitive toward people who selectively breed to preserve the desirable personality and appearance traits of pedigreed cats.

To protect the future of pedigreed cats, contact your city, county and state legislators and/or public officials. Challenge the motives behind coercive cat and dog breeding legislation. Be aware of the serious consequences on the positive activities of responsible people if restrictive laws are enacted. Respect the value of all cats, both pedigreed and random bred.

The Cat Fanciers' Association, its member clubs and pedigreed cat breeders are working to raise the status of all cats. Educational programs, assistance to humane shelters, support of feline health studies, public service announcements and other positive activities benefit both pedigreed and random bred cats.

We support alternatives to coercive legislation. Join with cat fanciers in promoting community programs to manage feral cats and to provide low cost neuter/spay, to educate the public on the nature of cats, to increase adoption rates and require sterilization of cats by shelters prior to adoption.

The Cat Fanciers' Association, Inc.
World's Largest Registry of Pedigreed Cats
PO Box 1005
Manasquan NJ 08736-0805
908-528-9797
#20039-93

Breeders must work together to combat laws that might restrict or even ban their right to breed pedigreed cats.

Making the Case for Breeding-Regulation Ordinances they write, "[O]pponents of breeding-regulation ordinances will be hard pressed to prove this baseless claim" that people who advocate "coercive breeding control legislation are animal rights radicals." The rebuttal to this actually lies within this document itself. The Fund for Animals is openly and actively against the breeding of cats and dogs—period. What's more, according to a 1993 report by the U.S. Department of Justice on the extent and effects of domestic and international terrorism aimed at animal enterprises, The Fund For Animals is listed as one of the "Animal rights organizations that claim to have perpetuated acts of extremism [in] the United States."

These kinds of attacks have pushed the cat fancy to begin to work together to work against laws that will eventually lead to the elimination of pedigreed cats and dogs.

As a responsible breeder, there are things you can do. First and foremost, you must maintain your cattery in as healthy and responsible manner as you can, and be proud of your breed and of being a breeder. You can also work with your breed societies and cat registries to weed out irresponsible breeders.

Be alert for anti-breeder legislation. Recently, the animal rights strategy has been to start a legislative initiative in a smaller town or county, get a model law passed, and then "export" it to other jurisdictions. It's much easier to get a law passed if the neighboring township has just enacted a similar one.

When you see anti-breeder efforts beginning, immediately contact local cat breeders, as well as dog clubs and all of the national registries. That will trigger the existing (and growing) network of formal and informal support for responsible breeders across the country.

As you can see, being a responsible breeder is a serious business—but a rewarding one. Do it right, and you can be proud of it.

Your Responsibility to Your Cattery Today

As a breeder, your first responsibility is to the cats you own. You are responsible for their life, health and happiness. However, you also have another responsibility, and that is to your cattery. While your cats are individuals, your cattery is an entity, and you are responsible for founding that entity, for its continuing existence and for deciding when it should be closed. These responsibilities are very closely intertwined: When you care for your cats you are caring for your cattery, and when you care for your cattery you are caring for your cats.

Your responsibilities to your cattery include maintaining the health of your cats and, therefore, of your entire cattery. This responsibility includes testing all cats who come into your cattery for infectious and contagious diseases. In addition, the responsible breeder makes certain there are no infestations of parasites or fungus in their cattery. If such an infestation should arise, prompt treatment is required. Cats or kittens who become ill are treated immediately in a responsible cattery. Inoculations are kept current, including rabies vaccines.

A responsible breeder maintains scrupulous cattery records. Pedigrees must be accurate and association paperwork should never be in such a state that it can be questioned. Breeding records must be reliable and birthing records must be accurate and maintained in a folder under the name of the breeding queen.

Whenever you sell a pedigreed kitten as a pet, you are selling both the reputation of your cattery and of yourself as a breeder. One kitten from each litter, at minimum, should be tested for contagious and infectious diseases before any kitten from that litter is released to a new home. No kitten should leave the cattery, under any circumstances, if they are under four months of age.

When a pet kitten does leave the cattery, he should be fully inoculated and wormed, and should come with a certificate from your veterinarian that the kitten has been examined within the previous week and found healthy. No kitten should ever leave the cattery without a sales contract, as well as any information that may be helpful to the new owner.

If at all possible—and this is critical to you as a breeder—no pet-quality kitten should ever leave the cattery unneutered. Early spaying and neutering has proven to be perfectly safe, so there is no longer an excuse for selling whole kittens and waiting for them to be neutered later by the new owner.

The **American Cat Fanciers Association**, one of this nation's largest registries of pedigree and household cats and sanctioning body for cat shows, is committed to the protection and promotion of all cats, pedigreed or otherwise.

WE BELIEVE:

- that the most effective method of reducing cat overpopulation and the needless euthanasia of healthy, adoptable cats is through education, not legislation.

- that members of the American Cat Fanciers Association and all others involved in the responsible breeding of pedigreed cats have a special obligation to promote ethical breeding practices, to include advice regarding neutering and spaying, which will reduce the number of unwanted kittens resulting from indiscriminate or unplanned matings.

- that the responsible breeding of pedigreed cats is of value to society because it preserves our domestic cat breeds and provides animals with desirable and predictable physical and personality characteristics. WE ARE OPPOSED TO ANY LAW OR REGULATION WHICH WOULD PREVENT THE EXERCISE OF THESE ACTIVITIES.

Your Responsibility to Your Cattery in the Future

In addition to the current concerns of the cattery, you must take into account the concerns of your cats in the future. Breeders tend to keep the very best cats, meaning those that are closest to the standard of perfection. Breeders also tend to keep the "worst" cats, meaning those cats we became so attached to that we just could not let them go to another home. We also keep those cats who may have been born with a congenital defect that rendered them unfit for sale, such as a heart murmur. For these reasons, most breeders will be running a multiple-cat household.

Your responsibility to your cats and your cattery extends for many years. Again and again, we hear about how people have learned to deal with the passing of a beloved cat. Unfortunately, we rarely hear about how people have made arrangements to take care of their cats if they die first. As important as that is for an individual, it is even more important for you and your cattery.

When we become incapacitated, or when we die, we want to make certain the cats we leave behind are cared for in the manner we want for them. Ensuring this can be more complicated than you think. Let's consider some of the more common questions people ask about this subject.

When Do I Have to Worry About My Cats?

Most owners of one or two cats do not plan for the possibility that their cats will still be alive after they have died. And, among those who do, the planning is fairly informal. For example, a study of elderly people living independently in Chicago showed that most of the pet owners assumed a family member or friend would take care of their pets after their death. However, fewer than 2 percent of them had made any legal provisions for funds to support their pets. And the situation is often no better among breeders and cattery owners.

You really need to be concerned about your cats in several different contexts, including planning for the possibility that you may die before they do, as well as planning for someone to provide care if you cannot.

And remember, the average life span of a cat increases every year, so we could be looking at making provisions for the all cats in a cattery for a decade or more after their breeding time has ended and you have closed the cattery as a breeding entity.

If you should be injured and hospitalized, does anyone else know you have cats and can they step in to care for them—immediately? If you are older or in poor health, you may find yourself under someone else's care, possibly with a guardian to help you manage your assets and take care of yourself. But that means someone else will be making decisions about your cats and the cattery, not you.

What Do I Have to Plan For?

Consider planning for the following:

- Immediate intervention if you cannot take care of the cats in an emergency.

- Long-term assistance or placement if you are indefinitely or permanently incapacitated.

- Your own death.

Each of these appears to be clear-cut, but they really overlap. For example, if you die and your cattery survives you, the issue is not just leaving money to care for the cats in the long term. What happens in the short term? Who feeds your cats today and tomorrow? And for how long and where?

Can I Order My Cats to Be Destroyed on My Death?

Probably not. Even though a pet cat (which is what all of your non-working or neutered cats are) is seen as having no monetary value, the courts that supervise the way estates are run have been reluctant to order pets destroyed by order of their now-deceased owners. And if you have a working cattery, the courts might view this as an asset and they will usually not order an asset, something with real monetary value, to be destroyed.

In any case, why would you want to do that to your beloved cats?

Can't I Just Leave Money to My Cattery?

In a word, no. We have heard the same stories you have about someone leaving millions of dollars (it always seems to be millions) to Fluffy. But legally, you cannot do that. Also, as any estate planner will tell you, trying to do something like that with a lot of money will only invite challenges to your will (and to the care of your cats) by those who could get the money if the cats were not "in the way." And the more money there is at stake, the more likely they are to try—and to succeed.

This is also true if the cattery is organized as a business, for example if it's incorporated. You cannot leave money to a business; in fact, you would have to leave the business (your cattery) to someone, who could then do whatever they wanted with it.

While the issue has not yet been taken to court, it would seem, based on the experience estates have had with breeding horse farms and the like, that a working cattery would not be closed down at once. Unless you have left specific instructions, the job of the estate executor or trustee is to liquidate the cattery in the most economical (and profitable) manner, as quickly as possible: In other words, to sell as many of the cats as possible as fast as they can.

Can I Leave Money in Trust to Care for My Cats?

If you are serious about estate planning, you have probably heard about trusts. For a number of fairly antique reasons, it has always been regarded as virtually impossible to leave money in trust for a single animal (or all of your animals), as opposed to creating a trust to benefit animals as a whole. Most state courts have refused to let pet owners set up trusts designed to care for their pets after the owner's death. The reasons for that have been extremely technical in nature, turning on two key problems: The laws governing the length of trusts are based on measuring human lives, not those of animals; and trusts must have someone to "enforce" them, that is, to complain if the wishes of the person who funded them are not met.

However, the laws governing trusts in many states have changed over the years, making these objections less important, if not removing them completely. Still, even in those states where such trusts may be valid, you must be careful not to "overfill" the trust—that is, you must provide an amount that is logically related to the kind of care and length of care needed.

In fact, the legal community is probably still a little short-sighted about this concept. If you go to your lawyer and ask to set up a trust to care for your cattery, you'll probably be told it is impossible. That's not so. It may be very difficult, but that is not the same as impossible.

Remember, in addition to providing money, you have to provide someone to care for your cats' welfare—the trustee. It should be someone you trust to look out for your cats.

Can I Leave My Cats to Someone?

Yes, but it does not end there. A cat is personal property. That means the person who "inherits" your cats can accept and care for them, accept and sell, destroy or neglect them, or refuse to accept them. It is that person's choice, and only theirs.

Can I Leave Money and My Cats to Someone?

This is probably the most common approach, and one that makes a lot of sense. Many people seeking to protect their cats (and other pets) leave money to a named person on the condition that the person care for the cats. While this arrangement seems to accomplish what the owner wants, the caretaker may challenge the provisions, often successfully. Even if the challenge is not successful, this does not end your need to plan.

Let us give you a bit of cold, hard, legal information. If you leave your cats to someone, say John, with money to care for them, that does not guarantee it will happen that way. John can take the cats and the money and care for them, as you intend. He can also take the cats and the money but use the money for his own ends; take the cats and the money and then give away, sell or destroy the cats; or he can just take the money and refuse the cats.

This is why it is critical that you speak with the person designated to receive the cats and the money, and be *sure* they will follow your wishes.

Who Might Be Willing to Take My Cats?

That's a tough one. First, start with where you got your cats. Since you bought them from a breeder, check the contract you signed. Some breeders agree to take back, or to help place a cat if you can no longer keep it. Even if that is not in the contract or you do not have a written contract, the breeder may be able to help you (or your estate) place the cat.

Now, turn to other sources. For example, if your cat is a fairly rare breed, you may be able to leave instructions to have a breed society contacted by the executor of your estate. The society would not be given the cats; however, it might prove useful in guiding your executor in finding new homes for them. Check with the breed society first. While none that we know of have set up formal systems to do this, some are already creating informal systems, and your call may provoke others into looking into this for your benefit and for the benefit of the breed.

Friends, family and the like, of course, should also be considered. But be careful and be realistic. Never assume that because your sister appears to love your cats, she will be happy to bring the entire cattery into her home with her three children and two dogs. Ask her, and then consider her answer very carefully. Other friends who have cats may be willing to take them, but again, check.

In any case, be realistic. If you are 55, do you really think it is a good idea to arrange for your 61-year-old sister to care for your cats when you die? Especially if the youngest cat is two years old now? That might eventually mean having a 74-year-old woman caring for a 15-year-old cat. Think about it—from both sides.

Another option is to arrange for your cats to be placed in a long-term or permanent care no-kill facility. A long-term facility cares for your cats while working to place them in a permanent home. A permanent care facility is just what the name implies.

Several issues are involved in the decision to use such facilities. First, as with any other option in caring for your cat, planning is vital. Most of these groups require you to contact them in advance. In addition, you will have to make specific financial arrangements with them. Second, you have to consider whether or not your cat will be happy living, for a short time or permanently, in such a facility. Some groups, among them the Humane Society, have argued that many of these facilities take in more animals than they can properly care for.

Another option is to contact groups that use companion animals for a number of positive purposes, such as therapy animals. These may agree to take your cats, usually if arrangements are made in advance. But the agreement may be conditional on whether your cats can be used for their purpose, each cat's age and condition, and other factors.

What Are the Most Important Things I Can Do?

Regardless of what option you choose in planning for your cats after your death or in case you are disabled, you have to make sure you have made arrangements with someone who you *know* will follow your wishes. That means you must take the time to find someone (or some group) you can rely on to do what you want done. But don't stop there. Contact them regularly. Make your intentions clear.

Also make sure others who know you understand that you have made arrangements for your cats. To be blunt, if the people who come across your cats after your death do not know what you have planned for them, they will do what they think is best. Your wishes may never be carried out, because you haven't made them known. Some people have a letter detailing their wishes prominently posted in their cattery at all times. It gives instructions about caring for their cats, and the name and contact information of the person to call should anything happen to them. This way, even a stranger, such as the police, knows who to call and what to do.

Take the following key points to heart:

- Right now, decide who will care for your cats if you become ill or die. Make sure they are willing and able to do this. Talk with them.

- Make sure someone you trust has access to the cattery (with a key) and that the local police, for example, know who to contact if there is a problem.

- If you are planning to have an organization care for your cats or arrange for their placement, check them out. Confirm any advance arrangements they need.

- If you want to use your will or create a trust for your cats, don't try and do it by yourself. It is a tricky area for skilled lawyers; for the unskilled, such efforts will almost certainly fail.

- Keep in mind this sad fact: The more money involved, the more likely it is that your relatives will challenge your will in court.

- Make sure others know about your cats and that you have already made arrangements for their care and disposition. Remember, if something happens to you, they need care and attention—immediately.

Another thing you must do is take steps to create and maintain a current (and easy-to-locate) system for identifying your cats. Just because you can tell the difference between two cats does not mean anyone else can do so. One way to set up such a system is to create a file for each cat in the cattery. The file should include, at a minimum, the following:

- A current photograph of each cat, showing any distinctive features. Also give a short description, using both official terms for colors (such as *sable*) and non-technical equivalents (like *brown*).

- A summary of any special problems associated with that cat. That could range from the fact that it is diabetic and needs daily shots of insulin (what dosage?) to the fact that it needs to live with another cat (which one?).

- Basic information on its call name, registered name, registration papers and whether or not it is still whole.

- Information of interest to a potential new owner, such as whether it is a proven breeder.

- The name and telephone of the veterinarian(s) who have the current records on the cats.

- A copy of the official papers on each cat (keep the originals somewhere safe).

Then, to be extra safe, have someone who is not familiar with your cats see if they can identify them from these materials.

All these responsibilities to your cattery must be taken into account and accepted before you ever acquire your first breeding cat.

By now you know that breeding pedigreed cats is not about winning rosettes, is not about titles and is not about making money. Rather, it is

Blizzard is evaluated by ACFA all-breed judge Ken Miller.

about preserving, protecting and advancing the breed you have chosen to work with. Becoming a breeder for any other reason is an error. If you are willing to devote your time and efforts to this important goal, you can become a responsible breeder—a term of real respect within the fancy. And if you do become a responsible breeder, that will be your true reward.

APPENDIX

Books

The books we have included here were the latest editions at the time this book was written. Several of them may be revised or updated in the next few years, so check for later or revised editions.

The Cat Fanciers' Association Cat Encyclopedia, edited by the Cat Fanciers' Association Inc., Simon & Schuster, New York 1993. This is a beautiful, comprehensive book dealing with most of the breeds recognized by the various cat registration bodies. The CFA standards of perfection for the breeds are included, as well as a section on the care of pedigreed cats.

The Complete Cat Book, by Richard H. Gebhardt, Howell Book House, New York 1991. A comprehensive guide to caring for and showing cats. Breed histories and Standards of Perfection are included. The author is past president of the CFA.

The Cornell Book of Cats, Second Edition, edited by Mordecai Siegal, Villard Books, New York 1997. If you can have only one book in your cattery library, this would be the book to have. It is a comprehensive guide to the care of cats, dealing with all aspects of care, all common diseases and parasites that affect cats, as well as sex and reproduction. This book is easy to understand and answers questions about all stages of a cat's life. It covers care of the cat from birth through old age.

Feline Husbandry: Diseases and Management of the Multiple-Cat Environment, by Niels C. Pedersen, DVM, Ph.D., American Veterinary Publications Inc., Goleta, CA 1991. This comprehensive book explains genetics, reproduction, infectious diseases, nutrition and toxicology. It also has an excellent section on cattery design and management. This is a very important book for you to have, as every breeder manages a multiple-cat environment.

Genetics for Cat Breeders, Third Edition, by Roy Robinson, Pergamon Press, Oxford, England 1991. This comprehensive book is a must for every breeder of pedigreed cats. This is the *only* source for genetic information specifically on cats, by the acknowledged expert in the field of genetics of pedigreed cats. Before you read this book, you must have a thorough grounding in basic genetics.

In the Spotlight: A Guide to Showing Pedigreed and Household Pet Cats, by Carolyn M. Vella and John J. McGonagle, Jr., Howell Book House, New York 1990. A comprehensive guide to exhibiting cats in the shows sanctioned by the United States cat registries.

Legacy of the Cat, by Gloria Stephens, Chronicle Books, San Francisco 1990. This book has an easily understood section on genetics and an explanation of the various breeds of pedigreed cats. What makes it unique is that the author discusses the personality of each breed, in addition to the physical appearance.

The Pieces of a Cat, by Carol Brown, Carlton Press, New York 1989. This is a basic book on cat anatomy, written in very easy-to-understand language. By understanding the structure of the cat, you will be able to identify any problems you may see and possibly avoid these problems in the future.

Veterinary Pharmaceuticals and Biologicals, published by the Veterinary Medicine Publishing Group, (800) 255-6864. This reference work is published every two years, with the latest issue published in December 1996. This is a key reference work for breeders. While its price (in 1996 about $80 plus shipping) may seem high, the coverage is comprehensive. In addition to providing current information on the drugs your veterinarian may be prescribing for your cats, it includes much more information, ranging from therapeutic diets and nutritional supplements to parasiticides and disinfectants. You also can find current information on many subjects, from the National Animal Poison Control Center to metric conversion charts. (To keep your copy current, take the printed information provided with any new drug your veterinarian prescribes and put it in the front of the book. That keeps all your reference materials together.)

Your Cat Naturally, by Grace McHattie, Carrol & Graf Publishers Inc., New York 1992. This beautiful book is an excellent introduction to the use of herbal and homeopathic remedies. There are numerous, easily understood charts and a list of suppliers.

HELP AND ADVICE

Blood Typing

Dr. Urs Giger, Department of Clinical Studies, Veterinary Hospital, University of Pennsylvania, 3835 Spruce Street, Philadelphia, PA 19104-6010 (215) 898-8076. This free service is supported by the Robert H. Winn Foundation and by several cat clubs that have generously donated funds for this study. When sending in a blood sample for testing, the majority of breeders enclose a small donation to help defray the costs of the blood typing.

Have your veterinarian draw a small blood sample, usually 1 ml (or 0.3 ml if you are testing a kitten less than three months of age). Use a purple top EDTA tube. Label the tube with the cat's name and wrap the tube in a paper towel or other suitable padding for shipment. Include in the envelope either your name and address or the name and address of your veterinarian so the results can be returned, the name of the cat, breed, age and sex. And enclose a copy of the cat's pedigree and mention that this cat will be used in a breeding program. Ship Priority Mail (two-day) Monday through Wednesday to the address mentioned above. You should receive your results within a week.

Disaster Response

CFA Animal Welfare/Disaster Relief Committee, (800) 979-0241 (this is a 24-hour pager number). In case of an emergency such as hurricanes, tornadoes or other possible evacuation situations in your area, contact this committee. They will respond to assist any cats in the area that may need assistance.

Poison Control

The National Animal Poison Control Center is operated by the University of Illinois, which runs two hot lines. The first, (800) 548-2423, will charge you a fee per case (charged to a major credit card); the second is (900) 680-0000 and charges for the time you are on the line (charged to your telephone bill). If you have to call the NAPCC, be ready to provide the following:

- Your name, address and telephone number.

- The substance(s) your cat has been exposed to, if you know.

- Information about the exposure, such as the amount, how long it has been since your cat was exposed, etc. Also, were other pets involved?

- Your cat's breed, age, sex, and weight and any medications it is receiving.

- The symptoms your cat is experiencing.

Shipping Cats by Air

The American Veterinary Medical Association has developed guidelines for traveling with pets. These guidelines, developed in cooperation with the Air Transport Association and the American Humane Association, are available from the AVMA Public Information Division, Suite 100, 1931 North Meacham Road, Schaumburg, IL 60173-4360, (708) 925-8070.

Telephone Consultations

Cornell Feline Health Center, College of Veterinary Medicine, VRT 7081, Ithaca, NY 14853-6401, (607) 253-3414, fax (607) 253-3419.

NATIONAL CAT PUBLICATIONS

These are the advertising offices, for marketing your cattery and your kittens.

Cat Fancy and *Cats USA*, P.O. Box 6050, Mission Viejo, CA 92690, (714) 855-8822.

Cats, PJS Publications, News Plaza, Box 1790, Peoria, IL 61656, (309) 682-7394.

I Love Cats, Grass Roots Publishing Company Inc., 950 Third Avenue, New York, NY 10022-2705, (212) 888-1855.

Cat World™ International Report, Ashdown Publishing, Avalon Court, Star Road, Partridge Green, West Sussex, RH13 8RY, U.K. Tel: 011-44-1403-711511, e-mail: ashdown@netmail.co.uk

NATIONAL CAT REGISTRIES

American Cat Fanciers Association Inc., P.O. Box 203, Point Lookout, MO 65726.
Telephone: (417) 334-5430; Fax: (417) 334-5540; Internet: http://www.acfacat.com

Cat Fanciers' Association Inc., P.O. Box 1005, Manasquan, NJ 08736-0805.
Telephone: (908) 526-9797; Fax: (908) 528-7391; Internet: http://www.cfainc.org

The International Cat Association Inc., P.O. Box 2684, Harlingen, TX 78551.
Telephone: (210) 428-8046; Fax: (210) 428-8047; Internet: http://www.tica.org

INTERNET SERVICES

The Internet is the newest way to find answers to many questions you might have about cats, feline veterinary medicine and breeding and care techniques. However, the Internet is active and constantly changing. Some of the sites that you may access today, you may not be able to access tomorrow.

In addition, there are currently over 100 different cat home pages to visit. Some of these home pages are there to promote a particular breed or advertise a cattery, but a few of them also have excellent advice for pedigreed cat buyers. We have listed some currently accessible sites for breeders and exhibitors. As you use the Internet, make a note of the sites you find useful so you can return to them again.

However, remember that the Internet is comprised of people who are able to hide behind the anonymity of their electronic nicknames. There have been well-known instances of fraud on the chat lines. Be extremely wary of any and all chat lines, home pages and private sources of information on the Internet. The information you are given may be wrong and, in some instances, can lead you to administer medications that can do deadly harm to your cat. Never follow veterinary advice given on the Internet until you have checked with your own veterinarian.

All of the home pages listed here are undergoing constant expansion and improvement.

American Cat Fanciers Association

http://www.acfacat.com

This site is for members, exhibitors and breeders who are involved with American Cat Fanciers Association (ACFA), a national cat registry. This site can also be checked if you are interested in going to an ACFA show either as a spectator or as an exhibitor. It offers show schedules, information of interest to breeders and exhibitors, as well as links to other sites.

Cat Fanciers' Association

http://www.cfainc.org

This site is for exhibitors and breeders who are involved with the Cat Fanciers' Association (CFA), a national cat registry. This site can also be

checked if you are interested in going to a CFA show either as a spectator or as an exhibitor. It provides a direct link to the Winn Foundation's
site.

Cat Fanciers Mailing List

http://www.fanciers.com/vetmed.html
This mailing list covers general medical topics, specific illnesses, reproduction and young kittens. Some examples of areas covered are clinical
signs of disease, feline leukemia virus, feline infectious peritonitis, cardiomyopathy, pregnancy and parturition, reproduction and newborn kittens. Many of these topics are addressed by the Cornell School of
Veterinary Medicine or by individual veterinarians.

We suggest you follow only the information offered by professional
experts. The advice written by other individuals may promote the use of
improper veterinary techniques or techniques best used only after checking with your own veterinarian.

Cornell Vet Web Resource

http://zoo.vet.cornell.edu/
This Web site provides information about Cornell University College
of Veterinary Medicine, its services and departments, and announcements.

Fanciers Breeder Referral List and Retired Friends

http://www.fanciers.com/breedlist/
The Fanciers Breeder Referral List is the largest online pedigreed cat
breeder's referral list today. If you are looking to purchase kittens or cats,
or need information about breeds, this is the Web site to visit. You have
the option of searching an alphabetical listing of breeds or searching for
breeds listed by U.S. state, Canadian province or country outside North
America. Using this site enables you to directly contact other breeders of
your breed. It is also an excellent source when looking to buy a kitten or
to sell one.

Retired Friends lists adult cats available for placement. These are usually older cats retired from active breeding programs.

Food and Drug Administration Center for Veterinary Medicine

http://www.cvm.fda.gov/

An explanation of the Center's activities and policies, Freedom of Information summaries on veterinary drugs, veterinary drug manufacturing and FDA approval guidelines.

The Fanciers List

fanciers@fanciers.com

Founded in 1993, the Fanciers List is a private, unmoderated mailing list intended for discussions or announcements specifically relating to showing and breeding cats. This includes such topics as feline veterinary medicine and home care, cattery management, the politics of cat shows and cat fancy associations, and the history and evolution of cat breeds. The list also serves as a social group for breeders and exhibitors.

The Fanciers List maintains a steady membership of approximately 500 people who are involved in the cat fancy in many ways. The members represent every major cat-related association, nearly every breed of cat and many countries around the world. Some of the most renowned feline experts are among them, including many cat show judges, board members of cat registries, cat geneticists, cat book authors and the like. Some members breed and/or show pedigreed cats; some put on cat shows or produce publications about cats and the cat fancy; some work with breed rescue groups and other organizations devoted to animal welfare; some practice veterinary medicine or participate in feline health research.

The Fanciers List helps bring together fanciers who work for the benefit of all cats and the people who love them. The List is committed to providing an open forum for all cat fanciers to discuss the issues that concern them. It is an aid to worldwide research, improving both our medical and genetic knowledge and our animal husbandry practices. Good factual information available on the Fanciers List helps individuals to make better choices and take better care of their animal companions.

Talking about our concerns and problems in a wide forum has helped us find practical solutions. This is a particularly powerful tool for sharing experiences with dreaded diseases, making our collective expertise available to the public at large.

To join the Fanciers List, send an e-mail message to **fanciers-request@ fanciers.com.**

The Fanciers List is also produced in digest form. The digest form will give you all of the messages clumped into a few, large messages per day. If you choose to join this version, contact **fanciers-digest-request@fanciers.com.**

The International Cat Association

http://www.tica.org
This site is for those members, exhibitors and breeders who are involved with The International Cat Association (TICA), a national cat registry. This site should also be checked if you are interested in going to a TICA show either as a spectator or as an exhibitor.

Winn Feline Foundation

http://www.cfainc.org./cfa/winn/winn.html
This service introduces the Winn Feline Foundation, a foundation affiliated with the Cat Fanciers Association that specializes in feline veterinary research. The site describes what studies are currently under way, what grants have been given for feline research and what studies have been completed.

The Winn Foundation has funded a few studies dealing with feline reproduction. The best way to track what projects are under way and what has been completed is through CFA's monthly publication, *Cat Fanciers Almanac.* The annual index is particularly useful in this regard.

VETERINARY SUPPLY CATALOGS FOR BREEDERS

The following is a partial list of veterinary supply catalogs that are used by pedigreed cat breeders. These supply houses sell everything from carriers and small cages to grooming equipment and equipment for your cattery and the delivery of kittens.

Many of these catalogs sell vaccines and syringes, so you can do your own inoculations (remember that some states prohibit this, and catalog companies can only sell vaccines where it is legal). The catalogs may also sell prescription medications. To order these, you must get a prescription from your veterinarian.

The prices in these catalogs tend to be very good, but some catalogs require a minimum order of $50 to $75.

Anicare	(800) 466-2642
California Veterinary Supply	(800) 366-3047
Care-a-Lot	(800) 343-7680
Canine Specialty Wholesale	(810) 939-5960
Dog Outfitter	(800) 367-3647
Drs. Foster & Smith	(800) 826-7206
JB Wholesale	(800) 526-0388
Jeffers Vet	(800) 641-2836
Omaha Vaccine Co.	(800) 367-4444
Re-viv-al	(800) 786-4751
R.C. Steele	(800) 872-3773
That Pet Place	(800) 733-3829

GLOSSARY

ACFA American Cat Fanciers Association Inc., a CAT FEDERATION.

ADRENALINE A hormone produced by the adrenal glands. Epinephrine, medical adrenaline, is used to treat ANAPHYLACTIC SHOCK. Epinephrine should always be accessible when vaccines are given to kittens or cats, in case they prove to be allergic to the vaccine.

ADULT For purposes of cat shows, a cat that is at least eight months old at the time of the show.

ALLELES Mutated genes.

ALTER A class where spayed and neutered cats are judged (see PREMIER). Also, a cat who has been surgically altered to prevent breeding (see NEUTER and SPAY).

ANAPHYLACTIC SHOCK A severe allergic reaction that can quickly lead to death.

ANOREXIA Loss of appetite.

ANTIBODIES A protein, produced by the immune system in response to the presence of a foreign substance such as bacteria.

ASPIRATED A substance, usually a liquid, drawn into the lungs. Aspirated liquids can lead to a form of pneumonia.

BREED CLUB A group of cat owners and exhibitors where membership is limited to owners of the breed in question. It may be independent or affiliated with one of the cat registries.

BREED STANDARDS Standards formulated by a CAT FEDERATION for use in judging a particular breed. These standards are the ideal for that breed. They are sometimes called Standards of Perfection.

CAT A domestic feline, of either sex, over eight months of age.

CAT FANCY A term often used to describe a CAT FEDERATION. It is also used in the broader sense of the entire community of those breeding pedigreed cats and showing both purebred and household pet cats at cat shows. There it is usually just called the "Fancy."

CAT FEDERATION An association of persons and clubs involved in breeding, showing and judging cats. Among its activities are sanctioning shows and registering cats (see REGISTRY).

CATALOGUE The official record of all cats entered in a particular cat show.

CATTERY A name registered by a cat breeder to identify the breeder's line of breeding. A registered cattery name always appears as a prefix to the name of a cat bred by that cattery/breeder.

CFA Cat Fanciers' Association Inc., a CAT FEDERATION.

COLOSTRUM A queen's "milk" produced during the first 48 hours after the birth of kittens. This very special substance is very high in protein and ANTIBODIES.

CONFORMATION The look or physical type of a cat, as measured against its BREED STANDARD.

CORONAVIRUS A family of related viruses, most of which are non-lethal intestinal viruses. One strain of the virus may present as FIP.

DAM The mother of a cat.

DECLAW To have the claws from the paws of a cat permanently removed, usually by surgery. Not every registry permits declawed cats to be exhibited.

DERMATITIS An inflammation of the skin.

ELISA TEST Enzyme Linked Immunosorbent Assay, a specific test that shows the presence of certain ANTIBODIES in the blood of a cat.

ESTRUS   Referring to the "heat" cycle of a QUEEN.

FANCY   See CAT FANCY.

FeLV   Feline leukemia, an infectious disease, caused by a virus that only affects cats.

FERAL   A non-domesticated cat, such as cats that live outside in a community but are not cared for by humans. This term is also sometimes used to refer to wild species of cats such as bobcats, tigers, etc.

FERAL BLOOD   When a wild cat, such as a bobcat, is bred into the lines of a pedigreed cat.

FIP   Feline infectious peritonitis, a disease that is presented by a coronavirus. FIP is the subject of many ongoing, and sometimes controversial, studies. Once thought to be highly contagious, it is now believed to be self-limiting, affecting some, but not all, cats exposed.

GENE POOL   The genetic constitution of a group of individual cats.

GENETIC CODE   A combination of letters and numbers designed to describe a cat in genetic terms. The purpose is to permit the cat to be classified properly for show and breeding.

GENOTYPICAL REGISTRY   A cat registry that classifies cats based on the breeds shown in the PEDIGREE, particularly the immediate parents.

HEMOLYSIS   Destruction of red blood cells, with the liberation of hemoglobin, which diffuses into the fluid surrounding the cells. When this occurs, the body is unable to retain hemoglobin and it is lost through the kidneys, giving the urine a red color (see NEONATAL ERYTHROLYSIS).

HERD MANAGEMENT   The practices necessary to maintain the health and well-being of a group of animals, usually a herd of farm animals but also a breeding CATTERY.

HIP DYSPLASIA   Abnormal development of the hip. Hip dysplasia is inherited and is a concern in some breeds of cats.

HOUSEHOLD PET   A non-pedigreed cat or kitten or a pedigreed cat or kitten being exhibited in a class with non-pedigreed cats or kittens in a cat show, abbreviated HHP. Some cat federations have a separate procedure for registering HHPs. Some federations also permit household pets to earn titles equivalent to those won by pedigreed cats. Household pets are usually required to be altered by a certain age and may or may not be permitted to be declawed.

INBREEDING   Mating cats that are closely related to each other, such as first cousin matings, father to daughter, brother to sister, and offspring to grandparents. Inbreeding can be an undesirable practice, since breeding closely related animals can accentuate existing genetic problems, even if they have not made themselves evident in past generations.

INBREEDING DEPRESSION   A decline in vigor or general weakness in a group of cats. It can be seen in factors such as declines in birth weights, a fall in average litter sizes, or even a greater propensity to illness. This is "due to the homozygous nature of an increasing number of genes with deleterious effects." (Roy Robinson, *Genetics for Cat Breeders, Third Ed.* Oxford: Pergamon Press 1991, p. 101-103.)

INDUCED OVULATOR   An animal in which eggs are released to be fertilized only after copulation takes place. Cats are induced ovulators.

INTACT   See WHOLE CAT.

KITTEN   A feline, of either sex, under the age of eight months. For purposes of cat shows, a kitten is a cat that is at least four months old but less than eight months old at the time of the show.

LINEBREEDING   A form of INBREEDING, involving breeding individuals within the same bloodline. Cats within the same bloodline differ from each other in most generations; common ancestors are only found further back in the breed's history.

LITTER   All of the kittens born of the same SIRE and DAM at the same time.

LITTER REGISTRATION   Officially recording the birth of a litter with a CAT FEDERATION, giving the date of birth, number of kittens, SIRE and DAM. Applications to register a litter are submitted by the breeder of the litter.

LONGHAIR   One of the two groups into which all cats are divided (the other is SHORTHAIR).

METASTASIZE   Spread throughout the body, as in cancer.

MUTATION   An obvious deviation from the normal which is genetically caused.

NECROPSY   An autopsy.

NEONATAL ERYTHROLYSIS   HEMOLYSIS of the newborn kitten, in which the red blood cells of the kitten are destroyed by the actions of maternal ANTIBODIES, which gain access to the kitten through the queen's COLOSTRUM. This can occur in kittens with Type A blood born to a QUEEN with Type B blood.

NEUTER   A male cat who has been castrated to prevent breeding. The surgery is called neutering.

OUTCROSS   Breeding one cat to another, unrelated cat.

PAPERS   One way to refer to a cat's certificate of registration and PEDIGREE form.

PATELLAR LUXATION   A displacement of the knee cap.

PEDIGREE   A document showing a cat's background for three, four or five generations. A three-generation pedigree includes the cat, plus three generations of forebears. A pedigree lists names, colors and registration numbers for each cat in the pedigree. Show titles are usually also listed.

PEDIGREED CAT   This usually refers to a cat whose heritage is known, documented and registered.

PHENOTYPICAL REGISTRY   A cat registry that classifies cats based on the physical look of the cat, but takes into account the breed(s) shown in its PEDIGREE.

POINTED   A cat on which the mask (face), ears, legs, feet and tail are clearly a darker shade than the body, but which merge into a lighter body color. Also known as color restricted.

PREMIER   In CFA, a class where altered cats are judged.

PROGRESSIVE RENAL ATROPHY   Also called PRA, a degeneration of the cells of the retina, leading to blindness as a cat ages.

PYOMETRA   An infection of the uterus.

QUEEN   A breeding female cat.

REGISTERED CAT   A cat that has completed the requirements for registration with one of the cat federations.

REGISTRATION   The initial recording of a cat's individual name and official ownership with a CAT FEDERATION. This also refers to the registration certificate issued by a CAT FEDERATION to the registered owner(s) of the cat.

REGISTRATION NUMBER   A unique number assigned by a CAT FEDERATION to identify one cat. Each federation issues its own set of registration numbers.

REGISTRATION RULES   The rules and guidelines set up by a CAT FEDERATION for the registration of cats, litters and catteries.

REGISTRY   One term used to describe a CAT FEDERATION, taken from one of its primary roles—registering the birth and pedigrees of cats.

SHORTHAIR   One of the two groups into which all cats are divided (the other is LONGHAIR).

SHOW   A series of rings where cats are judged, sponsored by a cat club. For a cat to earn a title with a particular CAT FEDERATION, the show must be sanctioned and licensed by that cat federation.

SHOW RULES   Rules formulated by a CAT FEDERATION governing all the aspects of how shows sanctioned and licensed by that federation are to be managed, including how the cats are judged and how titles are awarded.

SIRE   The father of a cat.

SPAY   A female cat who has had a hysterectomy to prevent breeding and heat cycles. The surgery is called spaying.

SPINA BIFIDA   Any failure of the vertebrae to close normally around the spinal cord.

SPRAYING   A male cat's habit of urinating anywhere, probably associated with establishing territory. Sometimes a female cat will also spray.

STUD CAT   A breeding male cat, also called a working male.

TICA   The International Cat Association Inc., a CAT FEDERATION.

TOXIC   Poisonous.

TOXOPLASMOSIS   A disease of cats generally associated with eating infected raw meat, caused by the presence of an intra-cellular parasite.

UPPER RESPIRATORY INFECTION   Infections affecting the upper respiratory tract, characterized by signs such as sneezing, coughing and nasal discharge. This term is sometimes abbreviated URI.

WHOLE CAT   A male or female who has not been altered and is still able to breed. Also called an intact cat.

.

INDEX

00176 4631